RACHEL R.

Significant

SIX
ORDINARY
WOMEN,
ONE
EXTRAORDINARY
GOD

A Study of
Women
in Jesus'
Genealogy

Significant

SIX ORDINARY WOMEN, ONE EXTRAORDINARY GOD
A Study of Women in Jesus' Genealogy

© 2020 Rachel Risner
All rights reserved.

ISBN 978-1-953016-00-3

To order additional copies of this resource, write to Bonfire Books, 5586 Township Road 381; Millersburg, OH 44654; email rachel@rachelrisner.com; order online at www.amazon.com or visit www.rachelrisner.com

Cover art Rachel Risner

Printed in the United States of America

Bonfire Books
5586 Township Road 381
Millersburg, OH 44654

DEDICATION

This study is dedicated to all women who are eager
to learn about being truly *Significant*.

MEET THE AUTHOR

Rachel Risner isn't exactly a motormouth, but when it comes to sharing what she's learning about God through the women in the Bible, she's got plenty to say. Studying their stories has changed her life, and she can't keep the life-changing truth to herself.

Rachel is an author and the wife of John Risner, lead pastor at MCA, The Church on the Hill, right in the heart of Ohio's beautiful Amish country. Her days as a mom of seven are filled with math lessons, potty training, soccer practice, ministering, and—when she can—sneaking away to clack at the computer or poke her nose into a good book (or better, *the* Good Book). She writes online at rachelrisner.com. *Significant* is her first in-depth Bible Study.

TABLE OF CONTENTS

Significant

AUTHOR'S NOTE

Friend! I am thrilled to have you along for the ride, journeying with me through the scriptures and stories of the women in Jesus' genealogy. My prayer is that this study would draw your heart closer to God, transforming us both to be more like Him. I have taken care in my writing to do my best to stay true to God's word and to use reliable commentaries to assure the most possible accuracy in its interpretation. But I am fallible. Anytime a human teacher is involved there is room for misinterpretation and error. I urge you to hold ***God's word alone*** in the highest regard. Only the Bible is without blemish. Because of this, I encourage you to grapple with the words in this text. Do not accept these teachings flippantly, but examine them for yourselves, using scripture as your measuring rod for truth. Know God's word for yourself and seek Him through your own serious study. Blessings to you as we embark on this journey together!

FOREWORD

A few years ago, I walked into Starbucks to meet a fellow writer and pastor's wife who wanted to chat about our mutual love for women's Bible studies. Little did I know then what a treasure I would find in Rachel Risner. Her love for the Lord and heart for women seeps from every pore in her body.

Helping her husband in ministry and homeschooling her seven children fill Rachel's days, and I appreciate her desire to keep first things first. Yet I also see in Rachel a soul ignited to write and teach the Bible with a heart to serve women. This drives her to use the time she could spend watching television or entertaining herself with her nose in commentaries or at her computer crafting sentences.

Over the past year, I've gotten to know Rachel well through an apprenticeship program for my ministry. I've heard her teach and met with her monthly for coaching. Rachel is the real deal. She loves the Lord and cares of about His agenda over her own. Her humility and teachability attracts people to her, and I know you are going to enjoy getting to know her more in these pages.

The Bible study you hold in your hands contains stories that inspire. Rachel brings biblical women to life so that when you turn the last page, you will feel like you know these women whose names appear in the genealogy of Jesus. They wrestled through many of the same identity issues we encounter, and had questions about their struggles just like we do. Yet we find they shared the bloodline of the Messiah and were used by God in significant ways.

Rachel helps us see how lives dedicated to God can become noteworthy even in the midst of our struggles and failures. Through this Bible study, you will find glimpses of your own story in the lives of Sarah, Leah, Tamar, Rahab, Ruth, and Bathsheba.

Rachel's unpacking of the biblical text will help you to see God's unique calling on your life. He is the One that brings great significance to even the most seemingly mundane tasks, routines, and situations. As we delve deep into Scripture with a fresh perspective on the lives of some of the women in the bloodline of Christ, we will uncover our own significance as children of God.

The truths in this book are invaluable, but I'm also thrilled that you will get to know my friend in these pages. Enjoy!

~Melissa Spoelstra, Award-winning Author and Speaker

INTRODUCTION

By Rachel Risner

Embarking on writing this study was one of the best decisions of my life. With seven children to homeschool and care for, the idea of writing an in-depth women's Bible Study seemed ludicrous—how could I possibly manage?

But my experience has been far from ludicrous—it has been one of my greatest joys.

Poring over the scriptures, my heart has been molded and transformed. My soul has been satisfied.

I've found myself mourning the fact that if only I were a better writer, I would be able to adequately teach other women the unspeakably encouraging, convicting, and humbling truths God has shown me as I've combed through the scriptures, learning about these women of the Bible.

But if I've learned anything throughout this study, it's that God can use the most unqualified woman in the most unexpected ways.

And so, my soul echoes the great hymn-writer Charles Wesley's lyrics:

> *O for a thousand tongues to sing*
> *My great Redeemer's praise,*
> *The glories of my God and King,*
> *The triumphs of His grace.*
>
> *My gracious Master and my God,*
> *Assist me to proclaim,*
> *To spread through all the earth abroad,*
> *The honors of Thy name.*

The Unlikely Six

If I've learned anything throughout this study, it's that God can use the most unqualified woman in the most unexpected ways.

Bully. Reject. Outsider. Prostitute. Pauper. Invisible—the world loves to give us names. Names that degrade and discourage us. Names that destroy us.

But what if I told you the women of the Bible we are about to study bore these labels accurately? What if I told you that the Bully, Reject, Outsider, Prostitute, Pauper and Invisible woman all went on to be arguably some of the most Significant women in history. Would you believe it?

Their seemingly insignificant lives would be used by our amazing God to change the course of history. You see, six women with train-wrecked lives were instrumental in bringing about our most precious Messiah. They were Jesus' foremothers.

Because of Christ, they were *Significant* beyond their wildest dreams.

Thicker than Water

"Blood runs thicker than water."

We have all heard it. The cliché means that family ties are tight, tighter than other connections.

This rings true in our everyday lives. We are more inclined to care for the needs of our own children as opposed to some stranger's kids. We are more loyal to our own husbands, rather than other men. We care for our own parents with a concern greater than that for the elderly in general. For many of us, family is a top priority.

God is no exception. Throughout the Bible, we see His special relationship with His people, Israel. The Old Testament chronicles the history of God's people--his family. Through thick and thin, obedience and sin, God stays true to His people Israel.

We see the father's heart God has for His people in Hosea 11, verses 1-4:

*"When Israel was a child, **I loved him**, and out of Egypt I called my son. But the more they were called, the more they went away from me...It was I who taught Ephraim to walk, taking them by*

> Because of Christ, they were Significant beyond their wildest dreams.

Choosing Jesus for the first time is as simple as telling Him, friend. Pray (talk) to Him, saying that you want to choose Him over everything else. Spill the beans...confess that you are ready to leave everything else behind, all wrong choices, and all distractions, so that you can choose Him each day.

Ask Him to take over, and release your life into His hands. As we surrender our lives to Christ, we let go of all that's holding us back–our fears, our worries, our doubt, our pride, even our own self-made plans.

What next? Learn how to study the Bible and dive into God's Word every day. It's the tool you need to help you choose Jesus today and always. Working through this Bible study book is a great way to start.

the arms; but they did not realize it was I who healed them. I led them with cords of human kindness, with ties of love."

God's people were not special on their own--not numerous, not strong, not intelligent. What set them apart was God's love for them, and their response of faith. Time and again scriptures tell us about our father-in-the-faith Abraham and his belief in God. *"Abraham believed God, and it was credited to him as righteousness," Romans 4:3.*

God used his people's faith in Him, feeble as it was, to bring about His purposes. Through them the **scriptures** would be written; through them **miracles** would be performed; through them **prophets, priests and kings** would rise and lead. And through Israel's bloodline, through their descendant Jesus, **all nations would have opportunity to be saved for all eternity** (John 3:16).

The good news—the best news ever—is that we can join the family! Jesus said in Matthew 12:50, *"For whoever does the will of my Father in heaven is my brother and sister and mother."*

And Galatians 3:7 says, *"Understand, then, that those who believe are children of Abraham."* If we have put our faith in the one true God, asking Jesus' blood to cover our sins and surrendering our lives to our Lord, we belong!

If we scoot on back to Romans 4 where it speaks about Abraham, we read in verses 23-25, *"The words 'it was credited to him' were written not for him alone, but also for us, to whom God will credit righteousness—for us who believe in him who raised Jesus our Lord from the dead. He was delivered over to death for our sins and was raised to life for our justification."*

Righteousness simply means **right living**—a life lived right with God's help. And justification is a fancy-sounding word that means **being made right**. Both can be yours if you choose Jesus today.

Why Study the Bloodline?

It can be confusing to know what it means to be significant. We feel like we have to be Serena Williams to be a significant athlete, like we have to graduate from Yale to be significantly intelligent, like our house has to look like Chip and Joanna Gaines' to be a significant homemaker, like our kids have to score a 36 on the ACT to be a significant mother, like we have to get 500 likes on our post to be significant among our Facebook friends, like we have to gain promotion after promotion to be significant at work. And we feel like failures when we can't live up to our own standards of significance.

But none of that is true. The women in Jesus' family help us understand how.

Throughout the pages of scripture God weaves a tale of heartache and love, pain and healing, sin and redemption. We know well the male roots of Jesus' family tree—Abraham, Jacob, Judah, and David. They are our fathers in the faith, power players in the story of God's people. Their lives teach us much.

But what of the mothers, those women lost behind-the-scenes? If we dive deep into the scriptures, we find that their stories speak volumes to us.

The *Significant* Bible study will focus on six women named in scripture that can be traced in Jesus' bloodline from Matthew 1: **Sarah, Leah, Tamar, Rahab, Ruth,** and **Bathsheba**. Some of these women's stories you may have heard, others seem to get lost in the thick Old Testament. Going deep into each of their narratives will show us how God used ordinary, human women to accomplish His amazing plan. And we will see that He can do the same with us.

God used ordinary, human women to accomplish His amazing plan.

Initially, we seem to share no common ground with Bible characters from long ago—our world is filled with iPhones, takeout, SUVs, and dishwashers. What could we possibly learn from these women from the ancient world?

These women are from all walks of life: some rich and others poor, some young and others old, some cherished and others rejected, some abusers and others abused, some ravishingly beautiful and others painfully unlovely.

But one common thread ties them all together—lives yielded to the one true God. And in that surrender God took what seemed like weakness and infused his strength. He took women who seemed insignificant, ordinary, and flawed and He used them each to play their part in accomplishing His greatest work: salvation for mankind. He made their lives *significant*.

Thousands of miles and thousands of years separate us from these women of the bloodline, but their humanity bridges the gap between us. Their struggles mirror our very own. Their jealousy, manipulation, deceit, despair, abuse, and fear look an awful lot like us.

In *Significant* we will unpack these six women's lives and learn how we too can have **beauty** of Biblical proportions, like Sarah. We can know, like Leah, the **fulfillment** of worshipping an amazing God. We will learn how to show the **mercy** of Tamar and go from forgotten to front-row seat. We will cultivate Rahab-like **courage**, and our past reputations will be shed as we become right with God. We will study Ruth, and see that God provides every need, inspiring **tenacious** faith. And we will learn how to go from invisible to **influential** in ways that really matter—like Bathsheba.

> The same God that had His fingerprints on their lives holds us in His hands.

The same God that had His fingerprints on their lives holds us in His hands. Let's dig deep into these women's stories to examine their lives, to learn and be encouraged, to grow in our own faith. Because these aren't just any women, they are Jesus' bloodline. Though at first glance they seemed ordinary, with God they were *Significant*.

How to Use This Book

This book is designed to be an interactive, 6-week study for you to embark upon with friends, with a Bible Study group, or individually. It could be done alone, but your experience will be enriched if you take at least one friend along for the journey.

Each of the six weeks will delve deeply into the life of one of the women in Jesus' bloodline from Matthew 1, going chronologically through the course of history. Whether the Bible women you are about to study are familiar to you, or not, going deep will help you be able to see them with fresh eyes, and learn that these six are ordinary women like you.

Each of the six weeks involves five days of homework. The study is designed to have assignments done individually. The group will gather together weekly, after the five days of personal study are complete—either online or in person. Women can hear a teaching (optional—see how to view these in the "Resources" section in the back of this book) and discuss their reflections from the week's study in small groups.

Though each day's work has been dubbed "homework" a more apt name could be soul-nourishment. True, doing daily assignments will take some amount of purposeful scheduling, but you will find that this becomes a highlight of your day.

The "work" of each day's study will become pleasure as you are refreshed and satisfied by stick-to-your-ribs, meaty Bible study that will sustain you through the busyness of your everyday life.

Be encouraged to take your time—Bible study sessions are not a race. Linger over the passages and give yourself the chance to take it all in. Getting messy may help too. Underline, circle, and dog-ear this book, if necessary. Whatever it takes to make your journey memorable!

Now let's get to it! Who else is ready to learn from God's precious word about how to be Significant? Let's go.

> Linger over the passages and give yourself the chance to take it all in.

Though at first glance these women seemed ordinary, with God they were *Significant*.

WEEK ONE

SARAH

Hot Mess to Matriarch

Day One
LIFESTYLES
OF THE RICH & THE PAGAN

Day Two
HAPPY CAMPERS

Day Three
FAMINE & FEAST

Day Four
HAGAR, THE HORRIBLE IDEA

Day Five
LAUGHTER,
THE BEST MEDICINE

Significant

DAY ONE: LIFESTYLES OF THE RICH AND THE PAGAN

MAIN TEXTS
Matthew 1:1-6,16
Genesis 11:27-12:6

"This is the genealogy of Jesus the Messiah the son of David, the son of Abraham" Matthew 1:1

Every epic tale has a prequel—Star Wars has *The Phantom Menace*, The Lord of the Rings has *The Hobbit,* and Narnia has *The Magician's Nephew.* These backstories fill us in on what happened before the story's climax—they set the stage for what comes next.

> Start each day's study right here! **Look over the main texts in your own Bible** before diving in to the workbook reading.

Jesus' story is no different. The Old Testament gives us the backstory for the main event—the coming of the Messiah. In order to better understand our Savior, to set the stage for His appearance, we will study His prequel.

Let's head over to Matthew 1:1, the first chapter and first verse of the New Testament. This is Jesus' genealogy—His genesis, His origin. Jesus family tree begins with, "This is the genealogy of Jesus the Messiah the son of David, the son of Abraham: Abraham was the father of Isaac." Breeze over verses 1-17 of Matthew 1 and make note of the women mentioned by name, filling in the following chart:

Verse	Woman mentioned
Matthew 1:3	
Matthew 1:5	
Matthew 1:5	
Matthew 1:6	
Matthew 1:16	

For our study of the first two women in Jesus' bloodline, we will need to do some digging. Notice that in Matthew 1:1-2 we don't find Sarah's name. We only hear of Abraham, Isaac, Jacob, and David. But she is there. She is lurking behind the scenes in this very important beginning of Jesus' beginning. If we dig deeper, we find how she fits into Jesus' bloodline. Check out Genesis 21:1-3 in the margin on the next page and circle Sarah's name:

> Now the Lord was gracious to Sarah as he had said, and the Lord did for Sarah what he had promised. Sarah became pregnant and bore a son to Abraham in his old age, at the very time God had promised him. **Abraham gave the name Isaac to the son Sarah bore him.**
>
> Genesis 21:1-3

There's no mistaking that Sarah belongs in Jesus' Genealogy. What is Sarah's relationship to:

Abraham—

Isaac—

So, we've established that Sarah is Abraham's wife, Isaac's mom. She's the very first woman, though not named specifically, in Jesus' bloodline that is found in Matthew 1. Now what? Well, before we dive into the details of Sarah's life, let's get to know her better by hearing her backstory.

Out of Ur

What better way to learn about Sarah's roots than to hear where she's from? Check out Genesis 11:31. Where were Sarai, Abram and Abram's family from?

Now I know what you're thinking: Ur sounds like some sort of guttural, cave-man grunt. Like these people were so primitive that they couldn't even give their city a two-syllable name. But before you jump to conclusions, I'll let you in on something—Ur was a happening place!

Ur was not just *a* happening place. For people in Mesopotamia in Sarah's day it was *the* happening place! Located in a prime spot right near the Persian Gulf and the Tigris and Euphrates Rivers, Ur was a hub for culture and trade.

Because of the prosperity Ur acquired in its position as a trade center, it was quite the cushy place to live.

Ur excelled not only in wealth, but also in knowledge. The mathematicians and astronomers of this region were the most advanced of their time. According to Answers in Genesis, Ur was "virtually the world's first civilization with a remarkable knowledge of astronomy and arithmetic."

Abraham and Sarah were born, raised, and lived the first 60 years of their life in Ur. They were right in the thick of the most advanced, opulent culture of their time. And God called them out of it.

Look at Genesis 12:1. What three things did God call Abram to leave?

Why? (see Genesis 12:2-3)

Do you see a theme here? How about blessing and increase? God called Abraham and Sarah to leave behind *everything* they knew, to be blessed and to bless others. And Abraham's response? Read Genesis 12:4-5 in the margin, circling the first three words.

Abraham and Sarah responded to God with *obedience*. God called them to leave their country of birth, their community, and their parents to head toward the Promised land of Canaan—and off they went!

Can you imagine what this might have been like for Sarah? Born and raised in the city, teeming with people and knowledge and comfort and culture, and called to who-knows-where? Called to leave everything and everyone she knew to venture out to "the land I will show you" (Genesis 12:1)?

Putting myself in Sarah's sandals, I think my talks with God might sound something like, *"God why can't You just bless me here? This is where my family is—my parents, my cousins, my neighbors, my friends. This is all I know! It's comfortable and familiar here. You're big enough to bring about Your purposes in my family, without me having to move. Just do that!"*

When has God called you to leave something important or familiar behind, for him? Describe how God used your obedience (or disobedience) and what happened as a result:

The Lord had said to Abram, "Go from your country, your people and your father's household to the land I will show you. 2 "I will make you into a great nation, and I will bless you; I will make your name great, and you will be a blessing. 3 I will bless those who bless you, and whoever curses you I will curse; and all peoples on earth will be blessed through you." 4 So Abram went, as the Lord had told him; and Lot went with him. Abram was seventy-five years old when he set out from Harran. 5 He took his wife Sarai, his nephew Lot, all the possessions they had accumulated and the people they had acquired in Harran, and they set out for the land of Canaan, and they arrived there.

GENESIS 12:4-5

God's plan for Abraham and Sarah was to leave Ur. Something about being in Ur was going to hold Abraham and Sarah back. God wanted them out of Ur to accomplish his plans. Often God does the same in our lives. God calls us to leave behind things that may seem good to us, in order to bring about His greater purpose in our lives.

Sometimes we must leave behind familiar places, close relationships, and comfortable situations. We have to ditch our own plans to embrace God's direction. And that, my friends, can be a scary, beautiful thing.

> Sometimes we must leave behind familiar places, close relationships, and comfortable situations...to embrace God's direction.

During his awkward, pimple-faced, squeaky-voiced teenage days, my husband felt a call. You see, he had always been painfully shy. As the youngest of the family and homeschooled all the way through, he had the luxury of being a mama's boy. As a tot, his older siblings tell of him always curling up on his mama's lap, thumb tucked into his mouth, whenever visitors came to the house. It was his comfort, his security.

But, at 15, he studied scripture faithfully and knew that God was calling him to boldness. As he learned about the patriarchs, prophets, and apostles standing up for their faith and proclaiming the gospel, he knew it was time to let go of the apron strings. So, he prayed for boldness, and he joined a friendship evangelism ministry.

Fast forward twenty years, and you'd never know the winsome, eloquent, fearless preacher I now call my husband, was once a backward, shy boy. God has a way of taking us out of our comfort zone to transform us for His purposes.

In my weakness and humanity, I sometimes resist God's direction in my life. I like being comfortable; I like familiarity and ease. But, like Sarah, sometimes God has to take me out of the comfortable, easy, familiar life in order to bless me, and to make me a blessing to others.

Sometimes we have to travel through the desert in order to arrive at the Promised Land.

An Idol Mind

What were God's reasons for taking Abraham and Sarah out of Ur? We can't be sure, but I have an educated guess at one of them—pagan religion.

Ur and all of Mesopotamia (later called Babylon) were crawling with false gods. Ur's main god was Nanna, god of the moon, to which a great ziggurat—still visible today—would be built.

Several other gods were worshipped including Baal and Asherah. Protective amulets, false priests, temple prostitutes, household gods, pagan rituals, and sacrifices to idols were part of everyday life in Ur.

Why do you think Abraham and Sarah could find serving the one true God difficult in Ur?

Time and again in scripture God called his people to separate themselves from bad influences. Read 2 Corinthians 6:17 in the margin, circling God's instructions to his people. God warned his people to be separate to protect them. Repeatedly in the Old Testament God's people were tempted to disobey amidst the idolatrous cultures surrounding them.

"Come out from them and be separate," says the Lord. "Touch no unclean thing, and I will receive you."

2 CORINTHIANS 6:17

What parallels can you see between our culture and the polytheistic culture of Ur in Abraham's time? How can the culture we live in be a problem for followers of Christ?

While we may not have friends bopping by the local ziggurat to make sacrifices to the moon god, our culture has its own idolatries. Worshipping sex, fame, power, and financial prosperity are temptations we all face.

We glorify beautiful faces over beautiful souls. We admire talented people more than the God who gave them their talents. We seek security in the money we have earned, rather than the Lord who provided the job in the first place.

While God might not be calling you to move to Timbuktu and leave our culture, what are ways in which you can "leave behind" or avoid the pagan idolatries that surround you?

> Just like Sarah and Abraham left all that was comfortable, familiar, and easy, we too should be willing to leave behind anything that will keep us from the Lord's purpose in our lives.

I remember feeling the squeeze to fit in during my teen years by wearing immodest clothing. It seemed like the fashion trends I needed to follow to be beautiful were also ones that would not honor God. The glossy mags and store mannequins all looked so cool and trendy in their skimpy clothes—surely the Lord wouldn't mind if I pushed it a bit? In retrospect, I'm thankful for boundaries put in place by parents wiser than I. What a mistake it could have been to follow the culture's fashion sense (or lack thereof). I'm thankful to have left that potential pitfall behind.

In addition to listening to wise counsel, studying God's word is a great way to separate ourselves from an ungodly culture. The false ideas that the world whispers in our ear must be replaced with the truth. That's one reason why Bible studies like this are so important.

Throughout this study keep your heart soft to what the Lord is showing you through His word—the difference between the world's counterfeit idols and the one true God.

Just like Sarah and Abraham left all that was comfortable, familiar, and easy, we too should be willing to leave behind anything that will keep us from the Lord's purpose in our lives. May we all be steadfast in obedience to Him.

Drawing Conclusions

Before we move forward, let's take a moment to review visually. In the middle of the following box, draw Sarah—a stick figure is fine. On the left side of Sarah put everything from her past in Ur (comfort, pagan religion, etc.) and on the right, put the things God had in store for her. Add to this picture as the chapter progresses.

> We are sometimes called to leave behind familiar comforts to embrace God's path for us.

Share a simple prayer time with the Lord:

- Thank Him for what He is teaching you through His word.
- Ask for his strength and resolve to leave behind whatever is necessary to follow his plan for your life.
- Pray that he would continue to reveal Himself and His truth to you throughout the remainder of the day, and this study

Truth Takeaway– *"Then Jesus said to his disciples, 'If any of you wants to be my follower, you must give up your own way, take up your cross, and follow me.'" Matthew 16:24 NLT*

DAY 2: HAPPY CAMPERS

MAIN TEXTS
Genesis 12:1-9
Luke 16:19-31
Matthew 14:28-31
Mark 9:20-24

"Abram believed the LORD, and he credited it to him as righteousness." Genesis 15:6

So, we've set the scene for day two of this week of our study: Abraham and Sarah were born and raised in Ur, a city—but not just any city, *the* city of their time. One that is posh, progressive,

Week 1–Sarah, A Woman of Beauty   21

> Abraham and Sarah are enigmatic Bible ... so **plain**, so **ordinary**, so **flawed**—and yet **big-time players**.

and pagan. But God had better things in store for this power couple. Now we begin to see the story unfold.

What's So Amazing About Abe?

Not much is amazing about Abraham! And at the same time, plenty. Abraham and Sarah are enigmatic Bible characters that just seems so plain, so ordinary, so flawed—and yet big-time players in God's plan to save the world.

One thing we have to remember as we dive into the story of Abraham and Sarah is their religious culture is nothing like ours. We have God's word, written down for us to pore over as much as we please. We have thousands of years of church tradition and Bible scholarship to draw from and to read. We are surrounded by fellow believers who share our beliefs. We have Christ's death and resurrection, enabling us to have forgiveness and the Holy Spirit always with us—comforting and encouraging us, helping us in our need.

In Abraham's day, people had oral tradition. Parents passed down stories of God's faithfulness and provision.

Abraham and Sarah had come on the scene 10 generations after the flood, and though they didn't have scripture, they had something equally incredible, maybe even more so—firsthand experience with God. Check out their first recorded encounter in Genesis 12, starting in verse 1. Underline the first six words of this verse in the margin.

> The **Lord had said** to Abram, "Go from your country, your people and your father's household to the land I will show you.
>
> GENESIS 12:1

Stop right there. I don't know how you feel about this, but wow—just wow! Now check out Genesis 12:7 and underline the first five words of the verse in the margin.

> 7 The **Lord appeared** to Abram and said, "To your offspring I will give this land." So, he built an altar there to the Lord, who had appeared to him.
>
> GENESIS 12:7

God *appeared* to Abraham. God *spoke* to Abraham. Take a second to let that sink in. If this story is Sunday-School familiar to you, step back and imagine the amazing experience it must have been to hear God's audible voice, to be a friend of God (James 2:23). In the early days of the world, this is how God's followers knew him—a very real, tangible, audible, personal relationship.

I don't think it's a stretch to say that Adam and Eve (Genesis 3:8-9), Noah (Genesis 6:13), and Abraham's one-on-one physical encounters with God are not the normal experience for most of us. Abraham's relationship with God literally included audible conversations—many of them.

Let's push on to see what they can teach us.

Believing the Unbelievable

As we covered in yesterday's study, part of God's instruction to Abraham and Sarah included leaving behind their homeland, their friends and their extended family. And despite how difficult it must have been, Sarah and Abraham obeyed. So, we know *what* happened, now let's delve deeper into the *why*.

Let's review: What seven things did God say he would do for Abraham and Sarah in verses two and three of Genesis 12? (see verses in margin)

1.

2.

3.

4.

5.

6.

7.

"I will make you into a great nation, and I will bless you; I will make your name great, and you will be a blessing. 3 I will bless those who bless you, and whoever curses you I will curse; and all peoples on earth will be blessed through you."

GENESIS 12:2-3

Things are sounding pretty good for Abraham and Sarah right now. According to God, they've got some good things coming. Who doesn't want power (being a great nation), good fortune (blessing), fame (great name), to be a benefit to others (made into a blessing), to have their friends prosper (bless those who bless them), to have their enemies fail (curse those who curse them), and to have world-wide impact (bless all people on earth through them). Wowza!

¹⁵ All the land that you see I will give to you and your offspring forever.
¹⁶ I will make your offspring like the dust of the earth, so that if anyone could count the dust, then your offspring could be counted.

GENESIS 13:15-16

As if that wasn't enough, God gives Abraham assurance of his blessings, time and again. What specific promises does God give Abraham in Genesis 13:15-16, echoed in Genesis 15:5 (see margin)?

So not only are Abe and Sarah getting power, fame, good fortune, and world-wide impact—they get prime real estate, and kids and grandkids too. At this point, Sarah must be thinking, "Count me in!" What more could one possibly want?!

We know that Abraham's response to God's **instruction** was **obedience** (Genesis 12:4). What was Abraham's response to God's **promises**? The answer is found in a key verse, Genesis 15:6. Copy the verse here:

⁵ He took him outside and said, "Look up at the sky and count the stars—if indeed you can count them." Then he said to him, "So shall your offspring be."

GENESIS 15:5

Belief. Abraham's response to God's outlandishly generous promises was *belief.*

What about you? Take a moment to reflect. Would it be difficult for you to believe these kinds of audacious promises from God?

Those of us who are pessimists (or realists, as I like to think of myself) can imagine what our response might be. "Too good to be true!" or, "Yeah, but what's the catch?" or maybe even, "There's no way that could happen."

Some things just seem too sensational to believe. Like a tabloid headline about alien babies or batboys, or a glossy ad about easy steps to make millions in a month. While I have a healthy dose of skepticism when it comes to get-rich-quick schemes and dramatic headlines, unfortunately I think I might have an unhealthy dose of skepticism when it comes to believing what God's promised me.

I Don't Believe it!

Cynicism is a commonplace for us. Unbelief is our go-to response, especially when the promises seem too amazing. But Jesus cautions us against being skeptical of God's promises.

In Luke 16 Jesus tells the story of two characters, an unbelieving rich man and a poor beggar named Lazarus. Both are in the afterlife, the wicked rich man in torment, and the beggar in comfort. Abraham is there and shows the importance of faith. Listen in on the rich man's conversation with Abraham from Luke 16:27-31:

"(The rich man) answered, 'Then I beg you, father, send Lazarus to my family, for I have five brothers. Let him warn them, so that they will not also come to this place of torment."

Abraham replied, "They have Moses and the Prophets; let them listen to them."

"No, father Abraham," he said, "but if someone from the dead goes to them, they will repent."

He said to him, "If they do not listen to Moses and the Prophets, they will not be convinced even if someone rises from the dead."

Ouch. The rich man didn't believe God's promises through Moses and the Prophets, and literally suffered grave consequences—and his family was headed toward the same fate.

This passage has sparked some soul-searching in my life. Sure, I *say* I believe all of the things I read in God's word, but do I really? Does my life *truly* reflect it?

I can read Proverbs 22:6 that tells me if I plant seeds of faith in my children's lives they'll grow—but still worry about their

> Jesus cautions us against being skeptical of God's promises.

future walks with God. Or I can read verse 9 from that same chapter that tells me the generous prosper, and still feel like it's up to me to scrimp and save each scrap for my own family rather than share. I've got a lot to learn—Lord help me believe!

I hope it doesn't take a resurrected patriarch for God to get His messages through to me (I'm not even sure that would work. It might just scare the living daylights out of me!) Perhaps I'm more like the rich man's family than I'd like to admit.

> Perhaps I'm more like the rich man's family than I'd like to admit.

Another example of the danger of disbelief is the story of Peter's attempt at walking on water. Let's read the following verses from Matthew 14 and we'll get to the bottom of Peter's blunder, so we don't make the same mistake ourselves. In verses 30-31 circle the words that describe Peter's situation:

"Lord, if it's you," Peter replied, "tell me to come to you on the water." 29 "Come," he said. Then Peter got down out of the boat, walked on the water and came toward Jesus. 30 But when he saw the wind, he was afraid and, beginning to sink, cried out, "Lord, save me!" 31 Immediately Jesus reached out his hand and caught him. "You of little faith," he said, "why did you doubt?"

What happened to Peter when he focused on the circumstances of his situation, instead of trusting God?

Have you experienced this same result in your life? What happened?

When Peter took his eyes off of Christ, and looked around at the problems surrounding him, his situation began to seem impossible. Instead of trusting in Jesus and walking on the water, Peter began to sink. Instead of belief, he was filled with doubt.

I remember days years ago when I struggled with changing friendships. Closer-than-family friends suddenly seemed distant. I mourned the loss. And as I surveyed the situation, I felt like I was sinking. How could God take those relationships away?

But when I turned my eyes to Jesus, I got my bearings. I realized that I needed to hold those relationships loosely—to surrender them to God and look to Him to be my companion in my loneliness. On my own my faith was feeble. I could only walk on water if I reached out and took God's outstretched hand.

But Abraham didn't falter like me; he was on board with God's promises from the get-go—Sarah too. Leaving everything they knew? Sure! Sleeping in tents? No problem! Uncertain future? Not when you are certain that God has a good plan. It may seem small to us, but believing God's promises was a big deal for Abraham.

That's why Abraham was considered righteous.

BUT WHAT IF I DON'T BELIEVE?

If you're an inquisitive, anxious worrywart like me, you might just be shifting into panic mode right now. Maybe believing the unbelievable isn't your strong suit. I get it. Same.

But I have good news, my friend! We are not alone. God is right by our side when we falter, and He longs to help us. While our emotions might take us for a roller-coaster ride through the ups and downs of faith, we can always call out to God to increase our trust in his promises.

Jesus encountered just such a man, tossed by the waves of unbelief in Mark 9. Let's eavesdrop on their dialogue. Jump in with me halfway through verse 22 when the man calls out to Jesus for help:

"' if you can do anything, take pity on us and help us."

"'IF (emphasis mine) you can'?" said Jesus. "Everything is possible for one who believes."

Immediately the boy's father exclaimed, "I do believe; help me overcome my unbelief!" Mark 9:24

Our emotions might take us for a roller-coaster ride through the ups and downs of faith, but we can always call out to God to increase our trust in his promises.

I don't know about you, but I sure am glad for this man's example! "Help me believe!" is my heart's cry when I find myself lacking faith in God's promises for my life.

Every word of God proves true.

PROVERBS 30:5 NLT

Let's hit the pause button and consider which of God's promises we could use some help believing today. Below is a list of truths from Isaiah 43. Read through the list and star the one which you could use a boost to believe today:

God is with you—"When you pass through the waters, I will be with you" Isaiah 43:2.

You are His—"I have redeemed you; I have summoned you by name; you are mine" Isaiah 43:1.

You are loved & precious—"You are precious and honored in my sight...I love you" Isaiah 43:4.

God makes a way where there is no way—"See, I am doing a new thing!...I am making a way in the wilderness" Isaiah 43:19.

You are forgiven—" I...am he who blots out your transgressions, for my own sake, and remembers your sins no more" Isaiah 43:25.

Sometimes we know God's truth in our heads, but we struggle to believe it completely in our hearts. Admit your struggle to fully believe the truth you starred to the Lord, and cry out to God like the man from Mark 9. Ask Him to help you overcome your unbelief.

Abraham's faith as righteousness is a bedrock of Christianity. Romans 4, Galatians 3 and James 2 all make it clear that Abraham's belief in God's promises was a big deal. God was going to bless Abraham and Sarah. God was going to build a nation through them.

They believed it.

Flip back a few pages to your drawing of Sarah from yesterday. Add the things you learned about God's future for Sarah from today's lesson.

> Because faith is foundational to our walk with God, we can shift our focus from trying to trusting.

Share a simple prayer time with the Lord:

- Surrender any areas of unbelief you are struggling with today.
- Ask for the faith to believe God's promises.
- Pray that He would soften your heart to receive from Him through this study.

Truth Takeaway– *"We are made right with God by placing our faith in Jesus Christ. And this is true for everyone who believes, no matter who we are." Romans 3:22 NLT*

DAY 3: FAMINE & FEAST

"The Lord leads with unfailing love and faithfulness" Psalm 25:10

Follow the Leader, Wherever He May Go

In our short time with Sarah we have learned that, despite her settled beginnings as a city girl, she followed her God-fearing hubby Abraham into a life of wandering in foreign lands. We have found that Sarah and Abraham were **obedient** to God's calling to go, and that they **believed** God's incredible promises to bless them and make them a blessing to others.

Today, their story takes a turn for the worse, as we see their shortcomings surface. But first, one more spiritual victory for Abraham and Sarah—an active response to God in **worship**.

Read Genesis 12:7-8 in the margin. What did Abraham DO for the Lord in these verses?

After a significant experience with God, his people often erected structures of remembrance. These two sites within Canaan, the land God had promised to give them, were meaningful altars of worship for Abraham and Sarah.

MAIN TEXTS
Genesis 12:6-20
Genesis 20

7 The Lord appeared to Abram and said, "To your offspring[a] I will give this land." So he built an altar there (the site of the great tree of Moreh at Shechem) to the Lord, who had appeared to him.
8 From there he went on toward the hills east of Bethel and pitched his tent, with Bethel on the west and Ai on the east. There he built an altar to the Lord and called on the name of the Lord.

GENESIS 12:7-8

ALTARED MEANINGS

Abraham and Sarah, having come out of Ur, left the most progressive hub of the ancient world. But excelling in mathematical calculations and astronomy were not God's calling on their life. Following their wise God instead of walking in worldly wisdom was their calling.

So, Abraham built his first altar at the great tree of "Moreh," which means teaching, or teacher. Shechem means "shoulder" or "strength." Since God was teaching Abraham and Sarah the strong, true wisdom found in him, the tree of Moreh in Shechem, symbolized the strength of true knowledge. How is God's wisdom stronger, or better than the knowledge the world has to offer?

Do you have any altars of worship to the Lord in your life? How do you remind yourself of the truths that the Lord has taught you and the times that He has proven faithful?

There are lots of ways we can commemorate God's work in our lives. Writing in journals, creating works of art, decorating our homes with meaningful Bible verses, telling others our God stories, posting on social media, and highlighting special scriptures can all be ways that we memorialize God's faithfulness to us.

During this study, I will encourage you to erect your own symbolic stones of remembrance. You may do this at the workbook's prompting, or on your own. Look for the blank pages at the back of this book marked "Significant Encounters with God" for plenty of space to record your God stories.

Or, if you're more tech-savvy, use social media for collecting your stones of remembrance. This is pretty cool because it's easy to add images as well. Type #significantwomenofthebible after your post to add it to a collection of posts from women going through this study.

You can also make up your own unique hashtag for your God stories that you can click later to review them. The (huge) bonus of using social media is that others can see your God stories as well—you'll be testifying to others and collecting your stones of remembrance all at the same time—hooray for multitasking!

The Honeymoon is Over

Everything was going well for Sarah and Abraham: God was calling them and they were walking in obedience. They were going to be prosperous, famous, powerful and influential. Their family would be God's family. Things were on point for this God-fearing pair.

But hit the brakes before you put this dynamic duo up on a pedestal, because these two had a few fumbles on the horizon.

Abram's second altar was symbolic as well. Bethel means "house of God" and Ai means "desolate heap." He recognized that one must leave their life without God, a "desolate heap," behind in order to become a "house of God."

What happened next? Read Genesis 12:10 in your own Bible or in the margin.

Now there was a famine in the land, and Abram went down to Egypt to live there for a while because the famine was severe.

GENESIS 12:10

After following God's lead to Canaan, their Promised Land, Abram and Sarai fell on hard times. A famine swept over the land—and not just a little dry spell, but a famine so devastating that Abram and Sarai were forced to relocate. Talk about a chance to be hangry!

We can only guess what the couple must have been thinking. If I were Sarai, I may have doubted God's provision. I might wonder why in the world God asked me to leave my homelands and family behind, only to come to a desolate famine-stricken land.

Have you ever followed God's lead, only to have things seem to turn out for the worse? What happened?

When my husband was a teenager, he worked for a grocery store. It was a great job—he liked the work and it paid well. He got plenty of hours and even had opportunities to share his faith with coworkers. There was just one hiccup. The manager wanted to schedule John for Sundays.

Thinking that it would be no big deal to respectfully explain to his manager that he had a conviction against working on Sundays, John went into the manager's office to address the issue. John was hoping the manager would guarantee him the ability to follow his conviction. God blesses his people for doing the right thing, so He'd surely protect the job John loved, right?

Wrong.

There wasn't going to be any guarantee that John wouldn't be scheduled for Sundays, even though he was an honest, hardworking employee. This was a huge disappointment. Time for another job.

Sometimes even when you follow your convictions and make the right choices, things don't go your way. Following God doesn't mean you travel an easy road.

Desperate Times, Desperate Measures

Sarah was no ordinary woman. She was beautiful. Actually, she was so beautiful that as she and Abraham were travelling, Abraham feared for his life. Abraham and Sarah lived in brutal times and he thought that powerful men would see Sarah's beauty and kill him in order to have Sarah for themselves.

So, Abraham came up with a plan.

In Genesis 12:11-13 he said to Sarah, *"I know what a beautiful woman you are. When the Egyptians see you they will say, 'this is his wife.' Then they will kill me but will let you live. Say you are my sister, so that I will be treated well for your sake and my life will be spared because of you.'"*

And Abraham was right about Sarah's looks. Her beauty was so captivating that, even at the ages of 65 and 90 years old, powerful men wanted her for their own. (Hard to believe, right?) Sarah followed her husband's sinful plan and played along with the deception.

Read Genesis 12:14-16. What happened?

To Sarai (verse 15):

To Abram (verse 16):

Epic fail for Abraham. Instead of bravely defending his wife's honor, *he pretended not to be her husband*! He *willingly* gave her away—and gained from it. He was so scared for his own hide that he said, "Sure! Take her as your own! Just don't hurt me!!"

When Abram came to Egypt, the Egyptians saw that Sarai was a very beautiful woman. 15 And when Pharaoh's officials saw her, they praised her to Pharaoh, and she was taken into his palace. 16 He treated Abram well for her sake, and Abram acquired sheep and cattle, male and female donkeys, male and female servants, and camels.

GENESIS 12:14-16

The man who was supposed to be Sarah's protector and provider sold her. Some knight in shining armor.

Wasn't this the man who believed God? We've learned that the Bible says so, four times over. One of the craziest things about this whole story is that *it happened again.*

Fast forward a few pages for us, several years for Sarah. Abraham pulled the same scam with another powerful person, King Abimelek.

In Genesis 20, Abraham spelled out his hare-brained idea. In verse 11 he said, *"I said to myself, 'There is surely no fear of God in this place, and they will kill me because of my wife.' Besides, she really is my sister, the daughter of my father though not of my mother; and she became my wife. And when God had me wander from my father's household, I said to her, 'This is how you can show your love to me: Everywhere we go, say of me, "He is my brother."'"*

Did you catch that? Abraham pulled that whole "if-you-really-love-me-you'll-do-this-bad-thing" act. Yikes!

But before we peg Abraham as only the corrupt guy in this whole mess, let's not forget that Sarah was part of this scheme too. Sarah lied about her relationship with Abraham.

In Genesis 20:5 Abimelek pointed out how he was duped by both Abraham and Sarah. Read it in the margin, underlining what Sarah and Abraham said.

Now if you are thinking that Sarah's off the hook because she was only following her husband, think again. We are all responsible for our words and actions. Look up Matthew 12:36 and write it in your own words below:

> "Did he not say to me, 'She is my sister,' and didn't she also say, 'He is my brother'? I have done this with a clear conscience and clean hands."
>
> GENESIS 20:5

It is true that the Bible tells wives to respect their husbands (see Ephesians 5:33), but any Christian's allegiance belongs first and foremost to the Lord.

When we are faithless, God remains faithful.

Jesus told us that following God clearly comes first. Read Mark 12:29-31 in the margin.

Lovingly respecting our husbands is of utmost importance, but Jesus says priority numero uno is loving and obeying God Himself. If we love God with all our hearts, we won't listen when others try to lead us astray.

Surprised, Not Surprised

Despite Abraham and Sarah's faithless, fearful behavior God protected Sarah from any harm. Even when we are faithless, God remains faithful.

How did God protect Sarah from harm in Pharaoh's household? Read Genesis 12:17 and record the answer below.

First Corinthians 13:7 says that love "always protects." Even though her husband Abram couldn't be counted on for protection, the Lord protected Sarah. Read Genesis 20 and see how once again God laid the smack down to shield Sarah from harm.

What did God say to Abimelek in verses 3-7?

In God's response to both Pharaoh (disease) and Abimelek (serious warning and infertility), we see already how he was fulfilling his initial promises to Abraham and Sarah. Turn back to the seven promises of God you recorded from Genesis 12:2-3 yesterday and find which specific promise God was fulfilling.

Even though Abraham was scared, even though Sarah was sinful, God was still faithful to His promises to them. God was cursing their enemies. Can I get an Amen? How wonderful it is that our God's love and faithfulness to us is not dependent upon us. What a great thing it is to be loved by a Lord that treats us better than we deserve.

Not only that, He heaped blessings upon His followers—even after their disobedience. At the end of both of these less-than-desirable episodes, Abraham and Sarah made out like bandits. Circle all of the wealth they acquired from Pharaoh and Abimelek in the verses below (don't forget to add these to your sketch documenting Sarah's life that you began in Day One):

"He treated Abram well for her sake, and Abram acquired sheep and cattle, male and female donkeys, male and female servants, and camels." Genesis 12:16

"Then Abimelek brought sheep and cattle and male and female slaves and gave them to Abraham, and he returned Sarah his wife to him. 15 And Abimelek said, "My land is before you; live wherever you like." 16 To Sarah he said, "I am giving your brother a thousand shekels of silver." Genesis 20:14-16

I don't know about you—but if I wasn't a follower of God, and encountered people who lied to me and caused me to be afflicted with diseases and infertility, I don't think I'd be showering them with gifts and sending them on their way peacefully. Truly God was with Sarah and Abraham.

Are you surprised at God's faithfulness to curse Sarah's enemies, to protect her and to bless her abundantly, despite her blunder in following Abraham's plan of deception? Why or why not?

> What a great thing it is to be loved by a Lord that treats us better than we deserve.

No two of our paths are going to look exactly the same, but we can all see our faithful God's fingerprints on our lives—if we remember to look.

I was practically born with baby fever. I was that girl who always dreamed of being a mama. I daydreamed about rocking my own baby to sleep and pretended to raise my own orphanage filled with baby dolls. I changed their diapers, fed them bottles—I even shoved a round pillow in my shirt and pretended to be pregnant.

I even tried to talk my mother into having more babies—but that was a no-go. I'd have to wait to bear my own.

But as I grew older and read the story of infertile, discontented Rachel in the Bible, my stomach sank. Maybe I never would be a mama and get to cuddle babies and raise children of my own. The fear niggled deep inside me.

In my early teen years, the fear grew—I didn't want a family if I wasn't married, and teenage boys that were husband material seemed non-existent. I knew God didn't owe it to me to give me the life I desired. Would my dream ever become a reality?

> God was faithful to me even though I didn't deserve it.

Fast-forward 25 years later and my story of God's faithfulness is that He gave me not only the man of my dreams, but seven children to boot. My life is not a storybook—I deal with leaky diapers, temper tantrums, and times my husband and I don't see eye-to-eye. But at the same time, I recognize God's faithfulness in leading my life on the path He had for me. He was faithful to me even though I didn't deserve it.

Have you noticed God's faithfulness in your life? Chances are your story looks a little different than mine. Take a moment to record your own brief story of God's faithfulness to you. You can use the "Significant Encounters with God" section in the back of this book, or use Facebook or Instagram and add an image that represents his faithfulness with the tag #significantwomenofthebible.

These pages and posts will serve as our own altars of remembrance of God's faithfulness.

> We can trust in God because He is faithful, even when we're not.

Spend a simple prayer time with the Lord:

- Thank him for his faithfulness to His promises, despite our own failures.
- Ask the Lord to provide opportunities to share your story of His faithfulness with others.
- Pray that He would show you how to live faithfully in your own circumstances.

Takeaway Truth– *"For the word of the Lord is right and true; he is faithful in all he does." Psalm 33:4*

DAY 4: HAGAR, THE HORRIBLE IDEA

MAIN TEXT
Genesis 16

"The heart of man plans his way, but the Lord establishes his steps." Proverbs 16:9

Yesterday we saw God's faith**ful**ness despite Sarah and Abraham's faith*less*ness. God protected and blessed Sarah and Abraham even though they deceived Pharaoh and Abimelek. God's promises to bless Abraham and Sarah and to curse their enemies were proving true. We follow a God who is steadfast, even when we waver.

After experiencing God's divine protection and providence firsthand, Abraham and Sarah should be on a spiritual high, unshakeable in their belief in God's promises. But, as we follow their storyline, we see something quite different than unshakeable faith from Sarah and her husband.

We follow a God who is steadfast, even when we waver.

Promises (Un)fulfilled

One of God's exciting promises to Abraham and Sarah was that they would have lots of descendants. God had spoken *directly* with Abraham time and time again. In Genesis 12:2-3 God gave his initial blessing, "*I will make you into **a great nation** and I will bless you; I will make your name great, and you will be a blessing. I will bless those who bless you, and whoever curses you I will curse; and all peoples on earth will be blessed through you.*"

God affirmed the blessing in Genesis 13:16, saying that Abraham's descendants would be like the dust of the earth. In Genesis 15:5 what did He say Abraham's descendants would be like?

> I will make your offspring like the dust of the earth, so that if anyone could count the dust, then your offspring could be counted.
>
> GENESIS 13:16

Take a moment to add some stars to your sketch of Sarah's life from Day One.

In Genesis 15:5 God told Abraham and Sarah that their descendants would be as numerous as the stars in the sky. On any clear night, the unaided eye can see thousands of stars in the night sky. But astronomers say that there are 100 thousand million stars in our galaxy, the Milky Way. They also guess that there are millions upon millions of additional galaxies too, each with their own vast number of stars. The promise of descendants too many to count was surely an incredible one for childless Abraham and Sarah.

> He took him outside and said, "Look up at the sky and count the stars—if indeed you can count them." Then he said to him, "So shall your offspring be."
>
> GENESIS 15:5

These **three** times God had spoken *directly* to Abraham, telling him of this blessing with no strings attached. There were no conditions which Abraham would have to follow—none. God would make Abraham's family line the one out of which prophets, priests and kings would arise. God's word would be given, and Jesus, the deliverer of all mankind would be brought through Abraham's family—blessing all people on earth.

> There were no conditions which Abraham would have to follow.

This was an amazing promise, a covenant like no other. Abraham responded with faith. Genesis 15:6 says, "Abraham believed the LORD, and he credited it to him as righteousness." But Sarah and Abraham remained childless.

The Horrible Idea

For years Abraham and Sarah had been married, and for years they had believed God's promise that a great nation would come from them. But, for years, nothing happened. Sarah shared Abraham's excitement. The man she loved was to be blessed by God in incredible, historic ways—the only problem was, Sarah was barren.

Just as God had given Sarah a beauty unmatched by women, he had also made her barren. Sarah was in her seventies. She had lost hope that she would have a baby, and she was eager to see God's promises fulfilled. So, she took matters into her own hands.

In her years of embarrassing childlessness Sarah had grown impatient. Let's read what happened in Genesis 16:1-6.

"Now Sarai, Abram's wife, had borne him no children. But she had an Egyptian maidservant named Hagar; so she said to Abram, "The LORD has kept me from having children. Go sleep with my maidservant; perhaps I can build a family through her.'

"Abram agreed to what Sarai said. So after Abram had been living in Canaan ten years, Sarai his wife took her Egyptian maidservant Hagar and gave her to her husband to be his wife. He slept with Hagar, and she conceived."

Sarah realized she was barren even though God had promised to make Abraham's family great. So, Sarah decided to play god and persuaded her husband to become a polygamist. Cringe.

She believed in God's promise, but it just. wasn't. coming. soon. enough.

Does anyone wish they could have called up Sarah and said, "Friend, bring this crazy train to a halt!"? Yikes.

But is it *really* unlike our own faithless behavior?

In our gender-bender, sexually-liberated culture, we may struggle to see why polygamy is much of a problem. Multiple partners and serial marriage are commonplace in our day, as was polygamy in Sarah's. If you recall our lesson yesterday Abimelek collected wives like coins (Genesis 20:17). How is the culture of Abimelek's land described by Abraham in Genesis 20:11?

God had not designed marriage to be like this. God had created marriage to be one man and one woman, as recorded in the creation story where *"two shall become one flesh."* Sarah's plan didn't follow God's way.

We see the disastrous effects of polygamy as it passes down the family line in Abraham and Sarah's grandson Jacob, and in the lives of their descendants: Kings David and Solomon. These men's sins ranged from family-destroying **favoritism** to **murder** to **idolatry**—all as a result of their polygamous lifestyle.

Have you rushed God's plans for your life, or tried to do things your own way rather than waiting on God's way? Or do you remember a season of waiting that you endured?

God's timetable doesn't look anything like our own.

He slept with Hagar, and she conceived. When she knew she was pregnant, she began to despise her mistress. 5 Then Sarai said to Abram, "You are responsible for the wrong I am suffering. I put my slave in your arms, and now that she knows she is pregnant, she despises me. May the Lord judge between you and me." 6 "Your slave is in your hands," Abram said. "Do with her whatever you think best." Then Sarai mistreated Hagar; so she fled from her.

GENESIS 16:4-6

Waiting is so difficult.

I remember early in our marriage waiting for a career change for my husband. He had gotten a Social Work job habilitating adults with disabilities. There were things he loved about the job—the hours were wonderful and the patients were great to work with—but there was also this feeling in the pit of John's stomach that something wasn't right. God was calling him to be a pastor.

Surrendering to the call and following God meant surely He'd quickly place John in the right church, right? Wrong.

It took two long years of traveling the country and seeking the Lord to finally find the church God was calling us to serve. God's timetable didn't look anything like our own.

Sarah's Plan

While polygamy may have been a common practice in Sarah's day, Abraham was the first recorded righteous man to take more than one wife, thanks to Sarah's not-so-bright idea. What a horrible tradition to start! Sarah's plan backfired almost immediately because as soon as Hagar realized that she was pregnant, her relationship with Sarah was destroyed.

Read the account for yourself in Genesis 16:4-6, in the margin—noticing Sarah's words to Abraham. Underline the words that reveal who she blamed for her bad situation.

Sarah forced her maid to sleep with her husband, then shrewishly chewed Abraham out when he went along with her plan. Can we say emotionally unstable?!

At this point, a bewildered Abraham threw his hands up and said, in effect, "whatever you want, honey" and Sarah added "abuse of a maidservant" to her growing list of sins: impatience, faithlessness, manipulation, deceit, and false accusations—to name a few.

As if introducing destructive polygamous practices to her family wasn't an awful enough result of Sarah's plan—there was more. Rushing God's plan had huge consequences. According to Genesis 16:12, what would Abraham and Hagar's son be like? (Choose every correct answer):

> He will be a wild donkey of a man; his hand will be against everyone and everyone's hand against him, and he will live in hostility toward all his brothers."
>
> GENESIS 16:12

    a.) He would live in hostility toward all his brothers
    b.) He would have strong faith like his father
    c.) He would be a wild donkey of a man
    d.) His hand will be against everyone and vice versa

Ishmael, the child born to Hagar and Abraham resulting from Sarah's plan, was not the one through which God would choose to fulfill his promises to Abraham. He too would become a "great nation," but there would be unrest in the land among Ishmael's descendants and everyone around them. Things were royally messed up.

Let's not be naïve enough to think that forcing our plans instead of waiting on God's is without consequence. Pushing our plans is a slippery slope to disaster.

What consequences have you seen in your life or in the lives of your friends that have failed to wait on God's timing?

Pushing our plans is a slippery slope to disaster.

Sometimes we share Sarah's eager anticipation. We are excited to see God fulfill his promises in our lives, but not patient enough to wait for Him. Like Veruca Salt from Charlie and the Chocolate Factory, we want it NOW! We are going to do things *our* way, not God's. We try to force God's plans to match our own instead of willingly placing our lives in His hands.

When my sweet niece was about three years old, she decided she needed some grape juice. Never mind that her mama said now was not the time for grape juice. Never mind that the grape juice was still a frozen concentrate in the freezer at the top of the fridge—this little missy was determined. No waiting for mama's timing, she'd have it now.

So, she pulled a chair up to the fridge and climbed precariously up to reach the juice, unbeknownst to her mother.

Little fingers digging around where they weren't supposed to soon led to frozen grape juice concentrate crashing down on little toes, bruising her big toenail purple to match the juice. After many tears, she was comforted. But that purple toenail reminded her of her foolishness for weeks to come.

She'd remember to wait for the juice.

What are the situations in your life right now in which God might be calling you to show patience? What plans of yours might you need to stop in order to let God work in His timing? Write about it here, or draw a quick sketch that represents the situation.

> Perhaps you're trying with all your might to change a situation that God wants you to leave to Him. Stop now.

Maybe there's a person you want to change. You know they're not living like they should and you're tempted to help God out by nagging and grumping at them until they shape up.

Or it could be some difficult circumstances that don't suit you at work. Perhaps you're trying with all your might to change a situation that God wants you to leave to Him. Stop now—before you have a disaster on your hands.

Don't give up on Sarah yet—God surely didn't. While she may seem like a lost cause at this point, her story with God doesn't end here. Stay tuned for tomorrow's lesson and you'll be reminded that God can take a situation that seems messed up and hopeless, like Sarah's, and work his amazing plans.

> Sometimes God calls us to wait
> instead of taking matters into our own hands.

Share a simple prayer time with the Lord:

- Thank God for his plans and offer up your own to him.
- Ask for the wisdom to believe God's plan for your life, despite any impatience that you may be experiencing.
- Pray that God would continue to teach you how to wait on him.

Truth Takeaway–*"Wait for the Lord; be strong and take heart and wait for the Lord." Psalm 27:14*

DAY 5: LAUGHTER, THE BEST MEDICINE

"This is how the holy women of old made themselves beautiful. They put their trust in God..." 1 Peter 3:5a NLT

Old and Worn Out

Sarah and Abraham started off strong, leaving behind their hometown to follow God's call. They believed and obeyed God, heading out into lands they didn't know.

But their stellar beginning didn't last. Soon fear would overcome Abraham. He dishonored the God he once trusted by deceiving (and asking Sarah to deceive) the powerful, evil men they encountered. But God's protection and blessing proved steady even when Abraham and Sarah faltered.

MAIN TEXTS
Genesis 17:15-18:15
Genesis 21:1-7
1 Peter 3:1-6

God's protection and blessing proved steady even when Abraham and Sarah faltered.

> Then Abraham bowed down to the ground, but he laughed to himself in disbelief. "How could I become a father at the age of 100?" he thought. "And how can Sarah have a baby when she is ninety years old?" 18 So Abraham said to God, "May Ishmael live under your special blessing!" 19 But God replied, "No—Sarah, your wife, will give birth to a son for you. You will name him Isaac and I will confirm my covenant with him and his descendants as an everlasting covenant.
>
> GENESIS 17:17-19

God makes good on His promises.

Next it would be Sarah's turn to lead the couple's misstep. When God wasn't giving their promised offspring according to Sarah's expectations, she put family-planning on the fast track by talking Abraham into her polygamous plan.

Deceptive, fearful, worried, faithless, abusive...Sarah's life had been characterized by these bad behaviors. But God wasn't done with her yet.

After the whole mess with Hagar, God *still* wanted to use Sarah to carry out his plan. He said to Abraham in Genesis 17:15 "*As for Sarah...I will bless **her** and will surely give you a son **by her**. I will bless **her** so that **she will be the mother of nations**; kings of peoples will come **from her**.*" (emphasis mine)

This seemed just too good to be true. What was Abraham's reaction in Genesis 17:17-18?

What was God's response to Abraham in verse 19?

There wasn't any room for confusion this time. God spelled it out plainly for Abraham—the promises he'd made for Abraham's descendants would come to fruition through his and Sarah's yet-to-be-born son Isaac, which means "he laughs."

The Happy Ending—A Bundle of Joy

And guess what happened? Sarah had a baby. When the *only* possible way for her to conceive was a miraculous intervention by God—God gave Sarah her promised son. God makes good on his promises.

Sarah was old (Genesis 18:12). She had struggled with infertility during her younger days, but by this time she was no longer in her fertile years. That ship had sailed. In the NLT Genesis 18:11

says, "Sarah was *long past* the age of having children." Sarah's pregnancy was not some coincidence—it was a *miracle*.

Abraham (in Genesis 17:17) and Sarah (in Genesis 18:12) had both laughed in disbelief that God would actually give them their promised child. Now they held this special son, laughing with joy!

Read Genesis 21 in the margin. According to this passage, what did the Lord do for Sarah? Underline your answer.

God's dependability and trustworthiness can be contrasted to Sarah's behavior. When she overheard the angelic visitors telling Abraham she'd have a son, she had laughed. And when confronted about it, she had lied (Genesis 18:15).

Sarah lied.

God kept His promise.

God took Sarah's fear and disbelief and doubt, and he replaced it with a warm wiggling bundle of promises fulfilled—a sweet little bundle of joy.

But the joy Sarah experienced wasn't just the joy of motherhood. It wasn't about finally getting her way, and giving birth. The **joy she experienced was the joy of being part of God's bigger plan**—of being smack dab where God wanted her to be. She was fulfilling God's purpose for her as matriarch of his family.

> Now the LORD was gracious to Sarah as he had said, and the LORD **did for Sarah what he had promised**. Sarah became pregnant and bore a son to Abraham in his old age…. Abraham gave the name Isaac to the son Sarah bore him…Sarah said, "God has brought me laughter and everyone who hears about this will laugh with me."
> GENESIS 21:1-6

An Unlikely Legacy

With all of Sarah's missteps and mistakes, it's hard to know why God chose her to be the first mother in the family that would beget the Savior of the world. But what we *do* know is that God used her despite it all—and He can use us too.

Even though Genesis paints Sarah's life as filled with deception, manipulation, abuse, doubt and fear, the rest of scripture is speckled with praise for Sarah. In her legacy we *all* find hope.

Sarah wasn't just a mother for the Jewish nation, she's our mother too. Galatians 4 explains that Hagar and her children

> look to Abraham, your father, and **to Sarah**, who gave you birth. When I called him he was only one man, and I blessed him and made him many.
>
> ISAIAH 51:2

represent those bound by the law, trying to live by their works and their own effort, but those of us that choose salvation through Christ are Sarah's children—free. *"But his son by the free woman was born as the result of a divine promise...The women represent two covenants. One covenant is from Mount Sinai and bears children who are to be slaves: This is Hagar...Now you, brothers and sisters, like Isaac, are children of promise...Therefore, brothers and sisters, we are not children of the slave woman, but of the free woman. It is for freedom that Christ has set us free." Galatians 4:23-24,28,31, 5:1).*

Sarah's Daughters

Don't be confused about God's chosen people, Israel—this incredibly special family descended from Sarah. God had chosen His people for His purposes. Number each of the special purposes pointed out by Romans 9:4-5 in the margin. (I found eight—just in those verses.)

I know what you're thinking: what a cool and awesome thing...for them. Do you feel like the invisible step-child yet? The neighbor kid that just doesn't quite fit in to the family? Those of us that are Gentiles (non-Jewish) ethnicity might be feeling a little left out by now. Those of us "non-chosen" ones—but wait.

In Christ, we are Sarah's daughters. Romans 9 goes on to explain that it is not enough to be Jewish by race, one must choose faith in God. Verses 6-7 say, *"for not all who are descended from Israel are Israel. Nor because they are his descendants are they all Abraham's children."*

We aren't left out! When we choose God, we become chosen ones. Sarah wasn't a follower of God just because He chose her, she was a follower of God because *she chose him.* She may have lied, feared, abused and manipulated, but ultimately, she submitted to God's plan, placing her life in His hands and following His lead.

And we are her daughters when we do the same. Paul explains, *"it is not the children by physical descent who are God's children, but it is the **children of the promise** who are regarded as*

Theirs is the **adoption to sonship**; theirs the **divine glory**, the **covenants**, the **receiving of the law**, the **temple worship** and the **promises**. Theirs are the **patriarchs**, and from them is traced the human **ancestry of the Messiah**, who is God over all, forever praised! Amen.

ROMANS 9:4-5

Abraham's offspring," Romans 9:8. Our faith brings us into God's family (Romans 9:30). We are daughters of the promise when we place our lives in our good God's hands.

Ageless Beauty Secrets

If crow's feet and laugh lines are becoming a reality for you like they are for me, you are probably just as interested as I am in knowing the secrets to true beauty. Look no further, Sarah's beauty secrets can be found in 1 Peter 3:1-4 (in margin).

According to the verse 3, what beauty should we *not* be concerned about? Cross it off in the margin.

Anyone else feeling a little convicted about the hours they've spent shopping for just the right outfit or primping in front of the mirror? These aren't wrong, but if they're the *only* way we're cultivating our beauty, then we've got a problem. We've got to be sure we're spending the necessary time and effort cultivating beautiful hearts.

According to verse 4, in what *should* we be clothed? Underline it in the margin.

Now stay with me! I know that if you are anything like me, these verses can make you squirm (me? gentle?! quiet?!)—but hear me out. Let's see this through. 1 Peter 3:5-6 goes on to give two beauty secrets of the "holy women of old." What are they?

1.

2.

 These verses teach that a true beauty puts her trust in God and does right, accepting the authority of her husband.

Okay, I'll just level with you here. I think we both know that this passage raises some hackles. It's pretty counter-cultural to talk about a husband's authority in a society that wants us to shout, "I am woman, hear me roar!" Scripture says some things that aren't always easy to hear.

In the same way, you wives must accept the authority of your husbands. Then, even if some refuse to obey the Good News, your godly lives will speak to them without any words. They will be won over 2 by observing your pure and reverent lives.

3 Don't be concerned about the outward beauty of fancy hairstyles, expensive jewelry, or beautiful clothes. 4 You should clothe yourselves instead with the **beauty that comes from within,** the unfading beauty of a **gentle and quiet spirit,** which is so precious to God.

5 This is how the holy women of old made themselves beautiful. **They put their trust in God** and **accepted the authority of their husbands.** For instance, Sarah obeyed her husband, Abraham, and called him her master. You are her daughters when you do what is right without fear of what your husbands might do.

1 PETER 3:1-6 NLT

Some say that this passage is antiquated and outdated—that it's chauvinistic and sexist, and might as well be used for toilet paper.

At the other extreme, you'd find those that interpret these verses to mean that men are superior and women inferior. Some even use this concept as justification for abuse. Cringe.

I'm guessing you're somewhere in between these extremes, like me.

No scripture should be thrown out. According to 2 Timothy 3:16 it's God-breathed. So, let's press into this potentially-hard teaching, and see what life-giving help we can glean.

We make a mistake when we impose our modern-day culture's understandings onto this passage. We think of a submissive wife as being some sort of weird, non-thinking, robotic, Stepford wife. We feel like submitting means a harsh, punitive husband that lords it over his wife, and a woman who can't think for herself. The word "master" conjures up images of an evil southern slave master cracking his whip.

Let me be the one to say, our husbands don't want some weird, abusive slave/master relationship. And it's not what God had in mind.

John doesn't want me to refer to him as "Lord Risner." That would be really strange. What fun is it to hang out with a brainless person? I don't think many of us enjoy shooting the breeze with Siri or Alexa.

Men want us to be vivacious—to think, feel, and act for ourselves, to have personality and flair. To submit in a Biblical way doesn't mean laying down your God-given personality to become something you're not. This passage isn't talking about the off-putting idea of calling our husbands "Lord" with brainless obedience.

In reality, Biblical submission is about having a beautiful attitude of respect. It's acknowledging that God has called us to treat each other with kindness.

> All Scripture is God-breathed and is useful for teaching, rebuking, correcting and training in righteousness.
>
> 2 TIMOTHY 3:16

Some weird slave/master relationship is not what God had in mind.

When we give our husbands, our bosses, the law enforcement, the church leaders, even our president the proper respect we acknowledge our faith in our sovereign God. After all, He's the one who put things in place. We can "do what is right without fear" (verse 6), because our good God has instructed us to respect those over us—and following God's call is always the right move. No matter whether we're women who are married, widowed, single, or divorced we can show the inner beauty of faith in God and respect for others.

It's easier said than done, though.

I doubt I'm the only one who has noticed a lack of respect in our culture. Acting ugly isn't uncommon. And it's not just temper-tantrum-throwing toddlers and hormonal teens. It's women like me.

I never saw it coming, but I can be a woman of such disdain. Back when we were engaged, I was a doe-eyed girl who thought the world of her beau. Now, I'm embarrassed to admit, sometimes I look down on my husband when he doesn't do things like I would.

Like not asking the clerk in the hardware store to help him find the pet birdseed so he brings home wild birdseed instead of parakeet feed. Not a big deal. So why did I have such an ugly spirit about it? Why would I be condescending to the human I love most?

Or how about when a government leader seems to make a bonehead move. Why would I be tempted to make a snarky remark about her when I could use my words to lift her up in prayer instead?

Or what about when that ministry leader isn't making the decisions I think are best? Why do I feel like grumbling instead of writing a note of encouragement, thanking him for his heart to serve? Do you see how my lack of respect makes for inner ugliness?

> Biblical submission is about having an attitude of respect...it's a display of our faith in God.

The enemy knows the power of respectful Christian women to foil his plans—and so he wields the nasty weapon of our lack of respect. He really knows how to bait us. And I don't know about you, but all too often I go along with his plans and have a stony heart of contempt. But thankfully, we don't have to comply with the enemy's tactics.

When we're tempted to look down on our husbands for messing something up, let's be understanding. When we're tempted to treat men in our life with disdain for being unable to do something that comes easily to us, let's give grace. When those we're supposed to respect seem anything but worthy, let's call on God's help to show true inner beauty of a peaceful, quiet (because of trust in God) spirit of respect. Why? Because they deserve it? No. Because God commands it, and our obedience to Him brings Him glory.

That's true beauty. That's doing right without fear. It's letting go of the old, ugly, fleshly way, and clinging to our good God's plans for how to do life. That's the way to live as Sarah's daughters.

I get it. Respecting authority can be uncomfortable and downright unpleasant. But hear me in this: God knows what he's doing. He doesn't play games with us. He *knows* that this can be a scary thing for us (revisit 1 Peter 3:6). That's why all of this godly-woman stuff hinges on *trusting Him* (1 Peter 3:5).

> Please note that **abuse is NOT condoned or endorsed by the Bible**. If you are in an abusive situation, reach out right now for help from a friend or pastor. For more important things to remember, see "But what if my husband mistreats me?" at the end of this chapter.

Do we believe God's goodness enough to release control to him? To do what he says instead of what we want? I pray we do.

In the past what unbecoming attitudes or behaviors have you shown to your husband, if you are married, or to others you should have respected? (You know my birdseed story—cringe!

Our obedience brings God glory.

However, each one of you also must love his wife as he loves himself, and the wife must **respect** her husband.

EPHESIANS 5:33

Now it's your turn.) How might your behaviors or attitudes need to change to reflect the inner beauty God desires? (be specific)

Don't be discouraged if thus far your life has not followed God's inner beauty regimen. For crying out loud, look at Sarah! She followed Abraham into sin when she shouldn't have (Genesis 20:5) and manipulated Abraham into her horrible Hagar plan when she became impatient with God (Genesis 16: 1-4), then sassed Abraham up one side and down the other for the whole thing (Genesis 16:5). What a hot mess!

And yet, she eventually got it. After all she and Abraham had been through, she understood God's plan for her, and willingly, gladly accepted it. She learned to trust God and to show respect to her husband. She experienced the freedom of forgiveness for her past and the hope of a future with a good God. And what a bright future it was! So bright that the light of salvation would shine from Sarah's family for all mankind.

> A woman of true beauty trusts the Lord enough to let go of her own way of doing things, and lives with an attitude of respect for others, instead of disdain.

Share a simple prayer time with the Lord:

- Thank God for redemption, and second chances. Thank Him for His desire to use you, no matter how much you have failed.
- Ask for the steadfastness to trust God and to respect others, despite any fears or uncertainties that you may be experiencing

"But what if my husband mistreats me?" and other hard questions

Life isn't always a bed of roses, and our marriages are no exception. Marriages provide an opportunity for blessing, but also for difficulty. When we study the roles of husbands and wives there are a few important things to remember:

❖ Abuse by either partner is **not** condoned, nor endorsed by the Bible
❖ Roles of authority within marriage **do not** imply a hierarchy in value—neither spouse is better than the other; both are precious in God's eyes
❖ God calls husbands to love wives as Christ loves the church— willing to sacrifice even his very life for her
❖ God allows for divorce in some situations
❖ There will be times when couples mistreat one another. This is a chance to extend the love of Christ, even in the case of an unbelieving spouse. See 1 Corinthians 7:10-16).

If you are in a difficult situation in your marriage don't go it alone. Get help!

- Pray that He would continue to clearly reveal to you how to faithfully follow His plan for your life.

Takeaway Truth—*"You are her daughters if you do what is right and do not give way to fear." 1 Peter 3:6*

A Tangible Reminder—Choose a symbol of beauty—perhaps an old lipstick tube, a bracelet, or a makeup brush—and put it somewhere where you will see it throughout the rest of the week. When you see it, be reminded of Sarah's real beauty—that of her quiet, trusting spirit. Remember that despite the many (many!) failures in Sarah's life, God worked in her heart and in her life, and brought beauty from her mess. As you see your reminder, pray that God would cultivate a beautiful spirit within you. If you are willing, share a pic of your object and what it means to you on social media with the hashtags: #significantwomenofthebible #stonesofremembrance. Or record about the experience in the back of this book.

Pause for Praise—Whew! We've come a long way in our study this first week. You have done a great job of digging into scripture to see what we can learn from Sarah's story about being *Significant*—that God makes beauty from our mess. Before you wrap up your study for this week, take a few moments to praise our awesome God. I suggest you find the music video for Gungor's *Beautiful Things* on YouTube and watch with a worshipful heart. If you are a more traditional gal, try *Amazing Grace*.

God brings beauty from our mess

LEAH

Unlovely , but Loved

Significant

DAY ONE: DADDY'S BAIT-N-SWITCH

FOLLOW THE GENEALOGICAL ROAD

Matthew's genealogy of Jesus tells us which women of the Bible can be traced in Jesus' bloodline. While Leah's name isn't mentioned there, with just a little research, we know she's part of the family. Let's piece it together for ourselves. Circle the men mentioned in Matthew 1:2: *"Abraham was the father of Isaac, Isaac the father of Jacob, Jacob the father of Judah."*

According to the following verse, which of Jacob's two wives was Judah's mother? Circle her name. *"Leah became pregnant and gave birth to another son. She named him Judah..."* GENESIS 29:35 NLT

Since Leah was named as Judah's mother, we know that she was a foremother of Christ.

"I will show love to those I called 'Not loved.'" Hosea 2:23

Facebook feeds, trending Tweets, and Instagram posts keep us hyper-aware of the events and achievements in the lives of our peers. Social media can be used for God's glory as women support and encourage one another. But it can have a tragic effect when we become unduly focused on ourselves, trapped by pride or low self-esteem. Can you relate?

I know that I can get discouraged when it seems like everyone's home is perfectly neat and tidy and trendy in their pictures online. Then I look around at my home and see the crumbs, fingerprints, dust bunnies, and honey oak trim. There's nothing wrong with my home—it's actually really wonderful—but there's something about the picture-perfect images I see online that can make me feel miserable about my homemaking skills.

This problem isn't new—Satan has been tempting us to play this comparison game for generations. This sinful tendency goes way back to the first book of the Bible—to Leah and Rachel. In Genesis we learn about these two sisters: one who lived in misery because she compared herself with her sister, and one who looked to God and found that his love was all she ever needed.

Leah Comes on the Scene

Last week we learned about Sarah and Abraham and the amazing way God showed himself faithful to them in the birth of their son Isaac. Now we are going to fast-forward two generations down the same family line. God's promise continued as he granted Isaac and his wife Rebekah twin sons, Jacob and Esau.

Unfortunately, Jacob made some bad choices. He had lived up to his name, which meant "deceiver" and tricked both his father and infuriated brother. Jacob fled for his life. But God wasn't done with this trickster yet. In Genesis 28:13-15 God spoke to

Jacob in a dream. Read his amazing promise to Jacob in the margin.

Sound familiar? God's same promise to Abraham, echoed two generations further down the family line. God promised that through Jacob—this deceiver, this fugitive—amazing things would happen and the whole world would be blessed. But Jacob is not the only character we will read about today—today we will learn about Jacob's wives and how he came to marry them. Give them a reality TV show because they were literally "Sister Wives," Rachel and Leah.

We meet them in Genesis 29, when Jacob came to stay with their father, his uncle Laban. Read verses 16-18 and record the details about Laban's two daughters below:

Leah—

Rachel—

This hardly seems fair, right?

I know that I can be quick to proclaim, "It's not fair!" when God seems to have dealt out the blessings unevenly. Just like my kids want to make sure each brownie in the pan is the same size, we want our lives to measure up to everyone else's. When our income doesn't match our co-workers'; when we have to shoulder more household responsibilities than our spouse; when everything comes easy to our siblings; when our talents aren't the same as our peers—in all these situations it can seem like we're getting a raw deal. Life seems unfair. But God is in control.

So here we have two sisters: Leah, the older daughter with weak eyes, and Rachel, the younger who was lovely and beautiful. Jacob didn't take long to decide that it was Rachel he was going to pursue, and pursue he did. He promised seven years of hard work for the chance to marry Rachel.

Jacob's Unlikely Labor of Love

Manual labor was Jacob's payment in exchange for the chance to marry his dream girl. This was uncharacteristic for Jacob, the deceiver, who was accustomed to using shadier tactics to get what he wanted. While his brother Esau was the quintessential

"I am the Lord, the God of your father Abraham and the God of Isaac. I will give you and your descendants the land on which you are lying. 14 Your descendants will be like the dust of the earth, and you will spread out to the west and to the east, to the north and to the south. All peoples on earth will be blessed through you and your offspring. 15 I am with you and will watch over you wherever you go, and I will bring you back to this land. I will not leave you until I have done what I have promised you."

GENESIS 28:13-15

Life seems unfair. But God is in control.

hairy, manly hunter, Genesis 25:27 refers to Jacob as something quite the opposite.

How does Genesis 25:27 describe Jacob?

Esau spent his days adventuring in the wild and killing beasts, but Jacob was known for cooking stew and hanging out with his mama. And Rebekah had taught him that deceit, not hard work, was the way to get what you want.

So, Jacob's offer of seven years of honest, hard work for Rachel's hand in marriage testified to how head-over-heels he was for her. It also spoke to his life-changing encounter with God. On his way to Paddan-Aram, Rachel and Leah's hometown, Jacob had made a vow to God. Unlike his forefathers who *responded* to God, Jacob's vow is the first recorded instance of man *taking initiative* in his relationship with God. He declared his trust in God and God's promises in Genesis 28:20-22. Underline Jacob's pledge in the margin:

Jacob wasn't giving God an ultimatum—he was counting on God to do these things. This was a proclamation of faith, and a promise to give God a rightful share of all that Jacob acquired.

And did you catch verse 20 of Genesis 29? Take a quick peek at it now. It sounds like it is straight out of a romantic book, *"So Jacob served seven years to get Rachel, but they seemed like only a few days to him because of his love for her."*

Does this line make you melt a little inside for Rachel?

Jacob was devoted. Not only had he left his deceitful ways behind him, but he was *glad* to work hard in order to marry his true love. Sounds like this was just about the right time for a "happily ever after" fairy tale ending, right? But those of you who know this story well, know that it was about to go more the direction of a daytime soap opera rather than a fairy tale. Jacob was about to get a taste of his own medicine.

Deceiver is Deceived—Daddy's Dirty Trick

After the seven years were up, it was time for the wedding feast. Jacob was elated to finally marry his dream bride. The only catch was that his new father-in-law Laban wasn't ready to marry off Rachel after all. You see, there was the problem of Leah. It was only proper to give Leah, the older daughter, in marriage first (or so Laban said)—but no one wanted her.

Leah wasn't lovely and beautiful like Rachel. Something was wrong with her eyes—they were either not working properly or just plain ugly. According to the Cambridge Bible for Schools and Colleges, "the eye was the chief feature of Oriental beauty." Leah was clearly flawed, and her father wasn't about to break tradition for her sake. So, in Laban's mind, the best thing to do was pull a switcheroo and trick Jacob into marrying Leah. And that's exactly what he did.

How would it make you feel if neither your father nor your husband seemed to want you? Have you been in a similar situation with a spouse, co-worker, neighbor or friend?

> Leah was clearly flawed and her father wasn't about to break tradition for her sake.

Maybe it's easy for you to think of an instance of rejection. Maybe not. I think of the classic schoolyard pick rejection I suffered as a kid.

Red Rover was the game of choice at my elementary school during recess and gym class—the game where two lines of children face each other, holding hands, and dare someone from the opposite team to try to run through their line, breaking apart their team. If you succeeded, you took one of their team members back with you and your team grew. If you couldn't break through, you were forced to join their team—and suffer some humiliation while at it. It's a great game for strong, burly kids. But for a runty kid like me, it was a clotheslining and a concussion waiting to happen.

So, when it was time to pick teams, you can guess who was picked last—me. It felt pretty crummy. But if that's what it feels like to be rejected by your friends, how much worse must Leah have felt being rejected by her family. That must sting.

Jacob was distraught and disappointed to be married to Leah, instead of Rachel. Laban, being the crafty man that he was, decided that the perfect solution was to have Jacob marry *both* daughters, as long as Jacob was willing to work *another* seven years to marry the second. Jacob, so desperately in love with Rachel, quickly agreed.

Jacob had two wives—the unlovely and unloved older sister Leah, and the gorgeous, sought-after younger sister Rachel. As the lives of these women unfold throughout this week of study, we will see in one sister an example of how *not* to behave in relationships with other women, and in the other how *to* respond to the love of our God.

I will show love to those I called "Not loved."
HOSEA 2:23

Reread Hosea 2:23 from the beginning of this lesson and Jeremiah 31:3 (both are in the margin). What would it look like for you to live today confident in these truths? How would rejection from others feel different if you truly believed these verses? Meditate on these questions as you copy one of these verses below. Take your time and use fancy handwriting, if you're artsy. Use the time you spend copying the verse as a special time with the Lord. If you're willing, snap a pic when you're done, and share with someone who might need a boost.

I have loved you with an everlasting love.
JEREMIAH 31:3

you are precious and honored in my sight, … I love you

ISAIAH 43:4

If you happen to be in the midst of a situation right now where you're feeling the sting of rejection, copy these verses (Hosea 2:23, Jeremiah 31:3, and any others that encourage you) onto notecards and place them in prominent places—like your bathroom mirror, your car's dashboard, on the fridge, your desk at work—to help you stand on the truth that you that you are loved.

Basking in the security of God's love helps me when I am feeling hurt by others. When I am criticized, I have a tendency to retreat like an injured animal and lick my wounds. In those situations, I am swept over with feelings of self-pity. But feeding on God's truths in His precious word helps me to realize that what others think of me and how they treat me isn't the be all and end all. God's got me—and what He thinks of me is the most important opinion of all.

> Rejection stings, but I can hold on to the fact that in God's eyes I am loved.

Share a simple prayer time with the Lord:

- Thank God for His love and acceptance, no matter how others treat you.
- Ask for his strength and resolve to handle whatever comes your way.
- Pray that he would continue to sustain you and reveal His truth to you.

Takeaway Truth– *"I have loved you with an everlasting love."* Jeremiah 31:3

DAY TWO: SISTER WIVES' DRAMA

MAIN TEXTS
Genesis 29:22-31
Genesis 16:7-13

"He was despised and rejected by mankind, a man of suffering, and familiar with pain." Isaiah 53:3

Often the way others see us doesn't match up with how we see ourselves. People treat us according to their perceptions.

My husband isn't the svelte athlete he used to be in his younger years (if you know him, don't laugh too hard that I used the word "svelte" there). He knows that he has room for improvement in his fitness level, but still has a tendency to see himself as an athlete. Running is his way of getting into better shape.

WHERE IN THE WORLD ARE WE?

In the first week of our study, we didn't really stop and discuss this, but when God called Abraham's family out of Ur, there were more than just Abraham and Sarah that went, initially. Abraham's father Terah and his nephew Lot left Ur also, and settled in a place called Harran—a pit stop on the way to God's Promised Land.

Genesis 11:31-32 says, *"Terah took his son Abram...to go to Canaan. But when they came to Harran, they settled there."*

After Abraham's dad Terah passed on, God called Abraham to continue on, to Canaan (see Genesis 12:1-4). On the run from Esau, Jacob found himself in the land his grandfather once left, Harran.

In Genesis 29:4 the shepherds told Jacob they were from Harran when he arrived at the well where he met Rachel.

Harran was where Rebekah was raised, where Leah and Rachel grew up, and where they made their home with Jacob.

While out for a jog, a woman who was walking applauded him, "great job!"

What was meant as encouragement became a watershed moment. Suddenly, he realized he looked more like a couch potato needing a cheerleader rather than an elite athlete that you'd expect to be out for a jog. It was a funny example of something that can be much more hurtful—when others treat us a certain way based on how they see us.

We left Leah yesterday in the unenviable spot of being unwanted. Her defect of "weak eyes" made her so undesirable that her father resorted to trickery to get rid of her, and her husband was nothing but disappointed upon their marriage. Ouch. Rejection stings.

> He was despised and rejected by mankind, a man of suffering, and familiar with pain.
>
> ISAIAH 53:3

Perhaps you have felt the sting of rejection, just like Leah. It hurts when others push us away, when they don't want us, or care about us. But we are not alone in our times of pain—Christ himself knows the pain of rejection. Read the prophetic description of Jesus offered in Isaiah 53:3 in the margin. Circle the ways Jesus was treated, and how he is described.

How does the knowledge that Christ suffered rejection console you when you're feeling pushed away or excluded?

God may not take away our pain, but… he walks with us through it.

Some of the ways that God has called my family to live are countercultural. My husband and I have a larger family. Having seven kids has been one of the greatest joys of my life. But it's not something everyone understands.

When my children and I are out in public together we get plenty of sideways stares—sometimes even rude comments. Since others don't have the same calling, they sometimes feel like they should oppose us. But when I feel hurt or discouraged by others' reactions, remembering how Christ was treated puts things in perspective. He suffered so much more—surely I can endure a few unkind remarks and gawking glares.

We are not alone in our rejection. God is with us. God may not take away our pain, but He knows what it is to suffer greatly, and He walks with us through it. Unfortunately, Leah had not yet fully learned this lesson.

The Honeymoon that Never Was

A honeymoon is supposed to be a sweet time of love, one when husband and wife—giddy with excitement—have overwhelming joy in their marriage. But, for Leah, the honeymoon was over before it had even begun.

We don't know the behind-the-scenes of Leah and Jacob's wedding—whether or not Leah was privy to her father's plans—but we do know that her marriage started off on the wrong foot. Jacob didn't want her. Did Leah know that Jacob thought she was Rachel? Did she know the disappointment Jacob would feel the morning after their wedding night, upon finding he had married Leah instead? We just don't know. But we do know that, the morning after Leah's wedding, a debacle ensued.

Jacob had consummated his marriage with Leah the night before, and now he was hopping mad at his trickster father-in-law. Read the account in Genesis 29:25-30 in the margin:

So the problematic tradition of polygamy passed down the Abrahamic family line. Remember the Sarah and Hagar disaster—the abuse, and the animosity between the descendants of Isaac and Ishmael? Sarah's generation saw some major problems, but the disastrous domino effect of following the practice of polygamy wouldn't stop there.

The problems with the Jacob's generation of polygamy would rival Abraham's—from favoritism to major family factions to the fallout they both brought upon Jacob's family. Jacob's marriages to sisters Leah and Rachel would be fertile ground for

When morning came, **there was Leah!** So Jacob said to Laban, "What is this you have done to me? I served you for Rachel, didn't I? **Why have you deceived me?"** Laban replied, "It is not our custom here to give the younger daughter in marriage before the older one. Finish this daughter's bridal week; then **we will give you the younger one also,** in return for another seven years of work." And Jacob did so. He finished the week with Leah, and then Laban gave him his daughter Rachel to be his wife. Laban gave his servant Bilhah to his daughter Rachel as her attendant. Jacob made love to Rachel also, and **his love for Rachel was greater than his love for Leah.** And he worked for Laban another seven years.

GENESIS 29:25-30

³⁰ So Jacob slept with Rachel, too, and he loved her much more than Leah. He then stayed and worked for Laban the additional seven years. ³¹ When the Lord saw that Leah was unloved, he enabled her to have children, but Rachel could not conceive.

GENESIS 29:30-31
NLT

When people treat us badly, and our situation seems hopeless and lonely, God sees us.

family problems to grow, with dire consequences. The generational drama continued.

Seen by God

It was bad enough that Rachel was so beautiful—and Leah undesirable—but to add insult to injury, Jacob was playing favorites. Reread Genesis 29:30 in the margin. Notice that says that Jacob loved Rachel more than Leah—some versions say, "much more."

But God saw Leah. The woman with weak eyes wouldn't be unseen by Her God.

Review the basic facts of this story with a quick True/False quiz:

T or F –God favored Rachel over Leah

T or F –Rachel struggled with infertility

T or F –Leah was unloved by Jacob

T or F –God made Leah unable to bear children   (Answers: F,T,T,F)

God saw Leah. Her suffering was not hidden from His eyes, and He took action on her behalf. When people treat us badly, and our situation seems hopeless and lonely, God sees us. He cares.

A few generations earlier, God had similarly seen a marginalized woman, and blessed her with the ability to have children. This may seem like an odd detour since we just studied Sarah last week, but looking more closely at God's relationship with Sarah's maidservant Hagar will shed light on His relationship with Leah.

In Genesis 16 Sarah, in her jealous rage, had abused Hagar so maliciously that Hagar had decided to run away. Desperate and alone, Hagar had come to a spring in the desert, where the angel of the Lord found her. Eavesdrop on their conversation in Genesis 16, in verses 7-13. Read the passage in the margin and answer the questions below:

In verse 13, what name does Hagar give God?

How does God bless Hagar in response to her suffering? (verses 10-11)

How would Ishmael's name remind Hagar of God's attention to her suffering (see your Bible's footnotes for verse 11, or the parentheses in verse 11 in the margin)?

Just like God saw Hagar and Leah, God hears our cry and sees us in our suffering.

Take a moment sometime today to write on your bathroom mirror Hagar's words from Genesis 16:13, "You are the God who sees me" using a dry-erase marker. This week, as you see yourself in your mirror, be reminded that you are never alone. God knows your troubles—God sees you.

Over the years my husband has struggled with severe back pain. Often it would flare up in debilitating ways at the worst timing. I remember once when I was only a few weeks postpartum, and he was laid up on the floor, unable to function without excruciating pain. I needed to care for him, our four small children (one of them a newborn), and bear the burden of running our household all by myself. We didn't have family nearby. I remember crying out to God with the weight of it all—how could I possibly manage?

But of course, the God who sees me came through in big ways. Before I knew it, the lawn was being mowed, meals were brought in, and the flowerbeds were being weeded and mulched. A huge weight was lifted off of my shoulders. God had seen me.

As you reflect on your life, what is the evidence of God's closeness—that He sees you? Write a short post on social media today, or share with a friend the evidence of God's attentiveness in your life. Add it to your altars of remembrance

The angel of the Lord found Hagar near a spring in the desert... 8 And he said, "Hagar, slave of Sarai, where have you come from, and where are you going?" "I'm running away from my mistress Sarai," she answered. 9 Then the angel of the Lord told her..."I will increase your descendants so much that they will be too numerous to count." 11 The angel of the Lord also said to her: "You are now pregnant and you will give birth to a son. You shall name him Ishmael (God hears) for the Lord has heard of your misery..."13 She gave this name to the Lord who spoke to her: "You are the God who sees me," for she said, "I have now seen the One who sees me." GENESIS 16:7-13

"You are **the God who sees me**"

by tagging it with #significantwomenofthebible online, or jot down some of your thoughts in the Significant Encounters with God section at the back of this book.

Psalm 34:18 says, *"The Lord is close to the brokenhearted and saves those who are crushed in spirit."* And not only does he save us—in his goodness, he blesses us too.

God blessed Hagar and Leah by making them fruitful. Hagar's descendants would be too many to count (Gen. 16:10). Leah would bear children, while Rachel remained barren (Gen. 29:31).

Children are a gift from the Lord; they are a reward from him.

PSALM 127:3 NLT

Living in our modern culture, we do not appreciate the windfall of a blessing that children would have been to these women. While children tend to be devalued as a burden and a hassle today, scripture calls them a reward. Now we think of mouths to feed and bodies to clothe, but women of Bible times knew that motherhood meant a chance for a better future. Hagar and Leah would have known this to be true. Motherhood was more than a blessing to women of their day—it was practical in purpose, assuring them value and security.

Even the most godless of men would have valued a woman that could produce offspring. In the days before IRAs and Social Security, having children meant a stable future. Children and grandchildren cared for their mothers. The blessing of children would have been profound for women in Hagar and Leah's day.

God had seen the weak-eyed woman. He'd seen the outcast on the fringes. The same God that saw Leah, that blessed Hagar, still loves and leads us today.

> We are seen by a God who knows
> pain and suffering firsthand, and cares for us.

Share a simple prayer time with the Lord:

- Thank God for His attentiveness—that he is the God who sees you both in the big and small circumstances of your life.
- Ask for eyes to see the ways that He is blessing you.

- Pray that He would draw close to you when you feel rejected.

Takeaway Truth–*"The eyes of the Lord are on the righteous, and his ears are attentive to their cry." Psalm 34:15*

DAY THREE: THREE STRIKES, SHE'S OUT

MAIN TEXT
Genesis 29:31-35
(including footnotes)
Judges 6:11-27, 36-40

"You are precious in my eyes, and honored, and I love you."
Isaiah 43:4

Caught in the Comparison Trap, Always Falling Short

Living in the shadows of her stunning younger sister was not easy for Leah. Not only was she the unwanted sister with the defective eyes, but she was stuck being married to the same man as Rachel. Talk about a tough situation.

We are always compared to our siblings—perhaps your sister was a better athlete, or your brother was smarter, or your step-sister always seemed to be the favorite. But for most of us the vying for attention stops when we grow up and move out of our parents' home. Not for Leah—she was stuck in Rachel's shadow, even as a married woman. She was keenly aware of her husband's lack of love.

But, as we learned yesterday, God saw her, and knew her sorrow. And God decided to bless Leah through childbearing. Genesis 29:32 says, *"Leah became pregnant and gave birth to a son. She named him Reuben."* Reuben sounds like "he has seen my misery" and means "see, a son." Leah saw God's hand at work in her life. She acknowledged God's sovereignty in her situation, giving him the glory.

What did Leah foresee happening after she had borne Jacob his first son? (hint, see Genesis 29:32b in the margin)

Leah was keenly aware of her husband's lack of love.

³² Leah became pregnant and gave birth to a son. She named him Reuben, for she said, "It is because the Lord has seen my misery. Surely my husband will love me now."
³³ She conceived again, and when she gave birth to a son she said, "Because the Lord heard that I am not loved, he gave me this one too." So she named him Simeon.
³⁴ Again she conceived, and when she gave birth to a son she said, "Now at last my husband will become attached to me, because I have borne him three sons." So he was named Levi.

GENESIS 29:32-34

Leah's comment shows us her awareness of God's attention to her situation. She knew that God saw her, and attributed the blessing of her son to God's providence. But one thing that Leah didn't quite yet understand is that God had bigger purposes for her life than a sappy love story. Her "surely my husband will love me now" lets us know that her heart still ached for Jacob's love, and she thought God had given her Reuben in order to get Jacob to love her.

Looking for Fulfilling Love in All the Wrong Places

While Leah thought that the romantic attention of her husband Jacob would make her happy, God had another plan—a bigger one. Leah thought that God had blessed her with children in order to win over her husband's love, but little did she know that God had so much more in store for her than the romance of a man.

Her story continued with the birth of another son. Again, she proclaimed God's goodness at her son's birth. See her words in the margin, from Genesis 29:33.

Again, Leah points to God's attentiveness to her situation (good job, Leah). In the naming of this second child, Simeon, which means "one who hears," Leah declared that God was noticing her plight. With Reuben, God had *seen* her and, with Simeon, God had *heard* her. Leah was wise to give credit to God for her success in childbearing. She was trusting in God's provision for her life, even though her marriage was unhappy. *But she still longed for Jacob's love.*

Three Strikes—She's Out!

A third time, Leah conceived and was blessed with the birth of a son. She was still holding on to hope that she would win Jacob's love through childbearing. We heard this in her exclamation after birthing their third son.

Leah named her new son Levi, which sounded like "attached" in her language. She was convinced that surely God had given her these three sons so that her husband would *finally* be head-over-heels for her. She had been waiting years to receive Jacob's love. She had loyally produced precious heirs for Jacob.

But it was not to be.

Leah was right that God had seen her misery; he had heard of her pain. She was right that God had chosen to bless her with three sons. But what she didn't see is why. She wasn't getting the "happily ever after" she expected. Leah felt inferior and rejected and longed for the love of her husband, not realizing that the love she really needed had been there all along.

Levi's birth wouldn't earn Jacob's affections. Leah had borne her husband three sons, but his love for her had not increased.

Though unloved, Leah's legacy through this third son would be great. God would do much more for His people through Leah's son, Levi, than she could have ever anticipated. (See the sidebar—Legendary Levites).

If only…

Leah saw God working in her life, but was still unclear on what He was doing. She thought God was giving her children in order to make her happily married to a loving husband. That was Leah's plan for her life. She had fallen prey to the human folly of, "if only…then I would be happy."

So often we do the same. We think, "if only I made more money, then I would be happy." Or "if only my life was easier…" or "if only I could have a baby, then I would be happy" or "if only I had a nicer house, then I would be happy." Maybe it's, "if only my husband would be more romantic…," or, "if only my children

While Leah suffered through her loveless marriage, God was stirring an amazing plan through her children. Leah had no idea the eternal impact her son Levi and his lineage would have.

God would deliver his people from the bondage of slavery in Egypt, using one of Levi's descendants. We read about this child in Exodus 2:1-10. His name was Moses.

Levi's descendant Moses was a key character in the story of God's people. God would speak to Moses in a burning bush (Exodus 3), use him to warn Pharaoh of the plagues (Exodus 7-12), use him to lead God's people out of Egypt (Exodus 12) across the Red Sea (Exodus 13), to lead his people through the wilderness (Exodus/Numbers), to give the ten commandments (Exodus 20), to build the Tabernacle and the Ark (Exodus 36-37), to give the law (Leviticus) and to lead God's people to the Promised Land (Numbers 13).

The Levites, the tribe of men descended from Levi, would go on to be a group specially selected out of God's people to be completely his. They would be the Jewish priests, with special duties and responsibilities.

God said of them: "…The Levites are **mine**" (Numbers 3:12) and "they are the Israelites who are to be given wholly to me. **I have taken them as my own**…" (Numbers 8:16).

God is doing something bigger, better, and more eternal than our own plans.

would be more obedient…" or "if only I had a really good friend…"or "if only I was really successful at work…" or "if only I was in better shape…"

But little may we know that, all the while, God is doing something bigger, better, and more eternal than our own plans.

What *if onlys* are there in your life right now?

How might you be missing the blessings God is giving you by focusing on the ways your own plans are failing?

There have been way too many times I've pined for my own *if onlys* instead of letting go, trusting, and waiting for the Lord's plans to unfold. I remember one time in particular there was this beautiful blue house in the country for sale…

At the time my growing family of eight was feeling the squeeze in 1300 square feet of living space in our little yellow house, with only one full bathroom and a postage-stamp sized city yard for six rambunctious children. We'd even given the master bedroom to our four daughters so John and I had only a small walkway around our king-sized bed in our extra-small bedroom.

We were thankful for our little home that had served us so well for so many years, but that bigger blue house in the country just seemed so perfect. I just couldn't resist driving by every chance I got.

It was just down the road from my husband's work, and right in the neighborhood of some of our good friends. And the price seemed like it would be a steal. *If only we could get that house!*

But just as soon as the sellers were hearing offers, a cash offer got it. And my dreams—of sipping coffee on the back porch and, 20 years down the road, of playing with our grandkids in the yard—evaporated.

I was so disappointed. I couldn't understand why I'd been able to get my hopes up, only to have the opportunity snatched right out from under my nose. Every time I drove past the beautiful blue house the disappointment washed over me again. But then...

Two years later, the Lord called us out of that community. Staying in the little yellow house and getting just a few more improvements done meant that much easier a move and that much more profit when it was time to go on.

If my plan had worked out, we'd have had the headache of moving twice, and trying to tackle all of the projects at the blue house in the country. We may not have had the buying power for our next move, had we bought that blue house. In the end, I'm so thankful my plans failed. I'm glad God gave me a beautiful *wait and see* in place of my *if only*.

I'm not the only one who has problems seeing God's good future for me. In Judges 6:11-27 the angel of the Lord spoke to an insecure, fearful Gideon about his future defeat of the Midianites. The Angel called Gideon a mighty warrior whom God was with (verse 12). See Gideon's reply in the margin, from verse 13. Gideon had a hard time believing the good God was going to do. He pined for Israel's victory over the Midianites with his own *if only God was with us...*

The Angel assured Gideon that Gideon himself would bring about victory over Israel's enemies. But Gideon couldn't see past his people's misfortune, and his own insecurities (Judges 6:15) which were so great that he repeatedly asked God for signs (Judges 6:17, 36-37).

Ironically, God would whittle Gideon's army down to a slim remnant (Judges 7) and bring about victory with insecure Gideon in command. Gideon's *if only God was with us*, turned

I'm so thankful my plans failed. ...God gave me a beautiful *wait and see* in place of my *if only*.

"...but if the Lord is with us, why has all this happened to us? Where are all his wonders that our ancestors told us about when they said, 'Did not the Lord bring us up out of Egypt?' But now the Lord has abandoned us and given us into the hand of Midian."

JUDGES 6:13

into a huge *wait and see how Israel will get the victory—and by the way, it's coming through you*. Funny how God has a sense of humor sometimes. He turned a faithless, weak warrior who demanded a sign into a victor—leading a small army in a big defeat of the mighty Midianites.

But after all God had done, Gideon would fail to worship the God who'd brought His people victory—even after all of the signs and all of the insecurities. Even then, Gideon would be distracted from giving God the glory by a glittering gold ephod he'd fashioned himself (Judges 8:27). Not a very happy ending, if you ask me.

Let's not be a Gideon—struggling to believe God's good to come, and worshipping the work of our own hands. Instead, let's praise the God who exchanges our pathetic *if onlys* for His better *wait and sees*.

God saw Leah's suffering; he heard her cry, and blessed her. While Leah was saying, "if only Jacob loved me...," God was waiting there, blessing her, loving her already. And His love story with her would be more beautiful than any love story with Jacob ever could be. His plans for her family were incredible. She only needed to wait and see.

> Gideon made the gold into an ephod, which he placed in Ophrah, his town. **All Israel prostituted themselves by worshiping it there,** and it became a snare to Gideon and his family.
>
> JUDGES 8:27

God is worthy of our praise because
our *if onlys* pale in comparison to His *wait and sees*.

Share a simple prayer time with the Lord:

- Give God your *if onlys.*
- Ask for eyes to see the ways that He is working in your life to bring about His better plans.
- Pray that He would continue to encourage you and surround you with his love.

Takeaway Truth--*"In their hearts humans plan their course, but the Lord establishes their steps." Proverbs 16:9*

DAY FOUR: FINDING LOVE AFTER ALL

MAIN TEXTS
Genesis 29:35
Genesis 30:1-2, 22-24
Genesis 35:16-18

"You will seek me and find me when you
seek me with all your heart." Jeremiah 29:13

Wretched Rachel

The enemy knows I have a bent toward comparing myself with others—and boy does he exploit it. As sick as it is, there are times when I feel superior to other women, because I get caught up in the comparison game. I see a kid screaming and spitting on his mom to get his way at the grocery and think, "My kids would *never* do something like that! She must not discipline her kid at all!" Or look at another friend and think, "I'm way more involved in church than she is. Does she even volunteer at all?!" Yikes.

But the enemy also pulls me in the other direction. He uses my inner comparison game to drag me into discouragement and self-pity. "She only gained 15 pounds during her whole pregnancy!" I think to myself, "I gained that much the first trimester!!"

We don't have to keep comparing ourselves to each other, and see other women as our rivals. We don't need to look around at others to make ourselves feel superior. We don't need to get sucked into self-pity when we don't feel we have it all together like other women.

If we play the comparison game—whether we end up feeling superior or inferior to others—either way we are actually losing, and the enemy of our souls is winning.

Maybe you can relate to the temptation of comparing children or weight, like me. Or it could be that for you it's envying others' relationships, careers, homes, or income. Does this comparison game more often cause you discouragement or pride and why do you think the enemy tempts you this way?

> If we play the comparison game, whether we end up feeling superior or inferior to others—either way, we are actually losing.

RACHEL TELLS IT LIKE IT IS

Why is the comparison game a win for Satan? Because when we get caught up comparing ourselves to others—**whether it causes pride or self-pity—in the end, it is all about *us***. And when the enemy has us fixing our eyes upon ourselves, that's just where he wants us to be.

Sadly, and ironically, Rachel's struggle continued until her death. And ultimately Rachel died bearing the children for which she so longed. The names she chose for her two biological sons are telling. Record their meanings here:

That's exactly where Leah's sister Rachel was stuck. Even though she had enviable beauty, and her husband's devoted love, it wasn't enough. She saw Leah's ease in childbearing and couldn't bear it.

Joseph means: (Genesis 30:24)

What are Rachel's jealous words from Genesis 30:1?

Ben-Oni means: (Genesis 35:18)

Rachel was desperate. She was devastated by her childlessness. The woman who seemed to have it all—breathtaking beauty and fairy-tale love—couldn't bear her barrenness.

Have you ever gone through a season like Rachel, when contentment eludes you?

After giving birth to her first son Joseph, Rachel proclaimed her desire for still more children, "May the Lord add to me another son."

And with her last breath, she named her youngest, "son of my trouble." Rachel's struggle for happiness was finally over, but tragically only because she breathed her last.

I have a child that went through a "bottomless pit" phase. No matter how much I gave her, it never seemed to be enough. If I gave her a cookie, before she even took her first bite, she'd look up at me with her sweet blue eyes and say, "Mama, may I have another?"

It always seemed to exasperate me. I found myself replying, "Why don't you eat that one first, then if you're still hungry, you can ask for more?!" But I realized that, so many times I can be like that with the Lord. God has given me more than I need, and yet I come to him with my laundry list of requests, asking, "may I have another?" without a grateful heart.

It's like the multi-billionaire John D. Rockefeller who, when asked how much money is enough, was quoted as saying, "Just a little bit more."

It's so easy to be like Rachel—to overlook God's blessings in our lives and to think we've just *got* to have everything *she's* got.

Leah and Rachel's story has a lesson for all of us.

"This Time I Will Praise the Lord!"

Yesterday we studied the birth of Leah's first three sons and how, with each, she hoped to earn Jacob's love. Leah hadn't found happiness where she'd thought she would. Jacob never loved her like he did Rachel.

But, unlike Rachel, Leah found the love that once eluded her in the place she least expected it. One simple verse tells how Leah finally found love.

Insert the middle of Genesis 29:35 below:

She conceived again, and when she gave birth to a son, she said,

So she named him Judah. Then she stopped having children."

Leah finally arrived with the birth of her fourth son. Instead of pining for her husband's love, **she responded to God with praise**. I absolutely love how *The Jesus Storybook Bible* tells it. If you happen to have a copy on your bookshelf, take the time to read it with your child or grandchild this week—you'll be glad you did.

When we are tempted to focus on the lives, children, fame, behavior, possessions, talents, wealth, or beauty of women around us, the right response is Leah's. Praise the Lord.

[35] She conceived again, and when she gave birth to a son she said, "This time I will praise the Lord." So she named him Judah. Then she stopped having children.

GENESIS 29:35

We don't need to waste our time whining and fussing about all of the things we think are wrong with our lives. We don't need to exhaust ourselves competing with other women.

Instead, we can focus on God. We can be thankful for God's love for us and for all he has done. We can echo the words of Leah from Genesis 29:35 when she said, *"I will praise the Lord!"*

If you notice yourself caught up in envious discontent make a conscious choice to praise. Even if you can't manage to sing, put on some music and ask the Lord to help you to have a grateful heart.

> It's ok if you aren't feeling particularly grateful—ask God to grow gratefulness in you.

I still remember my grandfather's customary mealtime prayer. He said, "Heavenly Father, give us grateful hearts for this, an expression of your great love for us." It's ok if you aren't feeling particularly grateful—ask God to grow gratefulness in you.

When we turn our thankful hearts to God in praise, suddenly our discontented longings will shrink. When we keep our eyes on Jesus instead of our peers, our hearts are more likely to praise the Lord instead of pine for what we don't have. Worship helps us realize that we can thank God in any circumstance.

Reflect on your current situation, taking a moment to praise the Lord—not only for the things that seem to be going well, but even for your struggles—surrendering to Him both the good and bad, the easy and difficult things about your life. Use the space below to write out a prayer, copy a verse of praise, or draw an artistic expression of your worship—choosing to praise the God who works good in every part of our lives.

If you'd like to share your expression of worship, post a picture on Facebook or Instagram with #significantwomenofthebible, or share with another in person. Take a few minutes to review your other collected posts—your stones of remembrance.

Rivals, or runners?

If we are able keep our eyes focused on Christ—living a life of worship—what happens in our lives is something amazing. It reminds me of a girl I know named Meghan Vogel.

Meghan and I grew up in the same sleepy little town of West Liberty, Ohio that boasts exactly three stoplights and one gas station. The high school doesn't have any state football championships, no baseball championships, no volleyball championships—let's just say we're not that great at playing ball. But boy, do we love to run.

West Liberty-Salem High School clenched the Boys Cross Country State Championship four years in a row back in the 70s and the whole town's had running fever ever since.

Meghan grew up with her mom having been a state champ with running in her veins, so when Meg made it to the State Track Championship her Junior year of high school, it was no big surprise. But what happened that scorching May day *did* surprise those who witnessed it.

Meghan qualified in two events: both the mile run, and the two-mile race. In her first event, the mile run, Meg dug deep and by the final straightaway had pulled away from the other runners, finishing in her personal best 4 minutes 58 seconds and securing a first-place state finish for a West Liberty-Salem track girl for the first time in 20 years. Joy shone on her face as the medal hung heavy around her neck on the podium.

Little did she know what else was in store for her that scorching spring day.

Before long, Meg found herself at the starting line again, this time for the two-mile race. The gun cracked and the runners circled, lap after lap. Then, just a few meters shy of the finish line Meghan noticed the runner in front of her collapse.

Little did she know what else was in store for her that scorching spring day.

When we fix our eyes on Christ, we realize that those around us—the ones that the enemy only wants us to see as rivals and competition—are really fellow runners in the race of life.

Rather than focus on competing and sprint past the fellow racer to the finish line—something she'd been training for years to do—Meghan stopped. She helped the other runner up, practically carrying the faint girl to the finish.

In one last act of sportsmanship, Meghan lifted her opponent across the finish line in front of herself, ensuring that the other runner would finish before Meghan. This meant a last place finish for Meghan, something that had never happened to her before in her life. When interviewers asked Meg after the race, why she'd done such a thing, she said, "That girl needed help, she worked hard and she deserved to finish too."

The ironic thing about all of this is that before long down-to-earth Meghan was receiving all kinds of attention—national TV interviews, ESPN articles, special recognitions and awards—all for her *last* place finish. She had just won a State Championship in the previous race—the mile run. She'd just set her personal best record, but what mattered more was the race in which she was willing to put someone *else* first, even if it meant she would place last.

For sure Meghan's mom raised her to be a strong runner, but Meghan's mom also raised her to love Jesus. And when we fix our eyes on Christ, we realize that those around us—the ones that the enemy only wants us to see as rivals and competition, are—really fellow runners in the race of life. Sometimes they need help, and they deserve to finish too.

We don't have to be like Rachel, seeing others as our rivals. Instead, let's be women of worship like Leah, secure enough in God's love for us that we quit striving to compete with other women and instead keep our eyes fixed on Christ.

We can live out Hebrews 12:1 that says, *"let us throw off everything that hinders and the sin that so easily entangles and let us run with perseverance the race marked out for us."* And when we reach that home stretch as we see someone stumble and fall, let's not blow by her like the world would have us. Let's use whatever strength God gives to pick her up and carry her with us toward the finish. Because let's face it, we all stumble. One day that exhausted runner will be me; one day that falling runner may be you.

And no matter what circumstance we find ourselves in, may we be like Leah, fixing our eyes on Christ alone, knowing we are loved and proclaiming, "this time I will praise the Lord!"

> When you worship God no matter the circumstance, you quit seeing other women as rivals and instead see them as fellow runners in the race of life.

Share a simple prayer time with the Lord:

- Thank God for his love that's been there all along. Pray that your life would remain laser-focused on Him rather than yourself, or others.
- Ask for a heart that's quick to praise God, no matter what circumstances in which you find yourself.
- Pray that instead of seeing other women as rivals, your eyes would be opened to opportunities to encourage each other along.

Takeaway Truth—"*Put your hope in God, for I will yet praise him, my Savior and my God.*" *Psalm 42:11*

DAY FIVE: THE LION OF THE TRIBE OF JUDAH

MAIN TEXTS
Genesis 37
Genesis 49:8-12, 31

"For it is clear that our Lord descended from Judah."
Hebrews 7:14

Hey, Judah: Take a Sad Song and Make It Better
The Beatles song *Hey Jude* talks about making a sad song better by falling in love with a girl.

This week, we've learned that with the birth of Leah's son, Judah, the sad song of her life made a turn for the better—but not through the romantic love for which she longed. Leah learned to stop looking for fulfillment from her marriage, and start praising the Lord—even when things didn't turn out the way she'd planned.

Leah had come full-circle. She had discovered the secret of praising God despite things not going her way. And, in doing so, she finally found her purpose. She let go of her plans and surrendered fully to Him.

> As much as Leah wanted the love and attention of her husband, God had bigger things in store for her.

You see, as much as Leah wanted the love and attention of her husband, God had bigger things in store for her. God saw Leah, and He loved her. His purpose was to make her a matriarch in the family line of Christ. And, not just anywhere in the family line, but as **the mother of Judah**. Today we'll see just why being Judah's mother was so significant.

Raising a Leader

Rachel and Leah, along with Jacob's concubines, would bear 12 sons for Jacob altogether. These were the forefathers of the 12 tribes of Israel—God's people. Among the younger sons was Joseph, a leader of Egypt who would play a crucial role in saving the family.

Even though Joseph was crucial to the family's survival, we see that Judah was the one God ultimately chose as leader and forefather of the Messiah. Again, and again throughout the narrative of Jacob's family, for better or for worse, we see Judah emerging as a leader for his family.

Genesis 37 shows us an example of Judah's leadership. Verses one to eleven set the stage. According to these verses, how did Joseph's brothers feel about Joseph? Why?

Judah's little brother Joseph had the reputation of being the family twerp, in his big brothers' eyes. He'd tattled on his big brothers (verse 2), had a beautiful coat—evidence of his father's favoritism (verse 3), experienced and shared grandiose dreams (verses 5-10), and was the envy of his brothers (verse 11). Joseph had found favor in their father's eyes, but Joseph's jealous, bloodthirsty big brothers were ready to kill him, to be rid of him once and for all.

But Judah spoke up. His words from Genesis 37:26-27 are in the margin.

"What will we gain if we kill our brother and cover up his blood? 27 Come, let's sell him to the Ishmaelites and not lay our hands on him; after all, he is our brother, our own flesh and blood." His brothers agreed.

GENESIS 37:26-27

Though his actions were deplorable—between selling his brother into slavery (Genesis 37:27) and then deceiving his father to cover his tracks (Genesis 37:32)—we don't know Judah's heart. It is unclear here whether his motives are selfish ("What will *we* gain...?") or merciful ("let's...not lay our hands on him...after all, he is our brother"), but one thing is certain: when Judah spoke, his brothers followed. He was a leader.

We will learn much (much) more about Judah's relationships—both his successes and failures—next week, as we study Tamar. But, for now, we see the part he plays in Leah's legacy as a forefather-in-the-flesh of Christ himself and a leader in his family. But before we shift full-throttle into Leah's legacy, let's do some thinking on our own legacies.

A Legacy of Praise

As we wrap up this week's study, I wonder how we're viewing our own legacies.

We've been learning about Rachel and Leah's struggle with envying one another, and talking about our own tendency to play the comparison game. We've also learned how Leah modeled for us a heart of praise to God in the midst of her life's disappointments. You may not readily see the connection to legacy there—but it runs deep.

The enemy whispers in our ear that winning at life—leaving the biggest mark—has to do with all those empty metrics we're so quick to use to measure our value. He wants us to believe the lie that being rich, famous, talented, accomplished, and beautiful are the ultimate goals—that those are the legacies worth leaving.

As Christians, we may think we see through empty legacies easily. We know that life's not about being rich. But may I suggest that we still get it wrong sometimes? We still tend to think of our legacies in terms of us—what *I* want to accomplish for the Lord: How many people did *I* help convert? How many years did *I* spend as an overseas missionary? What percentage of my salary did *I* give? But those questions are all about me.

We put the cart before the horse when we get our own long "to do" list for the Lord written without first realizing that offering a heart of praise is *the* thing we're supposed to do.

The first sentence of the Westminster Catechism, a 350-year-old collection of theological sayings to live by, sums up the purpose of humankind. It says, "Man's chief end is to **glorify God**, and to enjoy him for ever."

Not give large sums of money. Not do mission work. Not save souls—**glorify God**.

> When we get our priorities straight and **glorify God first**, all the other "to do"s for the Lord flow naturally into place.

When we get our priorities straight and **glorify God first**, all the other "to do"s for the Lord flow naturally into place. When we humble ourselves and worship Him, then He writes our legacy.

We saw this firsthand in Leah's' life—how she tried to strive after her husband's love, but found her satisfaction in surrendering her striving to the Lord, and being content to worship Him. In letting go—losing herself in the Lord—her true legacy was found.

This concept is echoed in Romans 12:1—the idea of being a living sacrifice. In contrast to the Old Testament ways of offering up slaughtered animals—an outward sign of obedience, being a living sacrifice is an inner obedience. It's a heart surrendered to

> Therefore, I urge you, brothers and sisters, in view of God's mercy, to offer your bodies as a living sacrifice, holy and pleasing to God—**this is your true and proper worship.**
>
> ROMANS 12:1

the Lord, willing to say, like Mary the mother of Jesus, *"I am the Lord's servant,"* Luke 1:38.

If we serve the Lord striving in our own strength and in our own way, we'll end up like Jesus' friend Martha—frustrated and flustered, missing out on the better opportunity to sit at His feet (Luke 10:38-42).

Take a moment right now in prayer to offer up your life and legacy to the Lord—your agenda, your hopes, your dreams, your "to do" list—give it *all* to Him. Offer yourself in worship as a living sacrifice, letting go and glorifying Him. As you humble yourself before the Lord, hold your palms open in surrender, asking Him to fill them according to His plans for your legacy.

After spending this time with the Lord, jot down any thoughts or ideas here, so that you can remember what the Lord brought to mind. What is God asking you to surrender in praise and what is He filling your hands with? You may not readily come up with answers to these questions. Continue to praise the Lord, even if nothing specific comes to mind.

> Offer up your life and legacy to the Lord—your agenda, your hopes, your dreams, your "to do" list—give it *all* to Him.

We may not fully realize the legacy the Lord is leaving through our lives of worship. Our time on this earth isn't over yet. But we can see what impact Leah's life of worship left—and it was incredible through her son Judah.

The Lion of the Tribe of Judah

You don't have to look far to realize the influential role Judah played in the history of God's people. Even today **Judaism** is what we call the faith of those that adhere to the Old Testament way of God's people, and their race is called the **Jews**. Both of these words find their roots in the name of Leah's son Judah.

Judah was also the geographical name of the southern kingdom in the time of the prophets of the Old Testament, when the land was divided into two kingdoms.

In Jesus' time much of his ministry occurred in the geographical region **Judea**, also named for Judah. It was the location of Bethlehem, Nazareth, Jerusalem, and the Mount of Olives.

Judah's role as a forefather is so prominent that **geographically**, **religiously**, and even **ethnically** God's people were known by his name.

At this point you may be scratching your head, wondering why God chose a man who sold his brother into slavery and deceived his father for such an important role in the story of His people (and just wait until next week if you don't know what other bad decisions Judah made—there are some doozies).

I am scratching my head too. Why not choose the golden boy Joseph? After all, he was super smart (Genesis 41:37-41), fled temptation (Genesis 39:10-12), forgave his brothers (Gen 45:3-4, 15) and endured adversity with an amazing attitude (Genesis 45:5-8).

God uses us *despite* our mistakes.

We can't know why God chooses as he does, but one thing we *do* know is that God can use us all when we hand over the reins to Him. Be encouraged by Leah's flawed son Judah that God uses us *despite* our mistakes. And use Judah he did. By the time Jacob was on his deathbed, Leah's son Judah had a change of heart. Jacob blessed Judah with an amazing, prophetic blessing. But why not his older brothers, Leah's elder sons? Genesis 49 reveals the dirty truth.

For it is clear that our Lord descended from Judah

HEBREWS 7:14a

Reuben was disqualified from his rightful blessing as firstborn because he slept with one of his father's concubines (see verse 4). Simeon and Levi were also passed over for the blessing because of their unreasonable vengefulness (see verses 5-6). Judah, on the other hand, made out like a bandit when it came to receiving his father's blessing. See for yourself in Genesis 49:8-12.

What three things did Jacob prophesy would happen to Judah's family in verse 8?

1—

2—

3—

Judah's descendants would rule. In fact, all of the rulers of the kingdom of Judah would be from his family line. The mighty warrior-king David would descend from Judah, as would the King of Kings, Christ himself.

What animal is used to illustrate Judah and the rulers from his family line? See verse 9 of Gen 49.

According to the following verses, what is a lion like?

Judges 14:18—

Proverbs 28:1--

Revelation 5:5--

A lion is strong, bold, and victorious. The Lion of the Tribe of Judah, Jesus Christ (Rev. 5:5), would "grasp his enemies by the neck" (Genesis 49:8 NLT), crushing the head of the serpent Satan once and for all (Gen 3:15). Praise the Lord!

If you're a doodler like me, a visual will help this lesson stick. Choose one of the following drawing prompts:

1. Draw a sketch of a lion trampling a snake. Be sure to label the lion with the descriptive words you looked up from the scriptures above. Also, label the serpent with the descriptive words found in John 8:44 (murderer, liar), Romans 16:20 (crushed), 1 Corinthians 15:54-55 (death, swallowed-up).

2. The *Leeland* song "Lion and the Lamb" about Leah's descendant Jesus proclaims, "every chain will break, as broken

"Judah, your brothers will praise you; your hand will be on the neck of your enemies; your father's sons will bow down to you.
9 You are a lion's cub, Judah; you return from the prey, my son. Like a lion he crouches and lies down, like a lioness—who dares to rouse him?
10 The scepter will not depart from Judah, nor the ruler's staff from between his feet, until he to whom it belongs shall come and the obedience of the nations shall be his. 11 He will tether his donkey to a vine, his colt to the choicest branch; he will wash his garments in wine, his robes in the blood of grapes.
12 His eyes will be darker than wine, his teeth whiter than milk.

GENESIS 49:8-12

Then one of the elders said to me, "Do not weep! See, the Lion of the tribe of Judah, the Root of David, has triumphed...

REVELATION 5:5

hearts declare His praise." Make a sketch of a breaking chain, as a result of praise.

Honored in Her Death

Leah endured struggles in life, but her husband Jacob honored Leah upon her death. Read evidence of how Jacob honored Leah in Genesis 49:31.

How was she honored?

Leah was buried in the Promised Land, where Jacob's parents and grandparents had been buried. Jacob had chosen this as his final resting place as well. Leah knew, just like the rest of the family, that her earthly death was not her end, and that the earth she was buried in was only a shadow of the promise to come.

Read how the writer of Hebrews explained it, in the margin.

Leah had gone from an unwanted weak-eyed woman to the mother of many. Her blood flowed through the veins of key men in the story of God's people—Levi, Judah, Aaron, Moses, Eli, John the Baptist, David, Solomon and the Lion of the Tribe of Judah, Christ himself. Leah was part of God's master plan to redeem mankind. Leah was loved. Leah was significant.

We know Leah's happy ending. We know how God used her to build his family through her sons Levi and Judah, even though she never won over her husband. Right now, whatever challenge in which you find yourself, take heart. Choose a posture of praise. God is doing an eternal work in your life. He's doing things you can't see. Take comfort in knowing you are in God's capable hands, just like Leah was.

> God's plans are much greater than anything we can dream up.

> A woman of true worship chooses to leave a legacy of victorious praise–giving God glory by offering up herself as a living sacrifice.

Spend some time in prayer:

- Thank God for His plans and purposes—that He has good things in store.
- Ask for eyes to see the ways that He is using you for His purposes, even when things don't seem to be going well.
- Pray for a heart completely surrendered to God, that He would develop in you persistent praise.

Takeaway Truth–"*See, the Lion of the tribe of Judah, the Root of David, has triumphed." Revelation 5:5*

A Tangible Reminder—Find a photo of a lion or small figurine of a lion and place it on your window sill at the kitchen sink, at your desk, or in another place where you will notice it throughout the week. As you see the lion, remember unloved Leah—how her years spent pining for her husband ended with a breakthrough of praise to God! Think of the ways your life has been a disappointment, and praise God anyway. Allow his love to wash over you and pray for his contentment, despite your feelings. Remember that even though Leah's life was not what she first desired, her legacy ended up being that of the Lion of Judah—a greater end than she could have dreamed! Know that the God who determined Leah's steps, directs yours as well. Share what God is speaking to your heart through Leah's story on social media with #significantwomenofthebible

#stonesofremembrance to curate your growth or use the blank pages at the end of this book.

Pause for Praise—Nice work persevering through Week Two! The Lord speaks to our souls when we seek him through his word. Through Leah's life, we are reminded of a God who loves us lavishly, even though we don't always see it. Looking at Leah's life, we also learn that God's plans are often much greater than anything we can dream up. Before you end this week with Leah, take a few moments to follow her example and praise our awesome God. I suggest you find the music video for Big Daddy Weave's *Lion and the Lamb* (I like the acoustic version) and watch with a worshipful heart. If you love hymns, try *Blessed Assurance* instead.

Think of the ways
your life has been
a disappointment,
and praise God
anyway

TAMAR

Forsaken to Foremother

Significant

Before beginning do an initial reading of Genesis 38, our main passage for the week

This is the genealogy of Jesus the Messiah the son of David, the son of Abraham:
² Abraham was the father of Isaac,
Isaac the father of Jacob,
Jacob the father of Judah and his brothers,
³ Judah the father of Perez and Zerah, whose mother was Tamar

MATTHEW 1:1-3

DAY ONE: TRADITION!

"So Isaac called for Jacob and blessed him and commanded him: 'Do not marry a Canaanite woman.'" Genesis 28:1

So, who is Tamar anyway?

Thus far in our study, we've examined the lives of Sarah and Leah—some of the better-known matriarchs. We learned their stories in Sunday School, and our aunts and sisters bear their names. We have long hailed their heroism and respected their positions in the Messianic family line—after all, they were the wives of big-time patriarchs Abraham and Jacob and mothers of Isaac and Judah.

But their lives were not so cut-and-dried.

As we've dug deeper into these well-known heroines' stories and aired their dirty laundry, we found their behavior and circumstances much more human than heroic. After all, Sarah's manipulative, bullying tendencies reared their ugly heads when she became impatient with God and jealous of Hagar and Ishmael. And Leah's looks left her unwanted, causing her father to treat her selfishly—spurring her to seek love and acceptance where it wouldn't be found.

But, with God's help, their lives took a turn for the better. Impatient Sarah became beautiful from within as her life showed respect for her husband and trust in the Lord. Looking-for-love Leah learned to praise God despite her disappointments. Their unlikely, happy endings have them each playing a crucial part in bringing about the long-awaited, much-needed Messiah.

Enter Tamar. Matthew 1:3 unmistakably named her as Jesus' foremother. Scan the first few verses of the New Testament from Matthew 1 in the margin. Circle the first woman to be mentioned by name in the New Testament.

But who in the world was this Tamar? Her R-rated story didn't find its way into too many children's picture Bibles, so our familiarity with her is not so great. She also shares the same name as King David's daughter Tamar (2 Samuel 13), which has created confusion for the modern reader.

Our Tamar's story is told in Genesis 38.

Before we get knee-deep in her tale, let me just whet your appetite a bit and let you know that with a quick reading of her story, it's easy to get it wrong. If you've breezed over Genesis 38 in the past, it's likely that you, like I, have jumped to some wrong conclusions.

As parents, even though we're loathe to admit it, we sometimes jump to the wrong conclusions about our children. It's like the story my children recount about Adelaide's unfair punishment.

One day after lunch each child was to clear their own dishes from the table. My oldest daughter, Adelaide, had cleared hers, but there were still dishes on the table. Thinking they were her dishes, my husband enacted some strict discipline to the child he thought was guilty—without giving her a chance to defend herself. It turned out the dishes were Helen's. Sometimes we're too quick to jump to conclusions—a fact none of my children will let my husband forget.

This week we're going to see how maybe we've jumped to unwise conclusions as

BUT IT'S NOT FAIR!

Some of us may bristle at the thought that such a sullied couple as Tamar and Judah would get the privilege of being included in the bloodline of Christ. It doesn't seem fair that a man of such integrity as Joseph would get passed over and a mess-up like Judah (and a deceiver like Tamar) be chosen as ancestors to Christ. But the right attitude of our hearts should be thankfulness.

What does Romans 3:23 reveal about us all? "For everyone has sinned; we all fall short of God's glorious standard" (NLT).

Since we all have sins in our past, Tamar and Judah's story should be one of **hope** for us. When our hearts are willing to be used by God, like Tamar and Judah, we can be used for his purposes despite our past mistakes.

But what's the point of living a life of integrity if God can use a mess-up? Perhaps you're feeling a bit like the prodigal brother (Luke 15:25-30) and feeling like it doesn't matter whether you choose the narrow road or not. Let me let you in on something—it matters! For more on that, check out Romans 6.

And remember that even though Judah's life had a happy ending, his rebellious early years left a wake of heartache, death, and suffering throughout the entire family. A great deal of pain could have been avoided if Judah had been a man of integrity from the beginning. The same is true in our own lives.

Get ready for a fresh reading of Genesis 38 that might just rock your world.

we uncover some surprising twists in Tamar's tale. If you have read through Genesis, you were probably shocked to find that Tamar's narrative is a tale of deception and seduction—one that had me quickly pigeon-holing her a floozy. Get ready for a fresh reading of Genesis 38 that might just rock your world.

Bible characters are so much more than one-dimensional cardboard cut-outs—hardly ever strictly heroes or villains. We've seen this first hand in our study of Sarah and Leah, and we'll see it again in this chapter on Tamar.

Sure, she made some pretty big whopping mistakes (like I said, R-rated ones!) but read further, and you'll be surprised to find out she also bears a likeness to her descendant, Christ. Spoiler alert: some pretty big stuff is about to happen in our study this week. I can't wait for you to hear this. Let's dive in.

The Canaanites are Off-Limits

Tamar was a Canaanite woman. In other words, she was born and raised in the Promised Land—and off-limits to God's people, Abraham's descendants. The Bible could hardly be any clearer about marrying a Canaanite. Underline Isaac's command in Genesis 28:1 that follows: *"So Isaac called for Jacob and blessed him and commanded him: 'Do not marry a Canaanite woman.'"*

The strong tradition of marrying within the family started way back with father Abraham, when Isaac reached marrying age. In fact, it was so important to Abraham that his son Isaac not marry a Canaanite, he made his servant swear an oath (Genesis 24:3-4). That's how Isaac ended up marrying Rebekah from Paddan Aram.

Isaac and Rebekah's older troublemaker son, Esau, had ignored this tradition, causing major problems for the family. If you thought your relationship with your mother-in-law was strained, be thankful she's not proclaiming, like Rebekah did in Genesis 27:46, *"I'm disgusted with living because of these Hittite women. If Jacob takes a wife from among the women of this*

Hittites were a type of Canaanites.

land...my life will not be worth living.'" We know from Rebekah's extreme words that she was not taking this tradition lightly.

Often the rules that God places in our lives which at first glance seem inconsistent with his character (ie. How can God promote exclusion of certain people when John 3:16 says that he loves the whole world??), are actually for protection

While hate groups and white supremacists twist scripture to support their prejudice, these passages aren't ultimately about race. Yes, God's people weren't to intermarry with Canaanites, but it wasn't about the Canaanites' race; the guideline was in regard to their culture and their gods. It was about keeping the Israelites on the right track by keeping them away from bad influences.

Just as a parent teaches a small child to hold hands in a parking lot, or to avoid touching a hot stove, so God gave his people loving guidelines for their own good—even though they didn't always like or understand the rules.

It seems pretty crummy to think about certain people being off-limits, but God had Israel's best interest in mind. See 2 Corinthians 6:14 in the margin. How can we interpret and apply these ideas to our culture?

> Don't team up with those who are unbelievers. How can righteousness be a partner with wickedness? How can light live with darkness?
>
> 2 CORINTHIANS 6:14 NLT

Growing up it seemed like this "unequally yoked" verse made its appearance in every book and magazine article about dating as a Christian teen—and rightly so. But this verse is about more than caution in romantic relationships.

Paul wrote these words to the Corinthian church because they were cozying up with false apostles. It causes me to pause and think about what partnerships with dark influences I might be allowing in my own life.

What about the reality show following trendy polygamist families that I watched? At first it seemed innocently fascinating. Then, in a moment of clarity I realized that I had invited an influence in my life that I didn't want there.

For you, it might be different. Maybe it's the secular psychology podcast that's ideas are a little off, and creeping into your thought life in unexpected ways. Maybe it's that neighborhood gossip that you've allowed yourself to hear, when you should've put a stop to it right away. Maybe it's the prosperity preacher you love to listen to, whose teaching is oh so inspirational, but not exactly biblical. Perhaps it's time for a change.

God knew that intermarriage with the Canaanites would bring harm to his people. He knew that, for his people to follow him wholeheartedly, they would need to stay away from the negative influences of others.

Allowing His people to intermarry with people that worshipped other gods would have been too strong a temptation for the Israelites. It would have been like putting a plate of Snickers in front of my three year old alongside a plate of broccoli and leaving him on his own, expecting him to make the right choice.

> Individuals from these excluded groups did have opportunity to be part of God's people.

But individuals from these excluded groups *did* have opportunity to be part of God's people. Because it wasn't about them personally, it was about their people's worship of false gods.

We'll meet a few women in this study who were smart enough to take that opportunity to leave the empty promises of their people's false gods behind, and boy did it pay off. Not only Tamar falls into this category, but Ruth and Rahab as well. We'll learn to follow in their footsteps.

As Shaky as a Fiddler on the Roof

Watch the opening sequence from Fiddler on the Roof and you'll be singing, *"Traditiooooooooooon!"* the rest of the day—you'll also get an understanding of the important role tradition plays within Jewish culture.

Traditions help people know how to live. They give routine and stability. According to the main character Tevye, "without our traditions, our lives would be as shaky as a fiddler on a roof."

How do your own family traditions provide comfort and stability?

My family always serves a dish we call, "Green Jell-O" at family gatherings. It's a concoction that includes—you guessed it, green Jell-O—with a variety of other mix-ins: cream cheese, canned fruit, mini marshmallows, nuts, and whipped topping.

As far as I know, none of us are consuming this dish—or really anything like it—regularly in our daily lives. And yet, every big holiday meal includes this side dish as a staple. Gotta have the green Jell-O.

Thankfully, the traditions God put in place for his people were more than just strange culinary concoctions. They were purposeful, and deliberate—put in place for his people's protection.

Unfortunately, people like me get caught up in the rule-following. We get carried away by the routine, even when the routine isn't accomplishing its original purpose. We eat the Jell-O even though we're not even sure we like Jell-O anymore. Just like the Pharisees, the rules become empty. The rules become religion.

I like my gold star—the satisfaction of knowing I didn't steal, commit adultery, or murder. Sure, I can follow those rules, but Jesus calls my bluff.

LAPP GREEN JELL-O
1 small box lime gelatin
2 c. boiling water
6 oz. cream cheese
1 ½ c. drained canned fruit cocktail
48 mini mallows
½ c. chopped nuts (opt)
2 c. whipped topping

Dissolve gelatin in boiling water. Add cream cheese, chunked, and let cool. Stir in fruit, marshmallows, and nuts. Fold in topping and chill.

Variations: use strawberry gelatin and strawberries or orange gelatin and pineapple

Like the rich young ruler of Luke 18 (see margin), Jesus urges me to go beyond the rules—he wants all of me. He wants me to follow him wholeheartedly.

How might you be in the habit of following rote rules, but holding back from completely following Jesus?

For me, following rules yet holding back sometimes has to do with giving money. I gladly tithe, and yet there are times when I begrudgingly rather than generously give when asked to go beyond normal tithing. Yikes.

Other times it's giving my time. I give of my time up to a certain point, but feel entitled to put my feet up at the end of the day. Sometimes I end up serving God into the night with a terrible attitude. Rule-following doesn't always make for a soft heart.

That's part of what makes Tamar's story so fascinating. Tamar was one of the *forbidden* people—one of the Canaanites, the idolaters. She wasn't a rule-following Israelite. And yet, God would use her as an unlikely foremother to Christ. How could this be? In our study this week, we'll see just how.

> Rules help us when they keep us from temptation, but following empty rules easily becomes empty religion.

Share a simple prayer time with the Lord:

- Thank him for his love and acceptance for you despite your upbringing.
- Ask for eyes to see the wisdom in God's word and the guidance he provides.
- Pray for a heart completely surrendered to him, that makes wise choices no matter what the temptation.

Takeaway Truth—"*The righteous choose their friends carefully, but the way of the wicked leads them astray.*" Proverbs 12:26

DAY TWO: FROM BAD TO WORSE

"The wages of the righteous is life, but the earnings of the wicked are sin and death.'"
Proverbs 10:16

Man on the Run

Have you ever seen a naughty dog slink away with his tail between his legs? That's reminds me of Judah where we pick up the story today. Judah was on the lam. He was having his own "Prodigal Son" (Luke 15:11-32) moment.

We learned that Judah led his jealous brothers in the conspiracy to sell Joseph (Genesis 37:26-28). Jacob's boys went down in history as the first recorded human traffickers.

Just following this, in Genesis 38, Judah skipped town. Perhaps Judah was filled with grief at what had transpired—after all, Jacob hadn't taken the news of Joseph's demise well (Genesis 37:34-35). Or, maybe Judah was just ready for a change of scenery. The text doesn't say.

Even though it doesn't give the "Why" Judah relocated, read Genesis 38:1-5 and record the information you *do* find below:

When:

Where:

Who:

What:

How:

MAIN TEXT
Genesis 38:1-10

34 Then Jacob tore his clothes and dressed himself in burlap. He mourned deeply for his son for a long time. 35 His family all tried to comfort him, but he refused to be comforted. "I will go to my grave mourning for my son," he would say, and then he would weep.
GENESIS 37:34-35 NLT

At that time, Judah left his brothers and went down to stay with a man of Adullam named Hirah. 2 There Judah met the daughter of a Canaanite man named Shua. He married her and made love to her; 3 she became pregnant and gave birth to a son, who was named Er. 4 She conceived again and gave birth to a son and named him Onan. 5 She gave birth to still another son and named him Shelah. It was at Kezib that she gave birth to him.
GENESIS 38:1-5

Young, headstrong Judah, finally rid of his pesky brother Joseph, headed off to find his fortune among the Canaanites. Unfortunately, Judah befriended Hirah of Adullam (a Canaanite) and married a Canaanite, without his father's consent...choices that proved foolish as the plot unfolded. With his wife Shua, he bore three sons Er, Onan, and Shelah at Kezib.

Judah would have been wise to heed Paul's advice in 1 Corinthians 15:33, *"Do not be misled: 'Bad company corrupts good character.'"* But, instead of following the wisdom and tradition of his family, Judah went his own way.

Judah's behavior is all too common. We all have times we want to go our own way. One day, my kindergartener, Mirielle, was setting the table. And while she's a driven personality and a very hard worker, she's also not one to be bossed around. She's a tiny little girl that likes to chart her own destiny.

Well Mirielle was certain that she could pour the drinks into the cups by herself—out of a heavy glass pitcher. I warned her that I thought the task was too difficult for her, the pitcher too heavy—but spunky Mirielle was having none of it. She wouldn't take help.

Despite my words of caution, a few minutes later the entire pitcher of water gushed over the table. Going your own way doesn't pay.

[6] Judah got a wife for Er, his firstborn, and her name was Tamar. [7] But Er, Judah's firstborn, was wicked in the Lord's sight; so the Lord put him to death.

GENESIS 38:6-7

As we study the lives of Judah and Tamar this week, we'll see the heartache Judah's family experienced as he walked his own way, but we'll also see how a loving God used unlikely Tamar to bring wicked Judah to a turning point—redeeming a broken situation for His glory.

The Wages of Er's Sin is Death

Tamar had the unfortunate circumstance of being married to an evil man. Read about Tamar's first husband, Er, in Genesis 38:6-

7. What happened to Er as a result of his wickedness? Circle your answer:

   a.) He was struck dumb and could not speak for a week
   b.) His crop was devastated by locusts
   c.) He was put to death
   d.) He became ill

Whew! I don't know about you, but being struck dead seems pretty extreme to me. How many people have you met that were so evil, God just did away with them? Becky cuts in line at the grocery store—BAM! Dead. Theresa fibs about her weight—ZAP!! She's a goner. Sandy speeds when she's late to an appointment—POW! RIP Sandy.

I know I haven't personally witnessed anyone struck down by God as a result of their wickedness. Maybe this passage should have the heading, "Evil Husbands: Extreme Consequence Edition."

We don't know exactly what Er did that was so wicked, and we can only guess what it must have been like to be married to such an evil man. Was Tamar relieved when Er died? Who knows, but being a widow was not desirable in Tamar's day.

Childless widowhood in ancient times meant certain poverty. With no husband or son to provide for a woman, she was left destitute, considered on the bottom of society. And to have no children to carry on the family line was shameful, and tragic.

But God didn't leave Israel's sonless widows in the lurch. He took care of His people, and He takes care of us. He provided his people with a plan.

The Levirate Marriage was a custom put in place within the Jewish people that provided for a widow by ensuring the furthering of the deceased husband's family line. Check out this custom as recorded in Deuteronomy 25:5-6 (in the next page's margin).

God didn't leave Israel's sonless widows in the lurch. God took care of his people, and he takes care of us.

If brothers are living together and one of them dies without a son, his widow must not marry outside the family. Her husband's brother shall take her and marry her and fulfill the duty of a brother-in-law to her. ⁶ The first son she bears shall carry on the name of the dead brother so that his name will not be blotted out from Israel.

DEUTERONOMY
25:5-6

Record the terms and details of a Levirate Marriage in your own words below:

A son-less widow was obligated to marry her brother-in-law and continue her deceased husband's family line by having a son through him. In a patriarchal society, this ensured the widow a place within the family. Her son would get his allotted inheritance and care for her as she aged. This tradition, though strange to us, was a widow's Social Security, her IRA—keeping her from helplessness and certain poverty. It also kept each family's property within that family.

Remember being a little kid and having that one place to sit that everyone fought over? Maybe it was next to a certain favorite sibling, or perhaps it was the comfiest chair, or the one with the best view of the TV.

In my family of origin, each of us kids loved riding in the front seat of the car. Heading out to the garage to run errands, we would holler, "I call the front seat!" and we tore off running to plop our bottom triumphantly into the seat and stake our claim.

Levirate marriage meant that even a pathetic, son-less widow had claim to a seat in the family, no calling, running, or triumphant bottom plopping necessary.

Ironically enough Judah, the one *unwilling* to keep the family tradition of not marrying Canaanites, *did* initially require his sons to follow the tradition of Levirate Marriage. He instructed his second son, Onan, to have a son with Tamar in Genesis 38:8: *"Then Judah said to Onan, 'Sleep with your brother's wife and fulfill your duty to her as a brother-in-law to raise up offspring for your brother.'"*

Onan was to have conceived a child with Tamar. The child of their union would ultimately belong to Er. But Onan made sure this child never existed, ramping up the gross factor of this uncomfortable story.

One Brother Like the Other

Poor Tamar goes from one evil husband to another! Ever feel like you can't catch a break? Tamar's been there.

Onan understood the birds and the bees, but wasn't happy about producing an heir for his brother. He wasn't willing to obey his father and carry out his obligations as a Levirate husband to Tamar.   But we know from scripture that God takes disobedience seriously. 1 Samuel 15:22 says, *"To obey is better than sacrifice, and to heed is better than the fat of rams."* Onan would learn this lesson the hard way.

In the margin, circle Onan's serious fate found in Genesis 38:10.

Watching Er perish hadn't scared Onan into right living. Instead, Onan followed his evil big bro's footsteps. And, sure enough, the Lord struck Onan down for his wickedness, just like Er. Tamar once again found herself widowed.

Why wouldn't Onan have wanted his brother Er's family line to continue? Part of the answer lies in Genesis 38:6.

What was the birth order of Judah's son Er, according to this verse?

For God's people, there was great significance to being firstborn. We see God's favor of the firstborn going all the way back to Genesis 4:4.

Throughout the Old Testament, we see the preeminence of the firstborn time and again, whether man or beast. As you remember, just last week we touched on Jacob's deceit of his

Then Judah said to Onan, "Sleep with your brother's wife and fulfill your duty to her as a brother-in-law to raise up offspring for your brother." ⁹ But Onan knew that the child would not be his; so whenever he slept with his brother's wife, he spilled his semen on the ground to keep from providing offspring for his brother. ¹⁰ What he did was wicked in the Lord's sight; so the Lord put him to death also.

GENESIS 38:8-10

⁶ Judah got a wife for Er, his firstborn, and her name was Tamar.

GENESIS 38:6

And Abel also brought an offering— fat portions from some of the firstborn of his flock. The Lord looked with favor on Abel and his offering,

GENESIS 4:4

brother and father, a ploy to get the much-desired blessing and birthright of firstborn Esau.

Try as we might, it's hard not to give our firstborn extra attention. After all, they're the only ones around initially. As a mom, I'm guilty as charged on this one. When my firstborn Jonas was a baby, my days were filled with pattycake and Jesus Loves Me—my world nearly revolved around him. He couldn't make a peep without me literally running to his aid. His baby book is thick with cute photos of everything from his first tooth, to his first bath, to his first visit from Grandma and Grandpa.

Meanwhile poor Matthias, baby number seven, has to holler over the commotion of the other six to get mama's attention. I love him just the same, but life is busier now. It's cringeworthy, but I doubt we can find ten good pictures of his first year. No thick baby book for him. Birth order makes a difference.

Deuteronomy 21:15-17 outlines the right of the firstborn. What does the firstborn receive, according to verse 17?

With Er and his descendants out of the picture, Onan would have received a double portion of his family's inheritance—a happy proposition for a wicked man like him. This sounded like a good outcome for selfish Onan, who took measures to make sure no other heir would be produced in Er's family line. But selfishly going against the wisdom of his father and the tradition of their people was not going to be tolerated by the Lord. Judah was now two-for-two on dead, selfish, sinful sons.

Christ warned against the danger of such selfish, evil behavior as Onan's in Mark 8:36. He said, *"What good is it for someone to gain the whole world, yet forfeit their soul?"* We should take accounts like Er's and Onan's to heart—God takes sin seriously.

In Tamar's story, Er and Onan suffered grave consequences of their sin, but Tamar too suffered in the aftermath of their deaths.

> If a man has two wives, and he loves one but not the other, and both bear him sons but the firstborn is the son of the wife he does not love, ¹⁶ when he wills his property to his sons, he must not give the rights of the firstborn to the son of the wife he loves in preference to his actual firstborn, the son of the wife he does not love. ¹⁷ He must acknowledge the son of his unloved wife as the firstborn by giving him a **double share** of all he has. That son is the first sign of his father's strength. The right of the firstborn belongs to him.
>
> DEUTERONOMY 21:15-17

Tamar was now twice-widowed with no sons to show for either marriage. Ever feel like nothing goes your way? Tamar knows your pain.

Can you relate to Tamar's hopeless situation? How can it seem unfair when we feel the consequences of someone else's bad behavior?

Tamar's life was beginning to look like a dumpster fire. While Tamar's situation may seem extreme to us, the truth is, none of us live in a vacuum. We all live in a fallen world, surrounded by sinful people. Inevitably others' poor choices will cause us pain and suffering—sometimes even through no doing of our own.

Perhaps you've suffered from your parents' unkind words. Maybe you've had to deal with your boss's poor management. It could be that you've dealt with a friend's betrayal, or a husband's poor judgement—and now you're suffering the consequences through no fault of your own.

We all encounter times in our lives when others mistreat us because of their own sinful behavior. We're not immune to the effects of the choices of others. But what can we do in response? How can we redeem these hopeless situations? No matter how we've been wronged, we all have decisions to make as we move forward. What steps can we take? How can we deal with the people who hurt us? What does God have to say? As we continue our study this week, we'll see ourselves in Tamar's story, and see that her actions, and the actions of her descendant Christ, gave us a real-life blueprint to follow. Stay tuned for practical help.

Tamar's suffering, as senseless as it seemed, wouldn't be wasted. God brought something unimaginably beautiful from

> Both Tamar and her descendant Christ give us a real-life blueprint to follow when we've been wronged by others.

God brought something unimaginably beautiful from the ashes of Tamar's life. And he does the same for us.

the ashes of Tamar's life. He does the same for us. Read the following verses from Isaiah 61:2b-3, circling the promises that the Lord will bring about for those who mourn:

> to comfort all who mourn,
> 3 and provide for those who grieve in Zion—
> to bestow on them a crown of beauty
>   instead of ashes,
> the oil of joy
>   instead of mourning,
> and a garment of praise
>   instead of a spirit of despair.
> They will be called oaks of righteousness,
>   a planting of the Lord
>
> Isaiah 61:2b-3

We are bound to suffer in the wake of others' sins, but God transforms our situation as we follow in His steps.

Share a simple prayer time with the Lord:

- Ask for discernment and wisdom for your life during the times when you suffer as a result of others' evil choices.
- Pray for a heart completely surrendered to him, that makes wise choices no matter what the earthly consequence.

Takeaway Truth—"*He defends the cause of the fatherless and the widow, and loves the foreigner residing among you, giving them food and clothing.'" Deuteronomy 10:18*

JUDAH'S PLACE OF REBELLION BECOMES A PLACE OF VICTORY

When Judah fled to Adullam to stay with his friend Hirah, he was making the foolish choice, befriending Canaanites and breaking relationship with his father and brothers. He was in a time of rebellion. Throughout this week you will see that time and again Judah's choice to go to Adullam, and the many other choices that ensue cause much heartache and pain for those closest to Judah. His selfish rebellion leaves hurt in its wake.

But one of the great things about our God is that he can redeem our places of rebellion. He can transform those past mistakes and pain into victories moving forward. And that's just what he did for Judah's descendants in Adullam. Adullam was near the valley of Elah, a location of great importance to Judah's descendant David. What monumental event took place in the Valley of Elah, according to 1 Samuel 17?

God brought about victory in a location that was once a place of pain, heartbreak, fear, and death. With God's help, David had defeated Goliath, and Adullam became a place of victory for God's people.

But David's time at Adullam was not done. He would return there in the future. When trouble surrounded David, he found refuge at—you guessed it—Adullam. Saul's maniacal jealousy of David led Saul to pursue David. He wanted to take David's life. Read the following passage, 1 Samuel 22:1-3, to hear about David's time hiding out at Adullam. Underline all of the people who found refuge in the cave there:

David left Gath and escaped to the cave of Adullam. When his brothers and his father's household heard about it, they went down to him there. All those who were in distress or in debt or discontented gathered around him, and he became their commander. About four hundred men were with him. 1 Samuel 22:1-3

The cave at Adullam was now a place of refuge for David, his family, and all who needed hope. David now had the support of his family and of 400 who needed him. His time in the cave was a time of praise, strengthening, and unity with his newfound following.

Later this week we will learn that rebellious Judah would come to repentance. Look up Proverbs 14:26 and copy it in the margin, affirming God's promise to the descendants of those who fear him.

David wrote Psalm 142, 57, and 34 at Adullam. He penned these words of praise from Psalm 57 while there:

Have mercy on me, my God, have mercy on me, for in you I take refuge. I will take refuge in the shadow of your wings… I will praise you, Lord, among the nations; I will sing of you among the peoples. For great is your love, reaching to the heavens; your faithfulness reaches to the skies. Be exalted, O God, above the heavens; let your glory be over all the earth.

May God transform our past places of rebellion into places of victory and praise, like Adullam was transformed for Judah's family. Do you have a testimony of God's transforming power? Take some time to share! Post about your past experience on social media or tell your story to a friend, remembering God's goodness. If you post online, tag your post #signigicantwomenofthebible #redemptionstory. Then follow the hashtag link to see others' stories as well. God's goodness is worth sharing!

DAY THREE: LADY IN WAITING

"There is no fear in love. But perfect love drives out fear."
1 John 4:18

Scaredy-Cat Judah

After two marriages to two wicked brothers ending in two men struck down by God, Tamar is in the crazy position of having yet another Levirate marriage to Er and Onan's younger brother, Shelah. We pick up the story in Genesis 38:11.

In this verse, what does Judah instruct Tamar to do?

> Judah then said to his daughter-in-law Tamar, "Live as a widow in your father's household until my son Shelah grows up." For he thought, "He may die too, just like his brothers." So Tamar went to live in her father's household.
>
> GENESIS 38:11

Why did Judah give this instruction?

According to the end of the verse, what is Tamar's response?

Judah didn't have Genesis 38 to narrate his family's story for him. He didn't know that God had stricken down his two sons because of their *own* wickedness. In his mind, the common denominator in the first two marriages of his elder sons was Tamar—and he was scared stiff that Shelah would suffer the same fate. He didn't want to lose Shelah too.

Instead of trusting God's way and continuing the family's tradition of Levirate marriage, Judah's fear caused him to slam on the brakes. God had told his people to have children. He instructed both Adam (Genesis 1:28) and Noah (Genesis 9:1) to "be fruitful and multiply." His promise to Judah's great-grandfather Abraham and his father Jacob was to make them a great nation, but God's plan to bless Judah's family had screeched to a halt. The kingly line of Judah was on pause because Judah the mighty lion cowered in fear.

Poor choice, Judah.

When has fear paralyzed you? Has it kept you from making the decision you knew was right?

> The kingly line of Judah was on pause because Judah the mighty lion cowered in fear.

When I was a little girl, I was the one who colored in the lines. I was careful to do what was right. But I still remember one day when fear kept me from obedience. As a child, I had an unreasonable fear of dogs. They terrified me. I just couldn't get over it.

One day I was over at a babysitters' house, and it was nearing the time when my mother was going to come pick me up. I was climbing a tree (to stay away from the dog) and the other children littered trikes and scooters about the driveway—then they fled the scene. I was the only one around.

The exasperated babysitter popped her head out the door and said, "Rachel, get down from the tree and clean up these bikes. I don't want them in the driveway when your mom gets here."

I didn't respond. I didn't do anything, except sit in the tree, nervous butterflies in my stomach. What could I do? I wanted to do the right thing, but the sitters' dog sat on the porch, smirking at me as if it knew my dilemma—and delighted in it. I just couldn't bring myself to obey. I sat on the tree branch unmoved.

The sitter opened the screen door again, even more exasperated, "Rachel! I told you to clean up those bikes! I'm going to discipline you if you don't obey!"

Thankfully, my older sister and the rest of the kids showed up and managed to take care of the situation. I never did obey. I was too afraid.

But sometimes our fears are much more serious than an old smug farm dog. What if my husband's job falls through? What if the person selling us the house is scamming us? What if they find out what I'm really like? What if I get cancer? What if she's late because she was in a car accident? What if my kids fall away from the Lord? Fears have a way of taking us captive, and transforming obedient faith into worry.

And yet, when our lives are in our good God's hands, our seemingly-serious worries are just as irrational as my childhood fear of dogs.

> There is no fear in love. But perfect love drives out fear.
>
> 1 JOHN 4:18

For me, faith is a continual process of letting go of my white-knuckled fears. I need to daily (hourly!) recognize the sovereignty and goodness of God. I need to be feeding on the good promises in His word, worshipping him, and spending time surrendering my fears to him in prayer. Following the Lord with faith instead of fear isn't easy. But it's right, and it is oh-so-good.

We see the serious consequences of not surrendering our fears to the Lord in Judah's life.

God was bigger than Judah's fears.

Judah balked at the promises God had made to his forefathers. He allowed his fears to squelch the promise of becoming a great nation. But God was bigger than Judah's fears. We will see how God made Judah a great nation *despite* his fears.

God replaces our fears with peace. Over and over in scripture we read the assurance, *"Do not fear!"* Filling our hearts and minds with God's truth is a practical antidote to our tendency to cower in fear.

The Forgotten Widow

With her former father-in-law, Judah, shipping her back to her parents, Tamar's life had reached a new low. Widows, together with orphans and foreigners, were lumped together throughout the Old Testament as those at the very bottom of society. In a world where property and income are handled by husbands, to be husbandless was tragic. It was a hopeless sentence of poverty.

To be returned to my parents' house as a young adult would have been deflating, to say the least. For eighteen years I looked forward to growing up and spreading my wings. I still remember the exhilarating feeling of moving out of my parents' home for college. Ah, what freedom! I couldn't wait to be a grown up.

Judah left Tamar with the impression that he would eventually marry her to Shelah with his instruction, *"Live as a widow in your father's household until my son Shelah grows up." Genesis 38:11.* Little did Tamar know that Judah was really leaving her in limbo—neither releasing her from her obligation to Judah's family (*"live as a widow"*), nor giving her the husband she deserved. Tamar was stuck waiting.

And wait she did!

But God was not happy about Tamar being neglected.

God does not take lightly the ill-treatment of widows and other marginalized people. Read His instructions in Exodus 22:21-22. Look on in verses 23-24 and see the consequence for mistreating widows. Paraphrase it below:

Do not mistreat or oppress a foreigner, for you were foreigners in Egypt. 22 "Do not take advantage of the widow or the fatherless. 23 If you do and they cry out to me, I will certainly hear their cry. 24 **My anger will be aroused**, and I will kill you with the sword; your wives will become widows and your children fatherless.

EXODUS 22:21-24

Though Tamar's situation seems hopeless as she waits in vain for Judah to fulfil his promise of marrying her to Shelah, she is not without options. Forgotten Tamar has an out.

Read Deuteronomy 25:7-10 and answer the following questions:

To whom shall a widow go when a Levirate marriage does not take place?

What will the elders do to help the widow?

What may the widow then do if the brother persists in being unwilling to marry the widow?

When a widow's in-laws refuse to provide for her through Levirate marriage, she has the right to the help of the elders in persuading the family to once again enfold her. And if they are still not willing to have her in the family, she can publicly insult her brother-in-law, spitting on him, and labelling his family so that his lack of loyalty to her is well-known.

Tamar never spit in Judah's face. She never humiliated him, though she had every right to do so. This was her Christ-like act of mercy.

God had serious consequences for those who neglected to care for these vulnerable groups of people. How does knowing the consequences for this offense help you understand God's heart for Tamar and other widows?

Because of the severity of God's punishment, we know of his deep concern for those that might otherwise be overlooked.

Now, Judah, whose birth inspired his mother to praise, had gone from human trafficker to rebellious son to liar to fearful widow-oppressor. And sadly, his sinful choices would continue.

The Waiting Game

Just like Sarah waited to conceive her promised Isaac, and Leah waited for married love, Tamar's life was on pause—through none of her own doing.

Notice a theme yet? The Lord uses seasons of waiting to grow us. Waiting often helps the Christian to be more like Christ. Time and again scripture calls us to wait

Having survived 48 days pregnant while post-due-date (during six pregnancies), I know the pain of waiting firsthand. It's tough. But imagine if your waiting was all someone else's fault—someone who was in the wrong. How hard it would be to keep a root of bitterness from growing in your soul. But somehow Tamar managed. How can we tell? By her actions.

Our culture's attitude toward others that have wronged us is "make them pay!" We are ambulance chasers and lawsuit-happy money grubbers. We hold grudges and take our commitments lightly. Hardcore, deeply-committed loyalty is foreign to us.

Tamar was treated so poorly; she legally had an out. She was justified in smearing Judah and Shelah's name (see sidebar "Tamar Avoids Adding Insult to Injury"), and yet she showed them mercy.

This reminds me of the bishop's act of mercy to Jean Valjean in the classic story *Les Misérables*.

In the novel (or movie), a kindly bishop had offered refuge for an ex-con, Jean Valjean. In return for his kindness, Valjean stole the bishop's silverware. When confronted by the bishop, Valjean beat the man and ran away into the night.

When the police bring Valjean back to the bishop, the bishop has every right to claim the silverware as his own, tell that Valjean hit him, and send Valjean packing off to prison.

But, like Tamar, the bishop lays down his rights. He chooses to show mercy. He tells the police that he has *given* the silverware to Valjean and wants to give him expensive candlesticks as well.

The bishop's mercy frees the criminal from his handcuffs, and he tells Valjean, "with this silver, I have bought your soul. I have ransomed you from fear and hatred, and now I give you back to God."

In the same way, God has shown kindness and mercy to us, freeing us from the handcuffs of our sin by paying Christ's blood as a ransom. He has bought our souls with his blood. And, likewise, we are called to treat others with this same kindness, even when they have mistreated us.

Tamar, chose not to spit in Judah's face and rebuke him publicly; we too can choose mercy.

Tamar's act of mercy and undeserved kindness should cause us to question our own attitudes and actions: Do I show this same soft heart of mercy? Am I quick to forgive, to repay injury with blessing? Or do I stew when someone cuts me off in traffic? Do I grumble when my family is ungrateful for the sacrifices I've made? Do I hold a grudge when someone has gossiped about

...while we were God's enemies, we were reconciled to him through the death of his Son

ROMANS 5:10

God has shown kindness and mercy to us, freeing us from the handcuffs of our sin by paying Christ's blood as a ransom.

Am I willing to lay down my rights to follow God's lead—even when it hurts?

me? It's so easy to have a hard heart—and *these are such small things!* If the Lord can't count on us to have a merciful heart when it comes to the small things, how in the world will we fare when faced with something monumental?

Am I willing to lay down my rights to follow God's lead—even when it hurts?

If my co-worker lies about me and ruins my career, and God calls me to bless her, will I have the strength to do it, even if I can barely stand the thought of her? What about the friend, who has betrayed me? How do I move forward?

How in the world will I manage these kinds of earth-shattering wrongs if I can't even deal with small day-to-day injustices done to me? We must pray for the Lord's help to have a soft, merciful heart. We need his strength to follow his lead when he calls us to mercy. We cannot do it on our own. As we are faithful in the small things, he will strengthen us to endure the hard things.

Take a moment right now to think about how you will live this out this week. What opportunities do you foresee?

If I have eyes to see them, opportunities to show mercy are all around me. When my children talk back to me, I can give gentle instruction instead of biting correction. When a driver cuts in front of me, I can give him grace instead of impatiently honking my horn and riding his tail. When my friend slights me, I can surprise her with a hand-written note or her favorite hot drink. When my husband is short with me, I can rub his shoulders in return. When a sales clerk is grumpy with me, I can be patient and thankful. Small opportunities for merciful living abound every day.

The mercy Tamar extended to Judah's family foreshadows the love of her descendant, Christ. He calls us to return blessing for harm. Read the following passage from Luke 6:27-31, circling the action words of how we are to treat those who mistreat us:

"But to you who are listening I say: Love your enemies, do good to those who hate you, bless those who curse you, pray for those who mistreat you. If someone slaps you on one cheek, turn to them the other also. If someone takes your coat, do not withhold your shirt from them. Give to everyone who asks you, and if anyone takes what belongs to you, do not demand it back. Do to others as you would have them do to you."

Tamar was wise to choose mercy over rebuke. We should do the same. Because Tamar showed mercy, she went from the margins to the main page of God's salvation story for mankind. Remember God's promise to Abraham from week one of our study? Genesis 12:3 says, *"I will bless those who bless you."*

In being a blessing to Judah's family, Tamar would herself be blessed. She would go from being a forgotten, Canaanite widow—a nobody—to being part of God's history-changing, redemptive plan for humankind. She would be a foremother to Christ, literally part of God's family.

> Tamar was wise to choose mercy over rebuke. We should do the same.

Christ calls us to show his mercy, even when we have been deeply wronged.

Share a simple prayer time with the Lord:

- Thank him for his hand of care, no matter how others treat us.
- Ask for strength to wait patiently on him.
- Pray for a heart completely surrendered to him, that returns good for evil.

Takeaway Truth—*"Wait for the Lord; be strong and take heart and wait for the Lord." Psalm 27:14*

DAY FOUR: TAMAR'S UNCONVENTIONAL PLAN

"For our light and momentary troubles are achieving for us an eternal glory that far outweighs them all.'"

2 Corinthians 4:7

Move Over Jerry Springer; This is Getting Weird

With years gone by, and nothing to show for all her waiting, Tamar realized Judah had been pulling the wool over her eyes. Verse 14 of Genesis 38 says, "[Tamar] saw that, though Shelah had now grown up, she had not been given to him as his wife." She had been waiting patiently, but she felt it was time for action.

Despite being misled and mistreated by Judah's family, Tamar *still* remained loyal to Judah's clan. Her loyalty never waned.

Can you think of a time when you were mistreated and were tempted to break a relationship as a result? What happened?

I know I can. For me when the choice is fight or flight, you better believe I long to choose flight! I am a peacemaker. Kum Bah Yah, don't-rock-the-boat, get-along-at-all-costs is my go-to method for dealing with conflict. No confrontation here. It's hard for me to understand others that aren't wired like I am.

A friend of mine decided it was time for some distance between us. I didn't know why, but she was really not happy with me. She didn't want anything to do with me. Flight time for Rachel. In my mind, if I could just avoid her altogether, there wasn't any chance for hurt. But God wouldn't let me off that easy. He wanted me to bless her.

It didn't make any sense to me. "Lord, why would she want me to bless her? She's not even going to want to talk to me. She'll be even more upset with me. It will just be a bother." I prayed. But God prodded.

I offered to help her with childcare, and to my astonishment, she accepted. Through that, God taught me that even when we feel like running from a relationship, it pays to listen to God's promptings, even when they don't make sense. He may have better plans than yours.

If I were Tamar, I probably would have felt like ditching Judah's family altogether. Time to fly. Hadn't she suffered enough already? But Tamar stuck it out.

> It pays to listen to God's promptings, even when they don't make sense.

Tamar did the math and quickly realized that, if Judah's lineage was to continue, it was up to her to make it happen. Judah's wife had died (Genesis 38:12) and Tamar's fiancé Shelah was still being kept from marrying by her controlling father-in-law, Judah. With Er and Onan dead, Tamar was the only foreseeable prospect to keep the family from dying out.

So, Tamar took matters into her own hands. Check out Genesis 38:14, and list Tamar's actions from that verse by filling in the blanks below:

1.

2.

3.

Why Timnah? Backtrack to verse 12 of Genesis 38, and you'll see who else was going that way. Who was it?

Let's press on through this weird-but-true text. Read on in Genesis 38:15-16 and see what crazy things ensue. Fill in the details of the story in this worksheet:

• Who saw Tamar?

• Who did Judah think Tamar was?

• Why did Judah think this?

• What did Judah say to the disguised Tamar?

"I'll send you a young goat from my flock," he said.
"Will you give me something as a pledge until you send it?" she asked.
¹⁸ He said, "What pledge should I give you?"
"Your seal and its cord, and the staff in your hand," she answered. So he gave them to her and slept with her, and she became pregnant by him. ¹⁹ After she left, she took off her veil and put on her widow's clothes again.

GENESIS 38:17-19

Tamar's plan, deceptive though it was, had worked! She had gone undercover as a woman of the night, hoping to capitalize on Judah's (or maybe Shelah's) celebratory time of shearing. Judah was tricked, fell for the bait, and propositioned her. And it only gets weirder from here, friends.

Check out verses 17-19 (in the margin) to see what happens next. Take note especially of what happens in verse 18b. Underline it in the margin.

Finish out this passage, reading verses 20-23 of Genesis 38.

Judah added solicitation of a "prostitute" to his ever-growing list of sins: human trafficking, deceit, disobedience, mistreating a widow—and *he knew it was shameful*. When he couldn't seem to find the mysterious woman to retrieve his seal, cord, and staff— possessions that clearly identified him—he gave up. He wanted to put the whole situation behind him. Little did he know, his visit to the woman by the road was much more than a one-night stand. It would change his life—all our lives—forever.

Now I know it seems like this plot we've just uncovered would make even Jerry Springer blush—after all, Tamar has now been married and widowed by two brothers, engaged to the third brother, and will now become a mother to the fourth and fifth brothers(!) But bear with me while we unpack this story by placing it in its proper setting.

In our day and age, such behavior is hardly imaginable! But, as we've been studying all week, Judah and Tamar's time was *very* different. Today, we marry for love. We choose our spouses based on our feelings. Back then, marriage was much more often for other practical purposes like reproduction, property ownership, and family loyalty. Tamar's behavior echoed her day's value of lineage and loyalty. Her actions, strange as they are to us, showed that she purposed to continue Judah's family line—aligning herself with his family and his God. Rather than smear his family, she furthered it—albeit in a way that seems highly unusual to us.

Remember how Levirate marriages put brothers-in-law together with their brothers' widows to further the family line? Fathers-in-law were also acceptable Levirate husbands. As we'll explore further when we study Ruth, the widow's new husband wasn't *required* to be her deceased husband's brother. Whichever willing family member was next-in-line was acceptable. So, really, it's not far-fetched that Tamar would end up with Judah. In fact, Judah *should have* offered himself as a Levirate since he refused to give Shelah.

Does putting Tamar's story in its historical context make a difference to you? Why or why not?

Tamar's behavior echoed her day's value of **lineage and loyalty**. Her actions, strange as they are to us, showed that she purposed to continue Judah's family line—aligning herself with his family and his God.

Understanding that Judah was an acceptable Levirate, coupled with the importance of the family line continuing, and the knowledge that no other prospect for progeny was in the picture help me realize the gravity of Tamar's actions. Even though I don't see myself seducing someone or marrying my in-law for any reason (ever!), I get it. To be an ancestress to the long-awaited Messiah was, well, the most important reason in ancient history to be a woman.

Living on this side of the New Testament I think it's hard for us to imagine the urgent need creation felt for Christ. Certainly we eagerly await the second coming of Jesus, but we have His spirit, His teaching, and His companionship. How much more must ancient followers of God longed achingly for His first coming.

As a child, I remember longing for something that seemed so distant—a holiday, a vacation, a birthday. Waiting in eager anticipation was both exhilarating and exhausting. If there were any way to accelerate its coming, certainly I would have made every effort to do so.

Tamar choosing to further Judah's family was a big deal. How could she be certain it would end well for her? If I were in her shoes, I might have chosen the safer route of hunkering down in my father's house longer, and missing out on God's big plans. Or maybe I'd have spit in Judah's face in frustration at his fraidy-cat inaction. But Tamar chose waiting, then mercy, then at the opportune time, action. Wow.

The Ends Don't Justify

Tamar's goal was immensely noble—to continue the family line and remain mercifully loyal to Judah's family was the right thing to do. Our family obligations are important to God! See 1 Timothy 5:8, in the margin.

But Tamar's *method* was anything but noble. Her desperation led to some foolish choices. Let's not let her good motives—

> Anyone who does not provide for their relatives, and especially for their own household, has denied the faith and is worse than an unbeliever.
>
> 1 TIMOTHY 5:8

which we *should* follow—influence us to follow her unwise actions. Deception is not a good idea.

Read about Paul's thoughts on using deception, even for the gospel cause, in 2 Corinthians 4:2 in the margin. While you read, cross out all of the negative techniques for ministry, and circle the proper way to share the gospel.

Christians are set free by the truth (John 8:32) and walk in the light (1 John 1:7). Satan is the father of lies (John 8:44). Trickery and deceit have no place in the life of a Christ-follower. We will discuss this more in Week 5 as we study the life of Rahab.

Though Tamar's cause was noble, and God certainly used her deceit to bring about good, we cannot use her example to condone or promote deceit in the life of the Christian. It would have been better for her to have found another way to get Judah to fulfill his family obligation (we will see an example of this in the story of Ruth and Boaz). Instead we can look to her example of patience, and mercy.

But aren't there times when we are just as bad as Tamar (or worse?), when we too deceive with what we think are good intentions? How about when we flatter others falsely, or when we tell white lies to make a situation improve, or say something untrue to make someone feel better? Tactful truth is the better way.

But, because of our miraculous God and despite her own sin, God used Tamar's willing, loyal mercy to the family of Judah to change the course of history. God would bring beauty from her ashes. In her heroic story we find an example—not of a perfect woman—but of a God who used flawed humans to carry out his perfect plan *despite* their own shortcomings. I don't know about you, but for me, that is a source of great comfort and hope.

If there's hope for a deceiver like Tamar to be used in huge ways, there's hope for me. She may not have had her methods perfected—far from it! But she had a heart of mercy for Judah

Rather, we have renounced secret and shameful ways; we do not use deception, nor do we distort the word of God. On the contrary, by setting forth the truth plainly we commend ourselves to everyone's conscience in the sight of God.

2 CORINTHIANS 4:2

In her heroic story we find an example—not of a perfect woman—but of a God who used flawed humans to carry out his perfect plan.

and a gritty loyalty to his family—a loyalty God used in amazing ways.

Tamar and Judah's story of flaws and redemption point not only to a powerful God—but also a broken humankind's aching need for a savior.

Sometimes even the most heroic of Bible characters make mistakes. We saw this with Abraham and Sarah, now with Tamar.

When Bible characters are praised for their heroism, it can be confusing. But they are flawed humans, just like us. We should emulate their good behaviors, not their mistakes.

A simple rule of thumb to tell if a particular action by a Bible Character should be imitated is to ask yourself, "what does scripture say about this kind of behavior?"

God allowed Tamar to conceive twins. But her womb nurtured more than two small, precious babes. In Tamar's belly grew the promise of something better. Something that would bring restoration to the lost cause that was Jacob's broken family. Some*one* that would save her from her sins and bring salvation for all mankind.

> God can mightily use even the most flawed of us that have a heart for His perfect plan.

Share a simple prayer time with the Lord:

- Thank him for his willingness to use even sinful people to accomplish his plans.
- Ask for strength to be loyal to the Lord's plan for you, no matter how impossible it seems.
- Pray for a pure heart, zealous for living with integrity in the light of truth.

Takeaway Truth—*"But we have this treasure in jars of clay to show that this all-surpassing power is from God and not from us." 2 Corinthians 4:7*

DAY FIVE: THE BIG REVEAL

"The hypocrite with his mouth destroys his neighbor, but through knowledge the righteous will be delivered."

Proverbs 11:9 NKJV

Judah's Hypocrisy

Judah and Tamar's story is about to go from *Jerry Springer* to *Days of Our Lives* in our first passage for today. Read Genesis 38:24 in the margin, underlining Judah's angry words.

If Tamar had truly acted as a prostitute—like everyone thought—she would have been committing adultery against Shelah. Living as Onan's widow meant she was betrothed to Shelah and expected to be faithful to him. She was still obligated to Judah's family, even though they had not given her a husband. So, when Judah found out about Tamar's pregnancy, he saw red.

Adultery was punishable by death, so Judah's consequence for Tamar *would* have been justified, had she been an adulteress. The irony here is that Judah was Tamar's sexual partner, and yet he is her accuser. Were their encounter adultery, he deserved death just as much as she.

Check out Leviticus 20:10 in the margin see what it has to say about adulterers:

Judah's anger resembled the angry mob of John 8. The hypocritical Teachers of the Law and Pharisees had caught a woman in adultery and brought her before Jesus to stone. Christ is not fooled by their "righteous" (hypocritical) anger.

What is his response? Read it in John 8:7b and put it in your own words here:

Jesus reminds the Teachers of the Law and the Pharisees that they are not innocent of their own wrongdoing, and therefore have no place condemning the adulteress.

How easily we tend toward the reaction of the Pharisees. It's easy for me to point out the struggle of another, to gather stones

> About three months later Judah was told, "Your daughter-in-law Tamar is guilty of prostitution, and as a result she is now pregnant." Judah said, "Bring her out and have her burned to death!"
>
> GENESIS 38:24

> If a man commits adultery with another man's wife—with the wife of his neighbor—both the adulterer and the adulteress are to be put to death.
>
> LEVITICUS 20:10

to throw without being honest with myself about my own sinful shortcomings.

I grumble about my children's bad attitudes by, ironically, complaining. I get frustrated with someone for running late, then find myself doing the same. I am offended that she's short with me because she's worn down, but I feel justified being grumpy when I'm tired. I think he should work harder but I should get a break. Maybe you can relate.

It's time to put down our stones.

What stones are you holding that you need to lay down? How might you be harboring a heart of hypocrisy like Judah?

It's time to put down our stones.

For the woman in adultery, a stone laid down meant no more condemnation. It meant a release from her death sentence—a newfound freedom. And since the wages of sin is death for us all, we—like the adulteress—have all been released from our own death sentences through Christ.

In the Bible, stones on the ground are also monuments of remembrance. For Tamar, for the adulteress, for us all—stones laid down can symbolize what the Lord has done in our lives (Joshua 4).

> For the wages of sin is death, but the gift of God is eternal life in Christ Jesus our Lord.
>
> ROMANS 6:23

The Truth Comes to Light

Verses 25-26 of Genesis 38 show a very different Judah than we've ever seen before. Thus far we've known Judah to be self-centered, rebellious, fearful, deceptive, and hypocritical.

Read Genesis 38:25-26. Answer the following questions after reading: What message did Tamar send to Judah?

What does Judah say when presented with the evidence against him?

Tamar didn't make a public announcement for all to hear. Instead like *The Scarlet Letter's* Hester Prynne, Tamar gave her babies' father the chance to fess up. Judah didn't respond with defensiveness or anger to Tamar's revelation, or make excuses. Judah took responsibility for his mistake.

Talk about a 180. One minute, Judah is calling for Tamar's blood to be spilled—the next, he is praising her righteousness. That's hypocrisy-turned-humility. The man who lived in selfish deception, rebellion, and fear, mistreating those around him, has suddenly shown a repentant, humble heart.

Tamar—the lowly Canaanite widow—was used by God as a pivotal character to help bring Judah to this turning point, the moment of repentance in this important patriarch's heart. Only God could have worked this miracle on such a hard heart.

Do you see the power of righteous living played out here? Do you understand what this means? This is huge! When we are faithful, and have a loyal, merciful heart heaping blessing upon those that insult and mistreat us, God can use us to bring about monumental change. Our obedience can lead to transformation in the lives of others. See the verses in the margin.

My heart's cry is that *that would be me*. My soul longs for *that to be you*—for us to be women like Tamar whose heart and priorities are *so in line with God* that our righteous behavior turns heads. That our faithfulness and loyalty to our Heavenly Father melts the hard hearts of those around us—all for His glory.

> Only God could have worked this miracle on such a hard heart.

Let your light shine before others, that they may see your good deeds and glorify your Father in heaven.

MATTHEW 5:16

Live such good lives among the pagans that, though they accuse you of doing wrong, they may see your good deeds and glorify God

1 PETER 2:12

Judah had wanted Tamar **burned alive**, but now it was he that was **burning with shame** over his own hypocrisy.

We read about the power of this "burning coals" phenomenon in Romans 12. See verses 17 and 20 in the margin.

What might it look like if you apply the "burning coals" philosophy to your life today?

Just the other day my husband had a chance to "heap burning coals." He was mowing our lawn, which borders a vacation rental property with several cabins. Just over a knoll, he found beer and soda cans littering our grass. Not cool.

He shut off the blade and dropped to his hands and knees to clean up the mess. He stuffed down feelings of revenge and a flaring temper, remembering his recent sermon on foot washing and humbly serving others. The Holy Spirit prompted him that this was a real-life opportunity to practice what he preached.

As he gathered the cans and planned to quietly cart them back to our garage, a sheepish young man hopped out of a nearby parked pickup. The red-faced twenty-something stammered out an apology—repentantly taking responsibility for the mess. The burning shame of the situation swept over the young man.

"No worries! I've got it," assured my husband with a smile. "Hope you have a great evening!"

It's contagious integrity—mercy breeds repentance.

We're about to get a close-up look at how the "burning coals" principle played out in the story of Judah and Tamar. It's huge.

By choosing to repay Judah's curse with blessing, a seemingly powerless widow turned the tides of Judah's life—and his family, and God's people, and us all—for eternity.

The Prodigal Comes Home

The rest of Judah's days would be lived out with a marked difference from his previous life. After his humbling encounter with Tamar, God would instill a deep loyalty within Judah's own heart.

The man who forsook his younger brother, fooled his father, and forgot his family's commitment to Tamar began behaving in ways hardly recognizable to those who knew the old Judah.

Judah's days of buddying up with the Canaanite Hirah of Adullam had been fraught with death and trouble—first losing his sons, then his wife, then seeking the bed of a shrine prostitute (or so he thought). But Tamar's life-changing mercy had Judah leaving his days among the Canaanites behind. The prodigal came home.

The God-timing was impeccable, as a severe famine had swept across the land, and Judah's family needed his help (see Genesis 42). The younger, rebellious Judah would have spurned his father's instructions to go to Egypt for help, but older, wiser, loyal Judah rose to the occasion when his father, Jacob (Israel), asked for assistance. Judah fell in line with his brothers to make the long, hard journey to Egypt for sake of the survival of his father's entire family (Genesis 42:3).

And, again, when the family needed more grain, Judah stepped up and convinced Jacob to allow Benjamin to come along to Egypt (Genesis 43:8-9). Believe it or not, the same Judah who once shook in his boots, fearing a helpless widow, now showed wisdom to lead his family well. Judah's persuasive words to his father show just how deep a heart-change he had after his encounter with Tamar.

What was reformed, humble Judah willing to do to reassure Jacob of Benjamin's safety during the brothers' second trip to Egypt, according to Genesis 43:8-9? Circle his words in the margin.

The prodigal came home.

Then Judah said to Israel his father, "Send the boy along with me and we will go at once, so that we and you and our children may live and not die. ⁹I myself will guarantee his safety; you can hold me personally responsible for him. If I do not bring him back to you and set him here before you, I will bear the blame before you all my life.

GENESIS 43:8-9

Fast forward a few verses, and Benjamin was in danger of being held back in Egypt. Judah's loyalty and integrity would be put to the test. What would the once-selfish Judah say when Benjamin was threatened with being detained? In Genesis 44:25-34, we find Judah's words to Pharaoh's assistant Joseph (Judah didn't yet realize his brother's identity).

Read verse 33 below, circling Judah's desperate pleas to Joseph:

Now then, please let your servant remain here as my lord's slave in place of the boy, and let the boy return with his brothers

The one who formerly sold his own brother into slavery was now completely repentant, willing to *himself* become a slave in order to save his brother. The one who once willingly brought misery upon his father was now *unable to bear the thought* of grieving his family.

Judah's actions proved his changed heart. Judah's repentance was the balm that healed deep, old wounds between him and Joseph. The broken family's story finds a happy ending in Genesis 45, where they are reunited and all are saved from the famine.

> Judah was showing a family resemblance to his descendant, Christ.

Judah was showing a family resemblance to his descendant, Christ. He now knew the true meaning of love. First John 3:16 says, *"This is how we know what love is: Jesus Christ laid down his life for us. And we ought to lay down our lives for our brothers and sisters."* God's people were restored, saved from starvation—all because a twice-widowed Canaanite chose to lay down her rights.

Leaving a Legacy of Loyalty

Tamar, a once forgotten Canaanite widow, would not leave this earth without leaving her mark. An unlikely foremother in the Hebrew nation both because of her nationality and her mistakes, God graciously rewarded Tamar's loyalty to Judah and his family by recognizing her time and again in scripture. While we may notice her faults and failures, God saw her Christlike heart and made her a heroine.

Remember shouting to your friend, "beatcha to the playground!" and running pell-mell to your destination? The feeling of victory upon arriving was sweet. There's nothing like being the first, right?

Tamar has the distinction of being the first woman mentioned by name in the New Testament and, likewise, the first woman mentioned by name in the bloodline of Christ in Matthew 1:3.

It may not seem significant to you that her name was listed in a genealogy—a long, long list. Perhaps you think this list is so boring it's worth skipping, but consider this: her name was important enough to be included. Not Sarah's, not Leah's...but Tamar's. Out of 42 generations listed in the genealogy with 42 men's names, only 4 women are named. *Four*. And Tamar is the first.

In Tamar's life, we are reminded that God accepts all, even if you come from a godless people. Though her story was unusual, and downright uncomfortable, she was more than a sum of her mistakes. She showed that though others abandon us, God never forgets us, and he can make beauty from even the most hopeless of situations. She models a Christlike heart of mercy, repaying evil with blessing, never flagging in her loyalty to God's people.

Stones once intended for punishment and death are laid down as stones of remembrance to remind us what an awesome, merciful, and gracious God we serve! And, as we end our study with Tamar, let us be inspired to be women of merciful loyalty. By the grace of God, may our lives show a righteousness that changes hearts like Tamar's did for Judah, setting others on the course to everlasting life. Let's live unselfishly for the cause of Christ rather than any other goal. Let us, like Tamar, strive to show the merciful, faithful loyalty of our Lord and King, Jesus Christ who first showed us his own perfect kindness in return for our evil.

Out of 42 generations listed in the genealogy with 42 men's names only **four** women are named... And **Tamar is the first**.

> A woman of true mercy can melt hard hearts, turning the tides of evil for good, bringing repentance to the wayward and giving glory to God.

> Let us, like Tamar, strive to show the merciful, faithful loyalty of our Lord and King, Jesus Christ who first showed us his own perfect kindness in return for our evil.

Share a simple prayer time with the Lord:

- Thank him that his truth sets free, and ask that he would help you live in the light.
- Ask for a deep loyalty to Christ, and to his calling on your life.
- Pray that your legacy would be one of God's grace for past mistakes and repentance moving forward.

Takeaway Truth—*"The people living in darkness have seen a great light; on those living in the land of the shadow of death a light has dawned." Matthew 4:16*

A Tangible Reminder

Find a stone to put in a prominent place—on your desk or windowsill—as a reminder. Just as the woman caught in adultery was shown mercy, and the rocks meant to stone her were laid down, we have been delivered from certain death and can lay down stones to remember our deliverance. Our rocks can also serve as a reminder of our own call to show mercy, laying down our stones of judgement or revenge.

When asked about why the stone is there, just like in Joshua 4:7, give testimony to the good mercy of God in your life. Share your stones of remembrance with a post to social media, using #significantwomenofthebible #stonesofrememberance to curate testimonies of God's goodness. Or be sure to share with someone in a conversation, text, or note as your own testimony to God's good mercy in your life.

Pause for Praise—A huge pat on your back for finishing Week 3 of the study! God blesses us as we seek him through his word. Though others may overlook us, God never does.

Looking at Tamar's life we also see firsthand the importance of merciful patience and treating others with respect—even when they don't deserve it. God never forgets us and he can make beauty from even the most hopeless of situations.

Before you conclude this time reflecting on the life of Tamar, take a few moments to ponder the perfect loyalty of our awesome God. I suggest you find the powerful lyric video for Lauren Daigle's *Loyal* on YouTube and watch with a worshipful heart. If you adore hymns, try *Jesus is All the World to Me* instead.

God can use our acts of mercy to melt
hearts of stone

RAHAB

Zero to Hero

Day One
RAHAB'S
SCANDALOUS BACKSTORY

Day Two
A PIVOTAL MOMENT
OF HOSPITALITY

Day Three
ESCAPING THE CORDS OF DEATH

Day Four
THE SCARLET CORD OF HOPE

Day Five
RAHAB'S LEGACY:
COURAGE, FAITH & HOPE

Significant

DAY ONE: RAHAB'S SCANDALOUS BACKSTORY

MAIN TEXTS
Matthew 1:3-4
Genesis 45:9-11, 20
Exodus 1:1-14
Joshua 2:1-7
Matthew 15:3-9

"So they went and entered the house of a prostitute named Rahab and stayed there." Joshua 2:1

A Quick Recap

Before jump right in to Rahab's story, let's recap what we've learned so far in this study. We are halfway through our in-depth exploration of the lives of six women in Jesus' bloodline found in Matthew 1. The reason we are digging into these women's lives is that they come from all walks of life—and made plenty of mistakes—and yet the Lord used them in powerful ways to further his family line. Through their family the scriptures were written, miracles were performed, and kings rose—most notably the King of Kings, Jesus Christ himself, through whom the whole earth could receive salvation.

Their lives are an example of God using the ordinary to do extraordinary things. They are heroic, and yet, as we read their stories, we are struck by their humanity. What God accomplished through their flawed lives is nothing short of a miracle. God has made us for significance as well. We can find purpose in Christ even when life feels ordinary.

So far, we've looked at the life of familiar Bible character, **Sarah,** foremother to the nation of Israel. We learned that, though she is truly an admirable woman, her life was filled with tragic mistakes. But God turned her hot-mess-of-a-life into a thing of beauty as he transformed her heart. Her sin would have devastating effects on her descendants, but ultimately, *she modeled for us a gentle and quiet spirit that is at peace and obedient because of her deep trust in God.*

We have also learned about **Leah,** who was rejected and unwanted by others—a situation in which we frequently find

God turned Sarah's hot-mess-of-a-life into a thing of beauty.

God's love for Leah was better than the love of anyone on earth, and so she praised Him.

God honored Tamar's merciful loyalty by making her part of his family.

ourselves. Leah strove to earn love from people. She thought that being cherished by her husband would bring her the fulfillment and acceptance she so earnestly desired. But, in the same way people disappoint us, Leah was disappointed when her husband Jacob never loved her in the way she wanted. At long last, Leah discovered that God's love for her was better than the love of anyone on earth. Through her life *we learn to praise God no matter what our circumstances and that, no matter how unlovely others make us feel, we ARE loved by God.*

Through **Tamar**'s unusual story we see the importance of mercy. Though mistreated and forsaken by her husband's family, Tamar remained devoted to God's people and God's purposes. Rather than choosing to disown Judah in response to his behavior—which she had every right to do—she chose to stay faithful to Judah's family, and to the Lord. Like her descendent, Christ, she returned blessing for curse. Her devotion to God's people and her heart of mercy would be used by God to melt the hard heart of Judah. God used her actions to change the course of Judah's life and heal deep wounds within his family—saving them all from starvation and famine. Though her methods of furthering the family line are not something we should emulate, ultimately God honored her merciful loyalty by making her part of his family. In her life we see a glimmer of *the perfect, steadfast loyalty and mercy of Christ, challenging us to live the same.*

Speeding Through Five Generations—the CliffsNotes Version

As we move down the family line in Matthew 1, after the generations of Sarah (Abraham), Leah (Jacob), and Tamar (Judah), we have a few generations about which we don't really know much at all.

Looking at Matthew 1:3-4, there were five men in the genealogy who were born in the generations between Judah and Salmon. What are their names? Find them in the margin.

We don't have the details of Perez, Hezron, Ram, Amminadab, or Nahshon's wives to glean much of anything from the foremothers' lives in these generations. Some sections of the genealogy don't give us much to go on.

These five generations were a crucial time in the history of God's people, however. So, we'll do a quickie overview of the years' events during these generations to give ourselves a refresher. Stay with me for today's longer-than-normal lesson, and we'll get our historical bearings before we move on to Rahab's story—the main focus of this week's study.

Tamar and Judah's story ended with a famine in the land and Judah and his brothers being reunited with Joseph in Egypt, where there was food. In the storybook ending, Joseph had proclaimed to his brothers: *"Hurry back to my father and say to him, 'This is what your son Joseph says: God has made me lord of all Egypt. Come down to me; don't delay. You shall live in the region of Goshen and be near me—you, your children and grandchildren, your flocks and herds, and all you have. I will provide for you there, because five years of famine are still to come. Otherwise you and your household and all who belong to you will become destitute... Never mind about your belongings, because **the best of all Egypt will be yours.**'" Genesis 45:9-11, 20.*

God had used what Judah and his brothers had intended for harm (selling Joseph to slave traders) for good! With Judah's change of heart, Joseph and his brothers had been reunited. It would be a fairy-tale ending. Their whole family would be saved!

But, in Exodus 1, we read that times were changing. What happened in the following verses?

Exodus 1:6—

Judah the father of Perez and Zerah, whose mother was Tamar,
Perez the father of Hezron,
Hezron the father of Ram,
4 Ram the father of Amminadab,
Amminadab the father of Nahshon,
Nahshon the father of Salmon,

MATTHEW 1:3-4

A GOOD MOVE FOR JACOB

Jacob and all of his sons relocated to Egypt to survive the famine. *"So Jacob and all his offspring went to Egypt, taking with them their livestock and the possessions they had acquired in Canaan. Jacob brought with him to Egypt his sons and grandsons and his daughters and granddaughters—all his offspring... All those who went to Egypt with Jacob... were seventy in all,"* Genesis 46:6-7,26-27. God was fulfilling his promise to Abraham.

Which specific parts of God's blessing to Abraham were being fulfilled? (Hint: look back at Genesis 12:2)

Because of Joseph's position of power, the family found favor with the Egyptians and prospered. This was surprising, as Jacob's family were both foreigners and shepherds—two things Egyptians would not have normally looked on with favor.

What did the Egyptians think of shepherds, according to Joseph in Genesis 46:34?

But God would continue to provide for his people, against all odds.

Pharaoh so valued Joseph that he showed Jacob's entire family unexpected favor. He said, *"settle your father and your brothers in the best part of the land"* Genesis 47:6.

So Joseph did—providing his family with prime real estate, and provisions to boot: *"Joseph settled his father and his brothers in Egypt and gave them property in the best part of the land, the district of Rameses, as Pharaoh directed. Joseph also provided his father and his brothers and all his father's household with food,"* Genesis 47:11-12. Jacob and his sons would live long and prosper in Egypt.

Exodus 1:7—

Exodus 1:8—

Exodus 1:11—

There was no longer a good relationship between God's people and the rulers of Egypt.

But God continued to carry out the blessing he'd promised to Abraham so many years before. The people of Israel continued to grow in number. Read Exodus 1:7, circling how the Israelites growth is described.

The Hebrew population was exploding, which was threatening to the new, not-too-fond-of-God's-people Pharaoh. He would put the Israelites in their place with an evil plan. God's people became enslaved. The Egyptians were harsh and demanding, but just as God never forgot Tamar, he didn't forget his people enslaved in Egypt.

God raised up Moses and sent him to Pharaoh with a message: "Let my people go." Moses was from the tribe of Levi, Sarah and Leah's descendants, and God used him to deliver his people out of slavery and back to the land he had promised Abraham and Sarah so many years earlier. You can catch that knock-your-socks-off, miraculous story in the first 14 chapters of Exodus. After the crossing of the Red Sea—the complete victory over Pharaoh's army—God's people "believed the Lord" (Exodus 14:31 NKJV). Just like their forefather Abraham, renowned for his faith, had "believed the Lord" (Genesis 15:6) and "he did not waver through unbelief regarding the promise of God, but was strengthened in his faith and gave glory to God, being fully persuaded that God had power to do what he had promised" (Romans 4:20-21), so God's people experienced a renewing of their faith.

But, even after their incredible deliverance from the oppressive hand of Pharaoh, God's people struggled to walk in obedience. Let's face it—they sound an awful lot like me.

I remember in the early days of our ministry, the struggle of keeping faith amidst the realities of life. We had left everything we knew behind to move a thousand miles away from our family. We felt the call of the Lord and happily followed in obedience—then the hard times came.

With an unprecedented plunge in the housing market came financial uncertainty in ministry. When members didn't have any income, tithes plummeted, and so did the church's financial health.

Suddenly our family's financial stability was at stake. How could the Lord call us so far from home, only to put us in such uncertain circumstances? There were moments I was so filled with worry that I wasn't so sure how I felt about following God's call anymore.

but the Israelites were exceedingly fruitful; they multiplied greatly, increased in numbers and became so numerous that the land was filled with them.

EXODUS 1:7

God's people struggled to walk in obedience. Let's face it— they sound an awful lot like me.

But despite my own doubts and fears, the Lord was faithful. Those years weren't easy, and His provision for us wasn't always in the ways I anticipated, but time and again—God showed himself faithful.

Likewise, Israel's wilderness wanderings would be filled with spiritual highs and carnal lows. God provided sweet bread from heaven and quail to strengthen and sustain his beloved people (Exodus 16). He miraculously produced water from a rock to quench Israel's thirst (Exodus 17), gave them the law to guide them in maintaining close fellowship with Him (Exodus 20-40, Leviticus, Deuteronomy), and delivered victory after victory over Israel's enemies (Exodus 17, Numbers 21 & 31, Deuteronomy 2-3).

But Israel's feeble faith faltered time and again. Their wilderness wanderings were filled with times of complaining (Exodus 17:3), idolatry (Exodus 32), disobedience (Numbers 20:1-12), and discontent (Numbers 21:5). But God's faithfulness did not depend on his people's fickle faith. He brought them to their Promised Land.

God's faithfulness did not depend on his people's fickle faith.

Are We There Yet?

At long last, after over 400 years of harsh enslavement in Egypt, and 40 years of both *victory* and *struggle-filled journeying* through the desert, God's people had arrived. The Israelites were on the cusp of finally entering the long-awaited Promised Land.

The Israelites had wandered in the desert for years because of their disobedience, but now Moses and the rebellious generation had passed away and Joshua was poised and ready to lead God's people into Canaan—the sweet Promised Land.

Like any shrewd military leader, Joshua needed to send in spies to do recon and scope out the land they were about to enter. This was a technique he learned from Moses, who had used spies years earlier, in Numbers 13-14.

Who were the two most faithful of Moses' spies, who gave a glowing report, according to Numbers 14:6-8?

Joshua knew firsthand the advantages of sending in spies because he himself had been a spy under Moses' leadership.

We now arrive at the first chapters of the book of Joshua. Joshua was about to send his spies into Jericho, a key city to overtake because of its location. Jericho was just across the Jordan River from the Israelite camp, on the very edge of the Promised Land, Canaan. We find Rahab, an unlikely character in the saga of God's people, and yet a pivotal person in God's plan for Joshua and the Israelites' entrance into the Promised Land.

Read Joshua 2:1-7.

God led the spies to the house of a prostitute to find refuge. But even though Rahab had a sullied past (her life would forever carry the label "harlot"), she proved her faith in God and her loyalty to his people by her actions.

While we certainly can't use Rahab's life to justify her harlotry—that would be far from wise—we will see that her past mistakes do not disqualify her from a life of faith.

In Jesus' words from Matthew 21, he pointed out that sometimes those with the biggest mistakes in their past are the very ones who are quickest to show a heart of faith. In verses 31b and 32, Jesus pointed this out to the religious leaders.

The religious leaders of Jesus' day were sure of their own righteousness, and sure that people such as prostitutes would have no place in the kingdom of God. Jesus' words were their wake-up call.

Joshua son of Nun and Caleb son of Jephunneh, who were among those who had explored the land, tore their clothes [7] and said to the entire Israelite assembly, "The land we passed through and explored is exceedingly good. [8] If the Lord is pleased with us, he will lead us into that land, a land flowing with milk and honey, and will give it to us.

NUMBERS 14:6-8

Jesus said to them, "Truly I tell you, the tax collectors and the prostitutes are entering the kingdom of God ahead of you. [32] For John came to you to show you the way of righteousness, and you did not believe him, but the tax collectors and the prostitutes did. And even after you saw this, you did not repent and believe him.

MATTHEW 21:31b-32

> Beware of the trap of thinking that just because we don't commit certain sins, our hearts are right with God.

As believers, we must be so careful to not have the hard hearts of the chief priests and the Pharisees. We need to cultivate repentant, humble hearts that realize their need for God and respond to Him with faith. Beware of the trap of thinking that just because we don't commit certain noticeable sins, our hearts are right with God.

Who are the Rehabs of our day? Who might we be quick to misjudge as unable to be used for God's kingdom?

It's hard to imagine God using Meth addicts, severely disabled people, the homeless, ex-cons, foul-mouthed celebrities, con artists, or any number of people who don't fit our mold of what a Christian leader looks like. Why are we wrong to jump to the conclusion that God doesn't use certain people?

In what ways are we ourselves similar to these people we may think of as "unusable" by God?

We may have a hard time admitting it, but sometimes as Christians we puff up with pride when we should really be humbling ourselves. Sometimes others' pats on the back trick us into thinking we're doing well, when really, we need prayerful heart checks to make sure we are repentant and humble.

Others may see us as the woman who has it all figured out—but if we're honest, we know we need a savior just as desperately as Rahab. May the Lord help us remember it.

Jesus had rebuked the Pharisees earlier in chapter 15 of Matthew with cutting words, *"And why do you break the command of God for the sake of your tradition? ... you nullify the word of God for the sake of your tradition. You hypocrites! Isaiah was right when he prophesied about you: 'These people honor me with their lips, but their hearts are far from me. They worship me in vain; their teachings are merely human rules.'" Matthew 15:3-9.*

In other words, we can't get so caught up in our own list of "dos" and "don'ts" that we miss the point—a heart that's devoted to God. We have to understand that even a prostitute can be a hero when it comes to faith. As we continue to follow Rahab's story, we'll see this firsthand.

> Like the Israelites of old, I can be faithless, but I serve a faithful God who sees the depth of my heart—and longs for my repentance and humility.

Spend a few moments with the Lord in prayer:

- Thank him for his faithfulness in your life, despite the times—like the people of Israel—you've stumbled.
- Ask him for eyes that are open to see the truths he's got for you this week in your study of Rahab.
- Pray that the Lord would guard your heart from becoming hard like that of the Pharisees, and instead give you a heart that is faith-filled, repentant, and humble.

Takeaway Truth—*"How then can we be saved? All of us have become like one who is unclean, and all our righteous acts are like filthy rags...Yet you, Lord, are our Father. We are the*

clay; you are the potter; we are all the work of your hand."
Isaiah 64:5b-6a, 8

MAIN TEXTS
Joshua 1:7,9,18
Joshua 2:1-11
Hebrews 11:31
James 2:25-26

DAY 2: A PIVOTAL MOMENT OF HOSPITALITY

"The prudent see danger and take refuge, but the simple keep going and pay the penalty."

Proverbs 22:3

Mission Impossible: Jericho

It was a super-secret mission that Joshua sent the spies on. The spies sneaked into Jericho to collect information on the Canaanites so Israel could be victorious. But the spies had to be careful not to be caught in enemy territory.

It's exciting and dangerous enough material for a suspense movie: evil enemies, coming destruction, secret information, hanging by ropes—it's practically Mission Impossible: Jericho. And these real-life infiltrators worked without harnesses or stunt doubles!

In chapter 1, Joshua is exhorted time and again with the same phrase, found in verses 7, 9, and 18. What is it?

> Rahab of Jericho, a Canaanite woman...is the first character in the book of Joshua to show a grand act of courage.

God's people are at a critical time in history, poised and ready to move into the Promised Land at long last. But battles lie ahead, and courage is necessary moving forward. What is interesting, though, is that Rahab of Jericho, a Canaanite woman—a prostitute no less—is the first character in the book of Joshua to show a grand act of courage.

Rahab is hugely important in this story. For God's people to safely take over Jericho and all of Canaan, they needed good information from the spies. As we will see in a minute, Rahab wisely supplied them with information that helped the Israelites succeed in battle. But she also provided refuge for the spies.

Perhaps you think that Rahab's actions were no big deal. You'd be wrong. In welcoming, hiding, and helping the spies, Rahab was committing *unthinkable treason* against her people and her king—she was turning her back on everything she knew. In brutal times like these, the punishment for such an act was sure to be severe, and yet Rahab's faith didn't flinch.

Hebrews 11:31 (NKJV) says she welcomed the spies with peace. Digging deep into the meaning of this word we find that it's not just a military-type peace—it's peace of the soul. Rahab had confidence in her salvation, even in dangerous circumstances, because she was so sure that she was choosing the right God. She knew the God of the Israelites could save her.

Rahab's city was replete with false religion. She would have been indoctrinated with idolatry from the cradle. And yet, Israel's God's reputation was enough to make her ready to jump ship from the pagan gods and seek refuge with the only real God.

> By faith the harlot Rahab did not perish with those who did not believe, when she had received the spies **with peace.**
>
> HEBREWS 11:31 (NKJV)

How convicting for me that a Canaanite prostitute like Rahab had enough faith to risk her life to align herself with God and his people. She knew so little of God and yet, she was willing to courageously put all her hope in him. Would I show that same courage in her shoes? I hope. But my track record isn't so great. Maybe you're the same.

I wonder how many times we could have shown courage in living for Christ in our day-to-day lives, and, yet we gave excuses and chickened out on serving God wholeheartedly:

I was in too much of a hurry to help that stranger.

I don't have enough talent to serve in that ministry.

I need time to myself to recharge; I can't be expected to care for those people today.

If I give to them, I'll just be enabling their dependency.

I can't talk to her about Christ, it would be too awkward.

...and our excuses go on and on. And opportunities to live courageously for Christ pass us by. Paul calls us to "wake up" in Ephesians 5:14. He goes on to tell us *why* in verses 15-16. Read these verses in the margin.

> This is why it is said: "Wake up, sleeper, rise from the dead, and Christ will shine on you."
> Be very careful, then, how you live—not as unwise but as wise, making the most of every opportunity, because the days are evil.
>
> EPHESIANS 5:14-16

It's time to serve the Lord, *today*. But if we can't even be faithful to Christ in the small day-to-day things, how will we do when faced with circumstances calling for true courage? What is one opportunity in your life right now where Christ could be calling you to show courage?

Maybe there's a hard conversation you've been dreading, or an apology you owe. Perhaps God has been calling you to serve in a way that's uncomfortable to you, and you've been avoiding it. Or maybe you're supposed to give something up, and you just can't seem to let go. I know it's not easy. But it's not too hard for God. Whatever it is, let's ask the Lord for the courage we need to follow him with abandon today.

> Let's ask the Lord for the courage we need to follow him with abandon today.

A Good Liar?

One thing that has caught the attention of many is that Rahab lied. Time and again it's sparked a debate in many-a-Bible study or Christian Ethics class. When questioned about the spies by the King of Jericho's messengers, Rahab deceived them. While the spies are still hidden, she tells the men: *"They left. I don't know which way they went. Go after them quickly. You may catch up with them." (Joshua 2:5)*. This is a bold-faced lie. Rahab herself had hidden the men. How could Rahab be hailed as a hero?

Those of you who know well the "Heroes of the Faith" chapter 11 of Hebrews know that it includes Rahab—in fact, she is the only woman other than Sarah to be mentioned by name in that chapter. It says, *"By faith the prostitute Rahab, because she welcomed the spies, was not killed with those who were disobedient." Hebrews 11:31*.

And Rahab is also praised in James 2:25. See this verse in the margin:

After reading these passages, you might start to think deception doesn't pose much of a problem for the believer, as long as you're doing it for the right reasons. I mean, Rahab lied and it was heroic, right? Nope.

"A lying tongue" is listed in Proverbs 6:7 as one of the seven things "detestable" to God. Even when it seems that good may come from some sin, it is not justified. Romans 3 teaches that we should never do evil that good may result. We'd be playing with fire trying to use Rahab's story as proof that lying is permissible.

If we look closely at the verses praising Rahab, we see that her lies are not the actions for which she was praised. Hebrews 11 doesn't applaud Rahab's lies; it praises her faithful actions. It commends her for welcoming the spies with peace, not lying to cover up their hiding.

Similarly, James 2:25-26 extols Rahab's honorable deeds: giving lodging to the spies, and sending the spies off in an advantageous direction. It doesn't praise her for lying to those chasing the spies.

In the same way, was not even Rahab the prostitute considered righteous for what she did when she gave lodging to the spies and sent them off in a different direction?

JAMES 2:25

Hebrews 11 doesn't applaud Rahab's lies; it praises her faithful actions.

Every good spy story needs a mole, right? A dependable informant—a double-agent on the inside is what's necessary to really get the one-up on your enemy. A good mole is exactly what Rahab was. Rahab had a reliable beat on the information circulating through the city as those coming and going stopped by her inn. She was shrewd enough to be all-ears.

Rahab told the spies, *"all who live in this country are melting in fear because of you. We have heard how the Lord dried up the water of the Red Sea for you when you came out of Egypt, and what you did to Siphon and Og, the two kings of the Amorites east of the Jordan, whom you completely destroyed. When we heard of it, our hearts melted in fear and everyone's courage failed because of you"* Joshua 2:9-11.

A God who parts waters and allows his people to walk through on dry ground would be intimidating to anyone! Moses' sister Miriam realized this right at the time of their Red Sea Crossing so many years earlier, and prophetically proclaimed, *"The nations will hear and tremble...the people of Canaan will melt away; terror and dread will fall on them,"* (Exodus 15:14-16). God had been with Israel through the Red Sea, and he would continue to be with them—even the Canaanites could see that.

In the same way that the Israelites had been delivered from Pharaoh's army and the cold waters of the sea, so they had been delivered from enemy armies. In Numbers 21, it recounts what happened to enemy kings Sihon and Og: *"The Lord said to Moses, 'Do not be afraid of him (Og), for I have delivered him into your hands, along with his whole army and his land. Do to him what you did to Sihon king of the Amorites, who reigned in Heshbon.' So they struck him down, together with his sons and his whole army, leaving them no survivors. And they took possession of his land."*

Such power, such victory would speak for itself—not for the glory of the Israelite people, but for the glory of their incredible God.

Give God's power and victory the spotlight in your life today. Post a testimony, picture or story of God's power and goodness on your IG account or FB wall and mark it #significantwomenofthebible. Or tell your testimony of God's goodness and power to a friend, relative, neighbor, or even store clerk today.

Rahab's story illustrates for us *not* how to lie for the sake of God's people, but rather how a deep faith in God proves itself in our actions (albeit in this case not every single action), and *that* in turn is our righteousness. Just to be clear: for Rahab those faithful actions were welcoming and helping the spies, not lying. (For more on this, review the sidebar in Day Four of last week's study, *Do as God Says, Not as the Characters Do*).

Melting in Fear

Thanks to Rahab's intel, the spies reported a sure victory based on the crippling fear felt by the people of Jericho.

News of the Canaanites' fear bolstered the courage of the Israelites. Not only did they have confidence, knowing that their enemies were frightened of them, but this also strengthened their confidence in the Lord.

How did the information Rahab gave the spies fulfill God's promise to his people in Deuteronomy 11:25 (in margin)?

Put yourself in the sandals of the people of Jericho. When faced with danger, do you react like Rahab—with decisive faith in God, even with so many unknowns? Or do we run elsewhere for comfort and security? We all face hard times—unforeseen obstacles and insurmountable difficulties. It's part of living in this fallen world. The crises will come, but in that crisis, is prayer our first resort? Or our last? Is Christ the strong tower to which we run?

God is calling us all to courage—not comfort. Rahab could have stuck with the people of Jericho. It would've been easy and comfortable to hunker down in her old lifestyle—to dig in her heels with the idols of Jericho for her security blanket. I'm wondering how we are answering the call to courage. Do we courageously leave everything behind and run to God? I'm not too sure we always do.

We may not think we're running to false gods when danger comes knocking, but how many of us find safety in our bank account? Or comfort in our refrigerator? Or sanctuary in our family relationships? Or our identity in our work?

These can all be good things, but just like the walls of Jericho crumbled, these false comforts can also all be taken from us in the blink of an eye. Our faith in God *must* be the bedrock upon which everything else in our life is built. Jonah knew this all too well as he prayed from the belly of the whale, "Those who cling to worthless idols turn away from God's love for them." Jonah 2:8. Hopefully it won't take a ship-wrecking storm and being swallowed by a giant fish for us to make the same realization.

> No one will be able to stand against you. The Lord your God, as he promised you, will put the terror and fear of you on the whole land, wherever you go.
>
> DEUTERONOMY 11:25

> Our faith in God must be the bedrock upon which everything else in our life is built.

Thankfully, we can learn from Jonah's aha moment in the belly of the whale. He went on to proclaim, "But I, with shouts of grateful praise, will sacrifice to you. What I have vowed I will make good. I will say, 'Salvation comes from the Lord.'" Jonah 2:9. Just after this proclamation, the fish vomited Jonah onto dry land. Let's make that same salvation proclamation.

Are you tired of being tossed by the stormy seas of life? Maybe for you it's worry, fear, or discouragement. Or maybe it's that pet sin you can't seem to shake. Tired of spending time in the belly of the whale, feeling like God's trying to get your attention for a lesson you don't want to learn? Don't be discouraged. Remember the power of our God—who parted the waters of the Red Sea, who defeated Israel's enemies on every side.

Or maybe you're blessed with a quiet season, a respite from the storms of life. Use this time to strengthen your faith before the next storm.

God was with the Israelites as they approached an unknown territory, and he's with us as well—to face our own unknowns. Whether it's an unknown financially, or with an employment situation, or a difficult relationship, or an overwhelming loss, or maybe a health struggle.

Whatever obstacles we face, we're not alone. The same mighty God that made the Israelites' enemies cower in fear, goes before us today.

How can we practically remind ourselves of God's power, to give us the strength we need to face the obstacles ahead of us and move forward in courageous living?

I know that for me, it's surprisingly easy for discouraging thoughts to creep in. Playing praise music throughout the day,

> The same mighty God that made the Israelites' enemies cower in fear, goes before us today.

placing opened Bibles in strategic places, decorating with inspirational verses (who knew shopping at Hobby Lobby could be faith-building? Ha!), asking a friend to pray with me, and scheduling time to intentionally serve others are all techniques I've used to keep me focused on the Lord and remind myself of God's power and sovereignty when life seems shaky.

> Living in courage doesn't mean pulling yourself up by your bootstraps, but taking strength from our mighty God.

Spend a few moments with the Lord in prayer:

- Thank him that he uses unlikely people, even us, to bring him glory.
- Ask the Lord for courage and strength to make the most of the opportunities you have to live for Christ.
- Pray that the Lord would give you a hunger for his word so that in, knowing it, you would know how to live with integrity.

Takeaway Truth—*"Be strong and courageous. Do not be afraid or terrified…for the Lord your God goes with you; he will never leave you nor forsake you." Deuteronomy 31:6*

DAY 3: ESCAPING THE CORDS OF DEATH

MAIN TEXTS
Joshua 2:8-21
Psalm 18:2-5
Psalm 116:1-6

"He rescued me from my powerful enemy, from my foes, who were too strong for me." Psalm (of David) 18:17

Deal? Or No Deal?

The same stories that had melted the people of Jericho in fear had also brought courageous Rahab to the point of being ready

Rahab knew Yahweh was her only chance.

The verses in James that praise Rahab make an interesting connection. James praises her for her actions when he says, *"Was not even Rahab the prostitute considered righteous for what she did when she gave lodging to the spies and sent them off in a different direction?" (James 2:25).* He used Rahab's actions to explain the relationship between faith and deeds. Because Rahab believed that Yahweh was the only way for her deliverance, she acted in faith. Her loyalty to the God she trusted was proven in how she hid the spies from the king of Jericho and sent the spies away from danger.

Interestingly, James also points to Abraham as an example of the connection between faith and deeds. In Week 1 of our study, we discussed how Abraham's faith was "credited to him as righteousness." James takes this a step further and teaches that true faith and deeds are inseparable—you can't have one without the other. He says, *"What good is it, my brothers and sisters, if someone claims to have faith but has no deeds?...Show me your faith without deeds, and I will show you my faith by my deeds." (James 2:14,18).* In other words: the true faith of a believer will be evident in their actions. What action of Abraham does James use to illustrate his point? (see James 2:21)

This chapter in James isn't the only one which uses both Abraham and Rahab as examples of Godly faith. Hebrews 11 also records the legendary faith of both Abraham (verses 8-19) and Rahab (verse 31).

There is great hope in these two lives of faith-filled deeds: one the Jewish forefather Abraham, handpicked by God; the other a hopeless Canaanite prostitute. The fact that both could be included in the "Hall of Faith" and in James' examples of faith and deeds shows that: *"righteousness is given through faith in Jesus Christ **to all who believe**. There is no difference between Jew and Gentile, for all have sinned and fall short of the glory of God, and all are justified freely by his grace through the redemption that came by Christ Jesus."* Romans 3:22-23. There's room in God's kingdom for all who choose to follow him.

to jump ship from her own people and pagan faith. Rahab was ready to hop on board with the one true God. Unlike the rest of her people, her strong faith was clear as she proclaimed to the spies, *"the Lord your God is God in heaven above and on the earth below!" (Joshua 2:11).* She even called him by his name, Yahweh.

Rahab knew Yahweh was her only chance.

Rahab was a smart enough business woman to know how to make a good deal—after all, despite being a woman, she managed to own her own business in an ancient patriarchal culture. She was savvy enough to help deliver the spies by giving valuable information and now shrewdly asked for the favor of deliverance for her family in return.

Check out her deal in Joshua 2:12-13. What did she ask?

The spies granted her favor without hesitation, as long as Rahab would abide by certain stipulations. They guaranteed Rahab and her family's safety with the following promise: *"'Our lives for your lives!' the men assured her. 'If you don't tell what we are doing, we will treat you kindly and faithfully when the Lord gives us the land...This oath you made us swear will not be binding on us unless, when we enter the land, you have tied this scarlet cord in the window through which you let us down, and unless you have brought your father and mother, your brothers and all your family into your house'" Joshua 2:14.*

Shrewd Rahab would make good on her promise. *"So she let them down by a rope through the window, for the house she lived in was part of the city wall. She said to them, 'Go to the hills so the pursuers will not find you. Hide yourselves there three days until they return, and then go on your way.'" (Joshua 2:15-16).*

A Shrewd Move

Making her move from godless woman of Jericho, to God-following Israelite-helper was the epitome of Rahab's shrewdness. Rahab's willingness to betray the king of Jericho and befriend God's people meant salvation for her entire household from the imminent attack of the Israelites. It meant joining forces with God's people.

Choosing God meant both safety from harm on this earth, and after death, in eternity. But maybe from your vantage point it seems like an obvious choice—what other option did Rahab

Maybe from your vantage point it seems like an obvious choice—what other option did Rahab have?

have when up against a God that parts waters in His people's path? Choosing God was the only path that made sense.

It is the same for us, and yet we so easily forget.

Urgently choosing to side with our Mighty Lord instead of the weak idols of this world should be a no-brainer. Like Rahab, for us not siding with God means our sure destruction. Without the eternal salvation only Jesus can provide, our lives are on the path to downfall, just like Jericho—crumbling walls and no safe place to hide. God's amazing gift of salvation is the only way.

And yet, is that how I live? Does my life reflect that truth? Sadly, not always.

I can be a pull-myself-up-by-my-bootstraps kind of woman. Sometimes too much so. Sometimes I forget the miraculous way God saved me—and I start to trust my own strength, instead of His. Sometimes I act like I'm good enough on my own. Sometimes I am tempted to think that my security can come from my bank account, my relationships, and my full refrigerator. It's foolish.

It's like the oblivious confidence of my curious one-year-old. My youngest, Matthias, just turned one, and he's a climber. Boy is he clumsy, but it doesn't stop him one bit.

He will climb up on the couch or ottoman, and triumphantly plop his rear end right on the edge. It tests our reflexes for sure. Many a family member has had to sprint over to steady him and keep him from falling. He thinks he's safe on his own, but really, he needs someone bigger to keep him from falling.

I do too, and maybe you're like me.

Are there any overly self-reliant attitudes in your heart today? Take a moment in silent prayer, seeking the Lord. Ask Him to reveal any sinful self-reliance. Thank the Lord for His mighty salvation and acknowledge your humble need for Him. Ask Him

> Without the eternal salvation only Jesus can provide, our lives are on the path to downfall, just like Jericho.

to help you reflect the way His mighty hand has saved you in your daily attitudes and actions. If writing your prayer would be meaningful, use the space in the margin to jot yours down.

Rahab was a strong woman for sure, but she knew that when it came to saving her family, she couldn't do it on her own.

Escaping the Cords of Death

A word study on the terms used to signify the cord and rope in Joshua 2 shed some interesting light on the story, and remind us of God's attentiveness even to the smallest of details. In verse 15, Rahab lowers the spies as she's sending them on their way using a strong, binding rope. The Hebrew word is "chebel." While "chebel" does mean a rope, cord, or band, it is sometimes used in phrases translated as "cords of distress, anguish, trouble or wickedness."

The word can be a symbol of captivity or subjection, such as in David's Psalm 18:2-5. See it in the margin, translated as "cords of death" and "cords of the grave." Rahab's descendant, David, penned these words when God graciously delivered him from his enemies and Saul. David knew firsthand what it felt like to be bound by the cords of death, and he also knew the freedom felt with deliverance.

Rahab, too, knew the cords of death. She knew that, without the help of Yahweh, the cords of the grave would surely entangle her. While she bound and lowered the spies out of the window using a strong rope, those actions would be the very ones that proved her faith in the God. And because of her faith, God would loose the cords of death from her own neck.

Christ himself likely spoke of the "chebel," or cords of death, the night he shared his Last Supper with his disciples. Reciting Psalm 116, which closely echoes Psalm 18, is part of the traditional Jewish Hallel—scriptures spoken on Jewish holidays by devout Jews in praise and thanksgiving. Christ probably spoke these words (see the margin) that Passover night.

The Lord is my rock, my fortress and my deliverer; my God is my rock, in whom I take refuge…I have been saved from my enemies. The **cords of death** entangled me; the torrents of destruction overwhelmed me. The **cords of the grave** coiled around me…

PSALM 18:2-5

I love the Lord, for he heard my voice; he heard my cry for mercy. Because he turned his ear to me, I will call on him as long as I live. The **cords of death** entangled me, the anguish of the grave came over me; I was overcome by distress and sorrow. Then I called on the name of the Lord: "Lord, save me!" The Lord is gracious and righteous; our God is full of compassion. The Lord protects the unwary; when I was brought low, he saved me.

PSALM 116:1-6

Could it be that although you are saved, you still carry a burden?

How fitting that Rahab's deliverance from "chebel" would be echoed in the words of her descendants: first David, then Christ.

David was delivered from his enemies, and Rahab from Jericho's destruction. Already we have emphasized our need to receive eternal salvation, but could there be something more from which you need to be delivered? Could it be that although you are saved, you yet carry a burden? Something holding you back from completely surrendering to God?

Maybe it's worry, or addiction—is escaping into a binge session of television, or spending too many hours in mindless Facebook feed, or comforting yourself with that tasty food too easy and too common? Maybe it's insecurity or anxiety. What about a need to be in control? Or perhaps you need to be delivered from your own selfishness or laziness. We all need the Lord's help to be freed from the burden of sin.

I know that often discouragement holds me down. Things don't always go the way I plan, which can lead to frustration. It can be big or small—from the little let-down of a toddler knocking over yet another filled-to-the-brim cup of juice, to the major disappointment of giving up on a super-sized unrealistic dream I was holding out for. Letting go of the situation and focusing on God's sovereignty frees me from the bonds of discouragement.

What do you need to be freed from today in order to follow God completely? Spend a moment in reflection and jot down any thoughts here:

Now imagine the cords of death untangling and loosening from you as you open your hands and release these things, praying for God's freedom and peace.

> God delivers us from our own Jerichoes when we call
> out to him for salvation—both from eternal damnation,
> and from the burdens of life that weigh us down.

Spend a few moments with the Lord in prayer:

- Thank him for his deliverance from the cords of death—the sin and burdens that bound you.
- Ask him for a faith so strong it is evident in your actions, like Rahab's.
- Pray that the Lord would give you wisdom to be spiritually shrewd in the way you live.

Takeaway Truth—*"As for God, his way is perfect: The Lord's word is flawless; he shields all who take refuge in him." Psalm 18:30*

DAY 4: THE SCARLET CORD OF HOPE

MAIN TEXT:
Joshua 2:21-6:27

"She has no fear for her household; for all of them are clothed in scarlet." Proverbs 31:21

It's Go Time

Thanks to Rahab harboring the spies, the intel she gave, and the escape she provided, God's people were poised and ready to finally make their move into the long-awaited Promised Land. It was Go Time.

The anticipation had to be electric. After generations of enslavement, years of captivity, miraculous escape, heavenly provision, and decades of wandering—the time had come. Joshua readied his men.

What did he tell them in Joshua 3:5? Paraphrase the verse below:

God parted the waters to make a way for his people—where there seemed no way. Just as the prophet Isaiah wrote: *"I will go before you and will level the mountains; I will break down gates of bronze and cut through bars of iron," (45:2).* God led his people as they entered their land.

Guiding God's people—going before them—was the ark of the covenant, the symbol of God's presence among the Israelites. And just as Peter stepped out of the boat and into the water in faith that with God's help he would not sink (Matthew 14), so the priests carrying the ark stepped into the Jordan River—at flood stage no less (Joshua 3:15)—certain that God would make a way. Underline God's purposes for His amazing miracle in the following list:

The Lord's purpose in this miracle was three-fold:
• For the **Israelites**: to make God's presence known among his people and give them confidence in a sure victory *"This is how you will know that the living God is among you and that he will certainly drive out before you the Canaanites, Hittites, Hivites, Perizzites, Girgashites, Amorites and Jebusites"* Joshua 3:10.

•For their **enemies**: to instill fear in the enemies of God's people *"when all the Amorite kings west of the Jordan and all the Canaanite kings along the coast heard how the Lord had dried up the Jordan before the Israelites until they had crossed over, their hearts melted in fear and they no longer had the courage to face the Israelites* Joshua 5:1.

• For **us**: as a testimony of God's power for all generations of all people *"He did this so that all the peoples of the earth might know that the hand of the Lord is powerful and so that you might always fear the Lord your God"* Joshua 4:24.

Clothed in Scarlet

For her salvation, Rahab was instructed to put a scarlet cord in the window. Though translated cord, the word used here is not "chebel," or "cord of anguish and distress" as we studied yesterday; instead it is "tiqvah." "Tiqvah" is translated as cord or line, but not one of distress—a cord of *hope*, expectation for a good outcome. This is not a cord tangling you, binding you, holding you down. It is not an instrument of captivity.

Think of a lifeline thrown to a drowning victim. It is a cord of *hope that rescues.*

It is the same Hebrew word used in popular verse Jeremiah 29:11. You also find it in Psalm 71:5 *"For you have been my **hope**, Sovereign Lord, my confidence since my youth."* And Psalm 62:5, *"yes, my soul, find rest in God; my **hope** comes from him."* Even though the literal definition of the word is "cord," it is used figuratively as "expectancy" and "hope" in every occurrence in scripture other than Joshua 2—32 times. The meaning would not have been lost on the reader of the original Hebrew text.

If you're an artsy person, I encourage you to pick one of these hope-filled verses, either Jeremiah 29:11, Psalm 71:5, Psalm 62:5 or another favorite verse about hope. Use the following space in the box to make a hope-inspired sketch.

You can use the concept of a lifeline, a cord of hope, or choose to copy a portion of the verse with fancy calligraphy—whatever would be most meaningful for you. If you feel so inclined, share a pic of your creation with a friend, via text or on social media as a stone of remembrance with #significantwomenofthebible. We all need to be reminded of our true hope in God the daily grind of life.

For I know the plans I have for you," declares the Lord, "plans to prosper you and not to harm you, plans to give you **hope** and a future.

JEREMIAH 29:11

> God had transformed a situation of pain, anguish, and captivity for Rahab into one of redemptive hope.

…all the members of the community of Israel must slaughter them at twilight. [7] Then they are to take some of the blood and put it on the sides and tops of the doorframes of the houses where they eat the lambs.…The blood will be a sign for you on the houses where you are, and when I see the blood, I will pass over you. No destructive plague will touch you when I strike Egypt.

EXODUS 12:6b-7,13

The scarlet cord in Rahab's window was a symbol of her hope in God—may our lives also show proof of our hope.

God had transformed a situation of pain, anguish, and captivity for Rahab into one of redemptive hope. What a beautiful picture of Rahab's faith as she hangs her scarlet cord, her hope of expectant salvation, out her window, knowing full well the Israelite's God, now *her* God, Yahweh, will save her!

The scarlet cord on Rahab's window delivering from death reminds us of the Passover Lamb's blood spread on the doorposts of God's people in Exodus 12, saving their firstborn from perishing.

God had given His instruction and His promise in Exodus 12:7,13. Paraphrase His promise from verse 13. What does it say?

This miraculous Passover is still celebrated today. Just as death passed over the homes of those with the lamb's blood, so death and destruction would pass over the house of Rahab.

Even as the scarlet cord saved Rahab's household from certain death, it also reminds us of the salvation bought for us by the Lamb of God, Jesus Christ's own precious scarlet blood. The red blood of the Passover Lamb foretells of the Lamb of God, Jesus. Read the following verses, **underlining** the phrases that refer to Jesus as a lamb:

"Look, the Lamb of God, who takes away the sin of the world," John 1:29.

"For you know that it was not with perishable things such as silver or gold that you were redeemed from the empty way of life handed down to you from your ancestors, but with the precious blood of Christ, a lamb without blemish or defect." 1 Peter 1:18-19.

"The great dragon was hurled down—that ancient serpent called the devil, or Satan, who leads the whole world astray. He was hurled to the earth, and his angels with him...They triumphed over him by the blood of the Lamb" Revelation 12:9,11.

Although the whole city was decimated, Rahab and her family were saved. They would never forget the danger from which they'd been delivered. And, yet, how often we take for granted our own equally real salvation from death. May we always remember the deadly danger from which we've been delivered.

Scarlet salvation from Yahweh had come to the home of Rahab.

Have you ever had a brush with death from which you were saved (health, natural disaster, near accident)? How does an experience of miraculous physical salvation—and relief thereafter—put into perspective your even more important eternal salvation?

> How often we take for granted our own salvation from death.

> The rest of the city was about to crumble into a rocky grave, but Rahab and her family knew real hope.

I remember one snowy, icy morning, back in my college days when my then boyfriend (now husband) and I were driving to a service assignment. He was driving carefully, but we were chatting lightheartedly, not realizing what danger lie ahead.

The two-lane road we were driving on curved slightly to the right so that the lane we were currently driving in lined up perfectly with the lane of oncoming traffic.

As the road curved, the icy conditions prevented us from following the curve. We were driving straight into oncoming traffic. A semi barreled towards us, without anything to be done about it.

John desperately called out, "help us, Jesus!" and at the last moment, our tires caught a dry spot and we swerved to safety. The heart-stopping moment helped us realize God wasn't done with us yet, and made me even *more* thankful for the security of heaven to look forward to.

In the famous battle of Jericho, Rahab and her family waited patiently with their cord of hope flagging out the window while Joshua and his 40,000 troops marched around the city, day after day. They were closed in, the whole city was on lockdown while the foreboding Israelite army marched, carrying the ark, blowing their trumpets. The city was doomed.

On the seventh day, when the army marched the seventh time and called their loud battle cry, the walls began to shake and crumble all around Rahab's house. What must that have been like for Rahab and her family, clinging to their cord of hope in Rahab's new God? Trusting the strangers Rahab had met only a few days earlier? The rest of the city was about to crumble into a rocky grave, but Rahab knew real hope. Like the woman of noble character described in Proverbs 31:21, Rahab had "no fear for her household; for all of them are clothed in scarlet."

Rahab was a liar; she was a foreigner; she was a prostitute—and yet she put her hope in God. Because of her steadfast faith though all the others in Jericho perished, she and her family were saved. She had blessed God's people, just like Tamar, and so she, too, would be blessed according to God's promise to Abraham in Genesis 12:3. *"I will bless those who bless you, and whoever curses you I will curse."*

Rahab's great faith was evident in that she had not seen and yet had believed. She was one of whom Jesus spoke in John 20:29, when he said, *"Blessed are those who have not seen and yet have believed."*

Her faith was steadfast enough to drive her to follow the spies' instructions exactly, flying her cord of hope and bringing her family salvation. You and I know the sweetness of salvation as well. May we never lose the wonder of it! And may that wonder motivate our right living.

I wonder about our obedience. Are we, like Rahab, following the right instructions? Is our faith in the God who parts the waters compelling us to righteous living? How might God be calling you to more faithful obedience today, either through what we're learning in this study, or other ways that He is speaking to you?

Perhaps the chapter on Sarah's true beauty hit home for you. Maybe you've been ugly on the inside, treating those you should've been respecting wrongly. Now, motivated by faith in the God that saved you from your crumbling Jericho, walk in the obedience His strength brings.

It could be that Leah's situation particularly struck you. Maybe you've been rejected by those who should've loved you best. Or maybe your life has been full of disappointments in other ways. Now you're convicted to respond to God with praise despite your despair.

Is our faith in the God who parts the waters compelling us to righteous living?

Or perhaps you've been wronged like Tamar, or are suffering a broken relationship. Maybe mercy and reconciliation are what God's calling you to next. Remember Tamar's actions and seek to return blessing for wrong, just like her descendant Christ.

Maybe you're feeling like Rahab, living in a godless culture and ready to say a courageous "goodbye" to the godlessness around you—including the ways your life doesn't look much different than those living for themselves. Maybe it's time to fly your red cord of hope and choose right living before the consequences of your own bad habits catch up to you.

Meditate on these possibilities as you close out today's lesson in prayer.

> Following Rahab's faith-filled footsteps means that the miracle of our salvation and the power of God compel us to hopeful obedience.

Spend a few moments with the Lord in prayer:

- Reflect on the miraculous salvation you've experienced
- Pray that it would spark in your heart a hunger for obedient living
- Pray that the Lord would bring to light what exactly He's calling you to do, and give you the strength to step out in obedience today

Takeaway Truth—"Therefore I am now going to allure her; I will lead her into the wilderness and speak tenderly to her. There I will give her back her vineyards, and will make the Valley of Achor (trouble) a door of **hope**." Hosea 2:14-15

DAY 5: RAHAB'S LEGACY: COURAGE, FAITH, AND HOPE

MAIN TEXT:
Proverbs 31:10-31

"Return to your rest, my soul, for the Lord has been good to you. For you, Lord, have delivered me from death, my eyes from tears, my feet from stumbling, that I may walk before the Lord in the land of the living." Psalm 116:7-9

The Unlikely Noble Woman

Courageous, faith-filled Rahab would walk before the Lord, just as the words of her great-great-grandson David suggest (Psalm 116:7-9, above). She was one of the few foreigners that lived out her days among the Israelites. According to Matthew 1, Rahab would marry Salmon and give birth to the man of integrity, Ruth's kinsman redeemer, Boaz. Their family line would produce the Kings of Judah, the great King David, and King of Kings, Jesus Christ himself.

Salmon the father of Boaz, whose mother was Rahab…

MATTHEW 1:5

Though labeled the harlot, Rahab's life showed characteristics of the woman of noble character from Proverbs 31. Several come to mind:

- Just as in Proverbs 31:13 which says *"She selects wool and flax and works with eager hands."* Rahab worked with flax; it was what she hid the spies under on her roof.

  hardworking

- Like the virtuous woman in Proverbs 31:20, *"She opens her arms to the poor and extends her hands to the needy."* Rahab opened her doors to the spies in need of shelter.
- In the same way that Proverbs 31:21 reads, *"When it snows, she has no fear for her household; for all of them are clothed in scarlet."* Rahab showed no fear for her household when she welcomed the spies with peace.

She knew aligning herself with the God of Israel meant salvation for her family. Unlike the rest of Jericho that melted in fear, she showed confidence. The scarlet cord she hung in her window signified salvation for her whole household.

- The woman in Proverbs 31:28 has children that, *"arise and call her blessed."* The line of children coming from Rahab rose up in kingly importance.

- And verse 30 states, *"Beauty is fleeting; but a woman who fears the Lord is to be praised."* Legend has it that Rahab was one of the most beautiful women in history, but as we've seen in our lesson today, she is most famous for her faith in action—her willingness to risk her life to help the spies and in doing so, the whole Jewish nation. With three New Testament passages speaking of her, she certainly went from a woman of ill repute to one that was praised!

Now go back and next to each bulleted point above, think of an adjective that reflects the virtue shown by Rahab and the Proverbs 31 woman. Label each paragraph in the margin next to the bulleted points. The first one is done for you.

Perhaps you came up with descriptive words like: *hardworking, generous, confident, praiseworthy, and faithful*—I know I'd like to live up to these.

Let's hit the pause button in our study and ask the Lord to impress upon our hearts how we can live out Rahab and the Proverbs 31 woman's godly qualities today. Brainstorm your ideas below (you may want to focus in on one or two main attributes):

Hardworking–
Generous–
Confident–
Praiseworthy–

Beauty is fleeting; but a woman who fears the Lord is to be praised

PROVERBS 31:30

Faithful—

Each of ours will look a little different because our daily lives are filled with different tasks and responsibilities. It could be that you've got that lingering chore you're putting off that you could accomplish and put your hardworking qualities to practice.

Or possibly you know of a gaping need that you can fill at work or at church, going above and beyond, giving generously of your time and talent.

Maybe you've been too scared to repair a broken relationship or reach out to a prickly personality, and God could be calling you to be a woman of confidence in that way.

Perhaps your level of faithfulness to God could use a boost and it's time for leveling up your daily devotions, finishing this study strong, then continuing regular Bible readings and prayer time habits after.

There are so many ways we can live out the courageous, faithful obedience of Rahab in our lives. Let's be inspired by the God who led his people across the Jordan on dry land and rescued the hope-filled prostitute who hung her scarlet cord out the window with her city crumbling around her. Go back and star or circle one idea from the list you created that you plan to prioritize pursuing.

If I've been impressed by anything in my study of Rahab, it's the transforming power of faith. How awesome that God can take one like Rahab who is entrenched in the life of sin, immersed in a culture where all she knows is godlessness—and grow in her a faith that is so strong it has the confidence to jump ship from her former life and latch onto God's people, to do the right thing even when it's dangerous. What courage!

When Courage Wore Pink Goggles

Let's be inspired by the God who led his people across the Jordan on dry land and rescued the hope-filled prostitute.

The Lord taught me a lesson in courage through my children. It was our first year of swim team, which meant a huge learning curve for the whole family—mama included.

We were at the pool, sitting on the bleachers before the first race when I noticed my daughter's eyes rimmed with tears. But that wasn't at all normal for her. She was my pull-yourself-up-by-your-bootstraps, git 'r done girl. She was the one who painted the foundation of our house at six years old with a toothy grin, exclaiming, "Thanks for planning this fun activity, mom!"

But this moment was just too much for her.

She was signed up to be the first leg of the first race. This wouldn't have been so overwhelming except that we had no idea what we were supposed to do that morning. And she only been to a handful practices. And she hadn't been able to practice starts yet. Ever. And we were in a humid, 90-degree room where the air was heavy with chlorine and the noise of 200 crammed-in people. It. was. crazy.

I put my arms around her narrow shoulders and held her close while we prayed for courage and strength for her race. She let out a deep breath.

She wiped her eyes, straightened her goggles, adjusted her swim cap, put her shoulders back, and stood as tall as her 8-year-old frame could. We found our way to the bullpen. She was ready.

A few minutes later she was gliding down the lane, her arms moving like clockwork, and my heart couldn't help but swell in my chest. She came dripping out of the water after the race with a huge smile on her face.

I hugged her and told her, "you did it! I'm so proud!"

Her grin went from ear to ear as she proclaimed, "that was fun!"

She had actually lost the race by a landslide, but had won a much bigger victory. That morning one small swimmer had shown big courage.

I couldn't help but think: so often in our lives we are called to do something uncomfortable, something overwhelming, something for which we feel painfully underqualified. But having courage doesn't mean that we are never afraid. It doesn't mean we never shed a tear.

I realized that morning that courage doesn't mean you have no fear. A courageous woman confides in the Lord, asks for his help, and then presses forward, knowing God is with her.

So often I believe the lie that courage means we have everything figured out—that we are completely ready for every obstacle. But that's not usually how it works.

What is God calling you to right now? Perhaps you are feeling inadequate and underqualified. Perhaps you are feeling overwhelmed. Your feelings are normal. Take your normal feelings to the Lord and ask him to give you an abnormal courage to press on and strain toward what's ahead. Ask him to give you the courage of the prostitute Rahab, who did the right thing even when it was dangerous.

And then let out a deep breath, put your shoulders back, stand tall and move forward, diving into your calling.

Who knows? You may emerge dripping on the other side with a smile, and say, "that was fun!"

(*originally published on rachelrisner.com*)

Who Are You?

I'm wondering of all the different Bible characters we've spoken of in this chapter, to which can you relate the most? Consider the following, putting a star next to the one that sounds the most like you:

> A courageous woman confides in the Lord, asks for his help, and then presses forward, knowing God is with her.

Maybe you're like the **spies**. You're trying to accomplish a daunting task for God and His kingdom and He's calling you to work with some unlikely people, like Rahab, to achieve His purposes. Perhaps you need a special dose of understanding and humility, and you could remember all God accomplished through Rahab despite her unsavory past.

Perhaps you're more like the **Pharisees** that Jesus addressed, and you don't even realize the condition of your hard heart. It could be that you've become caught up in empty rule following, and your heart is not in the right place. Learn from Rahab's sincere heart of faith, and pray that God would melt your heart of stone. Pray for faith that courageously acts in obedience to Him, going beyond the letter of the law.

Or are you like **Jonah**, having had your aha moment in the belly of the whale. Maybe the wind's been knocked out of your sails. You were on your own path and the storm has hit. God mercifully has you in the whale's belly—and you're praising God for it. Maybe you haven't yet been vomited onto dry land, but you're still choosing to worship in the midst of the typhoon.

Or are you like the **Israelites**, wandering in the desert through times of spiritual highs and carnal lows—and you're sick of it? You're ready to follow God's lead and cross the Jordan to enter the Promised Land once for all. Leave your complaints and unbelief in the desert and step onto the dry riverbed of the Jordan.

Maybe you're like the **people of Jericho**, and you're happy going your own way. You think you're fine without God, and you want to stay on your own comfortable path. You know God is powerful, but you're not ready to leave your familiar comforts to follow Him yet. You're living on borrowed time until the day of destruction, or until you have a much-needed change of heart.

Maybe you're like young **Rahab**. Maybe you've experienced the futility of other paths—albeit your idols probably look different than the gods of Jericho—and you know that you need the one true God. Maybe you're ready to make the courageous move, to hang that scarlet cord of hope in your window and cry out to Jesus to save you from the crumbling city of sin you find yourself in.

Wherever you are now, please known that God's not finished with you yet. He's not done with me yet. No matter where we find ourselves, we can cry out to God for help. We all need it.

Let's take a few minutes right now to reflect on all the Lord has done for us. With the walls of Jericho crumbling around her, the city threatening to be her grave, Rahab's faith—her cord of hope in Israel's God—enabled her to be delivered from death.

God delivers all those who cling to him with courageous faith.

When we put our trust in God, we, too, experience that same sweet deliverance from the crumbling city of sin and shame in which we used to dwell. Our own cord of hope, the precious scarlet blood of Jesus Christ, is our deliverance. May we praise the Lord that he brought us out of the darkness, out of our certain grave, into the light of day.

> No matter where we find ourselves, we can cry out to God for help.

A woman of true courage recognizes her need for Christ and lets go of everything else,
putting her hope in Him alone, and moving forward with boldness.

Spend a few moments with the Lord in prayer:

- Thank him for the testimony of Rahab's life—that, with faith in God, salvation can come to the unlikeliest of people.
- Ask him for the courage to let go of anything that would hold you back from Him.

- Pray that the Lord would give you strength and wisdom to live out your faith in any and every way the Lord may be calling you.

Takeaway Truth—"We have this hope as an anchor for the soul, firm and secure" Hebrews 6:19
"Now faith is confidence in what we hope for and assurance about what we do not see." Hebrews 11:1

A Tangible Reminder

Find something scarlet, and place it in a location where you will frequently notice it throughout this week. Just as Rahab hung her scarlet cord, which showed her hope in Yahweh, Israel's God, so do we hope in our God. She expectantly, confidently knew her deliverance was coming. We, too, expectantly receive salvation from our sins in this world and look forward to eternity with our Savior. If asked why your scarlet item is there, recount Rahab's courageous, obedient, hopeful faith—and explain how it's a reminder that we have hope through Christ's shed blood. Share your hope with someone else. Text or write someone, or go public with your scarlet cord of hope with a post to social media. Use #significantwomenofthebible #scarletcordofhope #stonesofremembrance to continue to collect your personal testimony to our all-powerful, saving God.

Pause for Praise—In Rahab's life, we are reminded that our pasts don't determine our futures. God rescues us from our former life of sin—no matter how scandalous. Looking at Rahab's life, we also learn the importance of courageous obedience and faithful hope—confidence when everyone around us is scared. We have also learned that God uses mightily those whose faith in him runs deep—no matter their past, God sees the heart. Before you end this chapter on Rahab, take a few moments to meditate on the hope we have in our powerful

God—hope enough to give us courage to obey. I suggest you find the powerful lyric video for *Glorious Day* (Passion) on YouTube and watch with a worshipful heart. If you enjoy hymns, try Fanny Crosby's *Safe in the Arms of Jesus*.

God uses mightily those whose faith in him
runs deep—no matter their past

WEEK FIVE

RUTH
Pauper to Princess

Day One
NO MOABITES ALLOWED

Day Two
GRIEVING AND GOING HOME

Day Three
OUTSTANDING IN THE FIELD

Day Four
MIDNIGHT
AT THE THRESHING FLOOR

Day Five
THE FAMINE'S
FAIRYTALE ENDING

Significant

DAY ONE:
NO MOABITES ALLOWED

MAIN TEXTS:
Ruth 1:1-4
Deuteronomy 23:3-6
Genesis 19:29-38
Numbers 22:1-25:3

"No Ammonite or Moabite or any of their descendants may enter the assembly of the Lord, not even in the tenth generation."
Deuteronomy 23:3

You Will Know the Ruth

As we trace the roots of Jesus' family tree, we don't have to go far down the family line beyond Rahab to discover another woman. In fact, we find another woman named in the very next generation. We know exactly who Rahab's daughter-in-law was. Read Matthew 1:5 in the margin, circling the women's names. In this verse, we find our next female character to study—Ruth.

Salmon the father of Boaz, whose mother was Rahab, Boaz the father of Obed, whose mother was Ruth, Obed the father of Jesse.

MATTHEW 1:5

Unless this is your first time cracking open the Old Testament, and unless you're new to the Christian faith, you've likely heard of the Biblical heroine Ruth. Her story is so noteworthy, so remarkable, that the chapters of the Bible that tell her story bear her name. In fact, she is one of *only two* women to hold the distinction of having a book of the Protestant Bible named after them, along with Esther.

But God has a way of opening up dusty old Sunday School stories for us in new ways when we take the time to have another look. Hold onto your hats, ladies! We're about to dive deep into the story of Ruth, mining for new treasures this week.

But, before we get too deep in Ruth's story, we'll take a look backward and see what was in her people's past, shaping who she was.

Just like our generation, hometown, and upbringing shape who we are—whether we're a Buckeye from Ohio, a Yankee from New York, or an Aggie from Texas—Ruth's roots were an important part of who she was.

In the days when the judges ruled, there was a famine in the land. So a man from Bethlehem in Judah, together with his wife and two sons, went to live for a while in the country of Moab. 2 The man's name was Elimelek, his wife's name was Naomi, and the names of his two sons were Mahlon and Kilion. They were Ephrathites from Bethlehem, Judah. And they went to Moab and lived there. 3 Now Elimelek, Naomi's husband, died, and she was left with her two sons. 4 They married Moabite women, one named Orpah and the other Ruth. After they had lived there about ten years, 5 both Mahlon and Kilion also died, and Naomi was left without her two sons and her husband.

RUTH 1:1-5

In Ruth 1:1-5, Ruth first appeared in the scriptures. Read this passage in the margin. What can we learn about her background—both her time period and her land of origin—from this brief passage? Circle, underline, or star any important details of Ruth's origins in the passage in the margin.

Moab's Sordid Past

Ruth was a woman from Moab who married into a Jewish family when they had fled their famine-stricken homelands to come to Moab in search for a better life. A Jew marrying a Moabite woman may not seem like any big hairy deal to you. Why would it? You wouldn't care much if your brother married a woman from Tennessee or your son married a lady from California.

But, to the Jewish people, being from Moab *was* a big deal—as you may have noticed in the verse kicking off this lesson, Moabite people were excluded from fully participating in Israel's worship—*forever* (that's the meaning of the phrase, "not even to the tenth generation"). Not only that, but Israel was prohibited from making peace treaties with Moab. Deuteronomy 23:6 says, *"Do not seek a treaty of friendship with them as long as you live."* Ouch.

Ruth's people, the Moabites, were given the strictest of restrictions by God.

God spells out the two reasons for excluding Moabites in Deuteronomy 23:4. Write them below:

1.

2.

This is really a bit of a head-scratcher. It's one of those Isaiah 55:9 times, when I have to chalk it up to God's "ways are higher than your ways and (God's) thoughts higher than your thoughts." (NLT).

Now I get it that not offering food and water to the Israelites, and attempting to call down a curse on them is not great. In fact, it's pretty downright rotten. I'm clear on the Moabites' foolish behavior. That's easy enough to understand. It's just the following few verses that get me confused.

You see, Deuteronomy 23 goes on to explain that the Moabites are to be excluded even more severely than the Egyptians (see verses 7-8). We're talking about the Egyptians, whose ancestors had enslaved God's people for 400 years. Even *they* were allowed to be enfolded after only the third generation.

Something about this exclusion of Moabites from worship, and inability of Israel to make peace treaties with them, just doesn't seem to jive with the God we know. It seems confusing. How can these be the words of the same God who tells us to "seek peace and pursue it" in Psalm 34:14? I mean, talk about holding a grudge! I thought God's mercies were new every morning?! (Spoiler alert: they are—Lam. 3:22-23).

I remember on one road trip finding some confusing rules. The traditional convenience store door post usually reads: "No shirt, No shoes, No service." We pulled into a gas station with a sign posted, "No shirt, No shoes, No pets, No service." I think the owners were a bit mixed-up. I don't think they wanted people to wear shoes, shirt, and bring pets inside the store. Thankfully God's rules, though sometimes confusing, are more well-thought out and worth actually following.

While we cannot fully know the mind of Christ (Isaiah 40:13), we *do* know that often God's laws and rules that don't make sense to us are often for our own protection. Just like it doesn't make sense to toddlers that they can't have candy for breakfast, lunch, and dinner ("but it tastes good, Mom!"), or play in the street unsupervised ("but it would be so fun!"), God knows what is ultimately best for his people—even when it seems to them like something else would be better.

We can't know for sure this side of eternity, but God likely warned the Israelites against the Moabites because He knew they were never going to be anything but trouble for Israel.

After all, that's what they'd been for Israel in the past.

Flip to Numbers 22 for a history lesson. We'll find some juicy tidbits there from Moab's past.

Breeze over Numbers 22:1-25:3. In this passage, we find that Balak, the king of Moab, got worked up when the Israelites

Do not despise an Edomite, for the Edomites are related to you. Do not despise an Egyptian, because you resided as foreigners in their country. 8 The third generation of children born to them may enter the assembly of the Lord.

DEUTERONOMY 23:7-8

> God knows what is ultimately best for his people—even when it seems to them like something else would be better.

moved in next door. At this point in history, God's people were wandering in the wilderness, preparing to enter His Promised Land—and their reputation preceded them, as it did in the days of Rahab. King Balak knew that, with their mighty God, Israel proved a formidable foe.

What does Balak plan to do, according to Numbers 22:5-6?

Balak knew it was time to pull out the big guns against the Israelites. And who better for the job than the mighty pagan prophet, Balaam? Balak called on bigwig Balaam—the LeBron James of pagan prophets—to curse the Israelites so that the Moabites would have a fighting chance against God's people. But Balak was in for a rude awakening.

What Balak didn't know was that God's blessing on His people can't be undone with a piddly curse—even one coming from a pagan powerhouse. Compared to God, Baal might as well have been a flea. Though Balaam was the MVP of the prophets of Baal, he simply could not curse Israel, no matter how hard he tried.

> Compared to God, Baal might as well have been a flea.

It was a Proverbs 16:9 moment. That verse says, "In their hearts humans plan their course, but the Lord establishes their steps." Balaam couldn't do anything apart from our omnipotent God, who wasn't about to let his people be cursed. Don't you love this mama bear behavior from God?

In the midst of his pagan ritual, Balaam could utter nothing but the blessings God placed on his lips. Balaam, despite his own donkey's pontification just a few verses prior (Numbers 22:28-30), was now the one whose speech was controlled by God. The owner of an eloquent donkey now had a God-given speech impediment.

Balak's plan for curse royally backfired as Balaam proclaimed, *"God is not human, that he should lie, not a human being, that he should change his mind...he has blessed, and I cannot change it. No misfortune is seen in Jacob, no misery observed in Israel. The Lord their God is with them" (Numbers 23:19-21)* and *"A star will come out of Jacob; a scepter will rise out of Israel. He will crush the foreheads of Moab...but Israel will grow strong." (Numbers 24:17-18).*

Note the destiny of Moab versus the future of Israel. Circle the promising outcomes for Israel in these verses, and underline Moab's sorry fate.

What was supposed to be a curse turned into a blessing. Balaam's curse accomplished the exact opposite purpose that Balak intended. God's people would be stronger than ever. Isn't it funny how God has an ironic sense of humor?

Unfortunately, despite Moab's inability to curse Israel, their influence still proved deadly. Despite God's protection, His people would fall to temptation.

What sinful behavior did the women of Moab entice Israel to engage in, in Numbers 25:1-3?

Who initiated this, according to Numbers 31:15-16?

When Balaam the sneaky snake couldn't call down a curse on Israel, he resorted to using the women of Moab to seduce Israel into idolatry instead. God's anger burned against his rebellious people, and death became the fate of Zimri, an idolatrous Israelite (Numbers 25:14) along with every non-virgin woman of Moab (Numbers 31:17).

Balaam experienced the miraculous firsthand, three times over—first in **his donkey's speech** (Numbers 22:28-30), then in **his encounter with the angel of the Lord** (Numbers 22:32-35), and finally **his God-given speech impediment**: (*"But I can't say whatever I please. I must speak only what God puts in my mouth,"* Numbers 22:38).

How could he possibly oppose God's people after so many miraculous encounters? I think the depth of Balaam's beef against God's people and his stiff-necked nature show us just

How easily we minimize the miraculous in our lives.

If we start at the very beginning of the Moabite people, their seedy history sheds some additional light on the bad reputation they carried in Ruth's day. We find the tale of their origin in Genesis 19.

Lot and his daughters were rescued by angels from the destruction of Sodom and Gomorrah (thanks, uncle Abe, Gen 18:16-33). But though Lot was righteous (2 Peter 2:7) he suffered some PTSD from his hometown's destruction by fire and brimstone (Gen 19:24-25) and his own wife's transformation into a pillar of salt (Gen 19:26).

So instead of settling in the town of Zoar, which God had provided as a safe-haven for him (Genesis 19:22-23), Lot took his newly-widowed daughters and fled. According to verse 30 of Genesis 19, where did Lot go, and why?

This living situation was not pleasing to Lot's daughters. Why? And what happened, according to verses 31-38? (Warning—this gets gross!)

Lot's fear led to isolation for his whole family. With no potential husbands on the horizon, Lot's daughters decide to get him drunk and commit incest in order to preserve the family line (Ew!). While the Levirate law allowed for remarrying within your deceased husband's family (Deuteronomy 25) it did *not at all* imply that you sleep with your own father. This story of fear and incest would be Moab's bad beginning.

This story can be a wake-up call for us. We may see fear as only a feeling—not especially dangerous. But in the story of Lot and his daughters we see their unhealthy, sinful behaviors were rooted in a life of fear. Fear leads us down a dangerous path. Let's ask God to replace our fears with faith.

why God had warned his people against the Moabites. They were determined to be a bad influence.

And, yet, there is within this character of Balaam a lesson for you and me. How easily we minimize the miraculous in our lives. How easily we forget the fabulous things God has done, and neglect to notice His fingerprints on our lives.

Balaam didn't remember God's miracles, and it caused him to sabotage the Israelites and suck them into sin. I should recognize the danger of forgetting about God's power and work in the past.

Seeing God at work in the Old Testament should cause me to pause and consider— how has the Lord worked in my life? When I step back regularly to see God's faithfulness to me, it gives me a more realistic perspective on my day-to-day discouragement and struggles. It bolsters my faith, and gives me the strength and endurance to press on in my walk with Him.

If I remember all of the great things God has done, suddenly waiting on that late person doesn't seem to frustrating, or dealing with that disobedient child doesn't seem so overwhelming, or pushing through the end of the workweek doesn't seem so daunting, or praying for that unanswered request doesn't seem so exhausting.

Oh, how I pray, friend, that our eyes would be opened to the astonishing works of God around us. Oh, how I hope that we have heaped up those all-important stones of remembrance, reminding us of God's faithfulness, mercy, love, and power.

What is something astonishing you can praise God for right now? Try to come up with at least one item for each of these areas:

Health–
Physical provision–
Spiritual needs–

You may want to add some of these to the Significant Encounters with God section at the back of this book.

I can praise God for victories of health—that two of my children born with potentially problem-causing birth defects are perfectly healthy and thriving.

I can praise Him for provision—that when the online realty map showed no promising home for us, He provided an unlisted gem that went above and beyond our expectations and needs. God went before us and made a way for us to find and secure our home.

I can praise Him for His live-giving word—that I have Bibles of every translation at my fingertips, along with all kinds of study materials to help me understand them.

If only we take the time to look for them, God's miracles are all around us, waiting to be noticed.

Take a moment to review your #significantwomenofthebible posts on Facebook or Instagram—and add a few more. Or flip back through this workbook and see the stories of God's faithfulness you've recorded in these pages throughout this study.

Remember the stories of God's faithfulness to Sarah, Leah, Tamar, and Rahab—and your own stories of His faithfulness. Praise God for your curated reminders of his majesty. Set a regular reminder on your phone or carve out time on your calendar to use these stones of remembrance to fuel your faith.

If only we take the time to look for them, God's miracles are all around us.

May we not ever forget what he has done. May we never have the hard hearts of Balaam and Balak.

How in the world could God possibly use a Moabite woman, one from such perverse people, to further his family line? Ruth's people's origins were rooted in fear and incest. Their women were known for seduction and idolatry leading to death. Her people were forever banished from publicly participating in worship. Ruth was one of the unlikeliest choices to be a foremother to Christ.

And yet, that's exactly what she was.

Come back tomorrow to read how it all plays out!

> Even when I don't understand everything God is doing, remembering the miraculous in my past keeps me focused and following God tenaciously today.

Share a simple prayer time with the Lord:

- Praise God for the astonishing things he's working around and in you.
- Give God any fears or worries you may be white-knuckling.
- Pray for a heart soft to his leading, and an eagerness to tenaciously follow him.

Takeaway Truth—"For there is no difference between Jew and Gentile—the same Lord is Lord of all and richly blesses all who call on him." Romans 10:12

MAIN TEXTS:
Ruth 1:1-18
Matthew 19:29

DAY TWO: GRIEVING AND GOING HOME

"Don't urge me to leave you or to turn back from you. Where you go I will go, and where you stay I will stay. Your people will be my people and your God my God." Ruth 1:16

Death in Moab

Review Ruth 1 verses 1-5 and test your knowledge with this pop quiz:

True or False	Ruth and Orpah were the Moabite wives of Naomi's sons.
True or False	The story of Ruth takes place when kings ruled Israel.
True or False	Elimelek and Naomi's family left their homelands because of enemy attacks.
True or False	Naomi's family was origially from Bethlehem, but spent time living in Moab.

These first five verses set the scene for Ruth's story. When judges still ruled Israel, before the days of monarchy (kings Saul, David, and beyond), Elimelek and his wife, Naomi, and their two sons, Mahlon and Kilion (Chilion), lived in Bethlehem, Judah. But, just as famine drove Elimelek's forefathers, Abraham (Genesis 12:10), Isaac (Genesis 26:1), and Jacob (Genesis 47:4), to migrate, famine also drove Elimelek's family out of their homeland in search of food—this time to Moab. Desperate times meant Elimelek's family took desperate measures.

The situation in Bethlehem was clearly desperate. Otherwise, Elimelek would never dream of moving his family into Moab, whose history was marred by its sullied, godless past—as we learned in yesterday's lesson.

Despite his flight to Moab, Elimelek would not thrive. Underline in the margin passage what happened to him, according to Ruth 1:3.

Even though she was now a widow and living in foreign lands, Elimelech's wife, Naomi, had hope for a future—her two sons,

In the days when the judges ruled, there was a famine in the land. So a man from Bethlehem in Judah, together with his wife and two sons, went to live for a while in the country of Moab. 2 The man's name was Elimelek, his wife's name was Naomi, and the names of his two sons were Mahlon and Kilion. They were Ephrathites from Bethlehem, Judah. And they went to Moab and lived there.
3 Now Elimelek, Naomi's husband, died, and she was left with her two sons. 4 They married Moabite women, one named Orpah and the other Ruth. After they had lived there about ten years, 5 both Mahlon and Kilion also died, and Naomi was left without her two sons and her husband.

RUTH 1:1-5

When Naomi heard in Moab that the Lord had come to the aid of his people by providing food for them, she and her daughters-in-law prepared to return home from there. 7 With her two daughters-in-law she left the place where she had been living and set out on the road that would take them back to the land of Judah. Then Naomi said to her two daughters-in-law, "Go back, each of you, to your mother's home. May the Lord show you kindness, as you have shown kindness to your dead husbands and to me. 9 May the Lord grant that each of you will find rest in the home of another husband." Then she kissed them goodbye and they wept aloud 10 and said to her, "We will go back with you to your people." 11 But Naomi said, "Return home, my daughters. Why would you come with me? Am I going to have any more sons, who could become your husbands? 12 Return home, my daughters; I am too old to have another husband... No, my daughters. It is more bitter for me than for you, because the Lord's hand has turned against me!" 14 At this they wept aloud again. Then Orpah kissed her mother-in-law goodbye, but Ruth clung to her.

RUTH 1:1-6-14

SIGNIFICANT

Mahlon and Kilion. For about 10 years, she and her sons dwelled in Moab, along with their wives, Orpah and Ruth. Then, the unthinkable happened, as tragedy struck Naomi's household once again. What happened, according to verse 5?

As poor and unfortunate a lot in life widows had in ancient times, many had the consolation of their sons to care for them. Desperate was the widow with neither a husband, nor a son—a situation in which Naomi, Ruth, and Orpah all three now found themselves. These were the hardest of times. Faced with these difficult circumstances, how would these three respond to the unexpected fork in their road? Let's keep going and see.

Naomi had faith in God—a God whom she knew would provide. What evidence is there from verses 6-9 that Naomi believed God would provide for her?

When Naomi had heard that God was caring for his people back in her homelands, she didn't hesitate to return (v. 6-7). So confident was she in God's provision for her that she urged her two daughters-in-law to return to their own families and look for new husbands (v. 8-9). She did this even though this was not easy for her.

Her attachment to her daughters-in-law shows: in her concern for them (v. 8), her affection toward them (v. 9), her weeping at the thought of their departure (v. 9, 14), and her repeatedly calling them "daughters" (v. 11-13). This ripping off the Band-Aid and parting of ways was not easy for Naomi, nor for her daughters-in-law.

Orpah obeys Naomi's urging and returns to her own family in Moab. To whom else did Orpah return, according to verse 15 of Ruth 1?

Escape from Moab

Going with Naomi back to Bethlehem was Ruth and Orpah's ticket out of a life of following false gods and into eternal life with the one true God. Returning to her own family meant Orpah was choosing to return to a Moabite life with Moabite gods.

In contrast to Orpah, shrewd Ruth knew a real God when she saw Him. Ruth wasn't about to miss her chance to get out of Moab, and pursue a relationship with Yahweh—even if that meant a tough road ahead.

We're all going to come to forks in the road in our own lives. As much as we'd like to just cruise along on easy street, scripture assures us that the only road worth travelling is anything but easy.

Matthew 7:13-14 says, "wide is the gate and broad is the road that leads to destruction, and many enter through it. But small is the gate and narrow the road that leads to life, and only a few find it." Circle the words that describe the path to life, and cross out the way to destruction.

If the path to life is hard to find and difficult to follow, how will we tread in its ways?

These verses can be intimidating. If the path to life is hard to find and difficult to follow, how will we tread in its ways? There's no question that we'll come to crossroads in our lives, and we'll have critical choices to make. As we delve deeply into Ruth's life for the remainder of the week, we'll see the exact steps she took to follow the narrow road, mapping out for ourselves our own course to life.

Despite Naomi's numerous pleas for Ruth to return to Moab (v.8, v.11, v.15), Ruth tenaciously "clung" to Naomi (v.14) and

While Naomi struggled to understand why God would allow her life to become so bitter, we don't hear the same tone from Ruth.

When we are in the midst of our suffering, it can be hard for us to see anything good coming from it. But God's plans are bigger than ours. His perspective sees so much more than our limited vantage point.

Think in terms of Naomi and Ruth's circumstances. If their husbands hadn't perished, and if no famine had come over Moab, what course would their life likely have taken?

How had God already used their hardship to direct their paths, even in the first chapter of Ruth?

As we continue to walk through the rest of Ruth's story, we will see God's fingerprints all over her life, a perfect example of a loving God, bringing beauty from a situation that seemed hopeless. In our own lives, it may not ever be clear why we suffer, but we can take comfort knowing we are in our good God's hands.

made her famous proclamation of loyalty. Copy your Bible's version of verse 16 below, or paraphrase it in your own words:

Though Ruth was doggedly loyal to Naomi, her commitment to move with Naomi to Bethlehem—a country and people unknown to her—showed an even greater loyalty to Yahweh. In fact, in her reference to "the Lord" (v.17) she used God's unique name "Yahweh."

Ruth made it clear—she wasn't just choosing Naomi's "god," she was choosing the only God worth choosing: Yahweh, the one true God.

Does shifting the emphasis to Ruth's choosing of Yahweh (as opposed to focusing on her loyalty to Naomi) change this Sunday-School familiar story's impact on you? Why or why not?

For me, focusing on Ruth choosing to follow Yahweh makes all the difference. As admirable as it is to help your mother-in-law, the highest calling of all is to follow God (sorry, Donna Risner). Realizing that Ruth's choice to stick with Naomi was a choice of faith gives me a blueprint for choosing Christ at my own forks in the road.

Much like Abraham and Sarah left their families, homes, people, everything they knew to follow Yahweh in Genesis 12, Ruth left everything she knew behind to follow God. Ruth's descendant Christ spoke about following God with such reckless abandon in Matthew 19:29. What does this verse promise?

We've all had to leave things behind us to follow Christ—whether sinful behaviors & bad habits, or certain comforts & conveniences that conflicted with God's calling on our lives. It's hard. Something inside us wants to cling to those familiar things.

I grew up the fourth generation on my family farm—the same rolling green hills that my dad frolicked on as a lad, the same patch of land my grandpa walked as a barefoot boy, the same rich dirt that my great-grandfather turned over and sowed with seed. And part of me always dreamed that my own kids would squish their toes in that same mud, lay in that same lush grass and stargaze, climb those same thick tree branches. A piece of me wanted to grow old there.

But God had different plans—and, I daresay, they were better.

God called my husband and I to raise our children elsewhere, ministering to other communities and living new places. I had to let go of the storybook ending I had been writing, and hand over the pen to God. Even though the plot has taken a different turn than I'd have penned, the tale He's writing is much better than anything I could've come up with. I'm on the edge of my seat to see what's next.

Sometimes we need to let go of the good to embrace what's better. That's how we pursue the narrow way.

Is there anything God has called you to let go of in the past, or is calling you to let go of now, to make room for His better plan?

> Sometimes we need to let go of the good to embrace what's better.

Have you handed Him the pen to write the story of your life? Write your thoughts here:

Ruth knew that sticking with Naomi meant journeying miles to an unknown land. She knew that it meant being an outsider, living scorned among people with different customs and different lifestyles. She knew that life as two lone widows was going to be a hard row for her and Naomi to hoe. But you know what else I think she knew? I think Ruth knew it would be worth it.

> Life will bring forks in the road—and while choosing the narrow path won't be easy, it will be worth it.

Share a simple prayer time with the Lord:

- Thank Him for His guidance in times of famine and feast.
- Ask that He would prepare you for the forks in the road you will face.
- Pray for an eagerness to hear from Him through his word.

Takeaway Truth—"Let us throw off everything that hinders and the sin that so easily entangles. And let us run with perseverance the race marked out for us." Hebrews 12:1

DAY THREE: OUTSTANDING IN THE FIELD

MAIN TEXTS:
Ruth 1:19-2:23
Psalm 68:5
Deuteronomy 24:19-22

"The Lord watches over the foreigner and sustains the fatherless and the widow." Psalm 146:9

"Is It You, Naomi?!"

Has a well-meaning friend ever told you, "Oh boy, you look tired"? What's meant as a statement of concern can sometimes seem like an insult.

Naomi wasn't offended when she arrived at Bethlehem and the city was a-bustle with news of her arrival. She milked it for all it was worth. When the women said, "Is this Naomi?" Naomi recounted her troubles.

> …the Almighty has made my life very bitter. I went away full, but the Lord has brought me back empty…The Lord has afflicted me; the Almighty has brought misfortune upon me.
>
> RUTH 1:20-21

After a difficult life in Moab and a long, hard journey back to Bethlehem, Naomi was ready for some sympathy from her friends. See her "woe is me" story in the margin.

How could Naomi feel so sorry for herself when she had the help, companionship, and loyalty of her incredible daughter-in-law Ruth? I might be offended if I were Ruth—after all Ruth had forsaken to be with Naomi, couldn't Naomi at least give her some credit? Naomi could have added the caveat—"but at least I have my Moabite daughter-in-law Ruth." But she didn't.

Even though Ruth had left everything to make the long, dangerous journey with Naomi, forsaking all she'd ever known and remaining loyal to her mother-in-law, Naomi could only dwell on her own misfortune. She was living up to her new nickname: Mara—bitter.

Naomi's entitled bellyaching actually sounds a lot like me.

Psalm 100

A psalm.
For giving grateful praise.

1 Shout for joy to the
Lord, all the earth.
2   Worship the Lord
with gladness;
come before him with
joyful songs.
3 Know that the Lord is
God.
It is he who made us,
and we are his;
we are his people, the
sheep of his pasture.

4 Enter his gates with
thanksgiving
and his courts with
praise;
give thanks to him and
praise his name.
5 For the Lord is good
and his love endures
forever;
his faithfulness
continues through all

So often I forget all of the blessings in my life, and instead see them as troubles. I'm guessing you've had moments like that too.

- When you're so exhausted from the demands of mothering tiny humans, that you forget they're some of God's greatest gifts to you.
- When your boss is so unreasonable you complain about your job instead of thanking the Lord for providing it.
- When your homework assignments pile upon you and you overlook the blessing of receiving an education.
- When caring for your aging parents seem so burdensome that you neglect to appreciate the role they played in raising you.
- When you rush from one celebration to the next in the holiday season, and in the flurry of activity, you forget that you're celebrating Christ.

If only our eyes would be opened to the blessings and work of God in our lives!

In moments of weakness, have you been a Naomi—quick to complain and focusing on what's wrong about your life instead of basking in God's blessings? What practical steps can you take to combat this tendency?

Self-centeredness is an affliction from which we all suffer. No matter how optimistic we are, each of us struggles with a complaining spirit at times. There are all kinds of solutions for the selfish spirit. One of the simplest is giving thanks.

Time and again—48 times in the NIV—scripture calls us to give thanks. Thankfulness has a way of recalibrating our complaining attitudes and setting our hearts aright. You can start by reading the Psalm in the margin right now—better yet, make a joyful noise and sing it!

God Provides

Just like God saw Leah, just like he remembered Tamar—so too God would provide for these two helpless, destitute women. Ruth and Naomi had a future beyond their wildest dreams.

According to Psalm 68:5, what is God's relationship to widows?

> A father to the fatherless, a **defender** of widows, is God in his holy dwelling.
>
> PSALM 68:5

God doesn't leave the helpless high and dry. In Psalm 68—depending on your version—God is described as widows' *defender, champion, protector, justice-giver,* and *care-taker.* What a precious promise to those who've lost a husband.

Naomi and Ruth's divine defender **provided**.

In his foresight, God had put in place a law that would feed Israel's hungry: the foreigners, widows, and orphans among them. See Leviticus 23:22 in the margin. Because God had been generous with his people, they were to be generous to others (see also Leviticus 19:9-10, Deuteronomy 24:19-22). This was important enough to God that scripture records it many times. There would be no mistake about God's heart, and His expectations on this matter.

> When you reap the harvest of your land, do not reap to the very edges of your field or gather the gleanings of your harvest. Leave them for the poor and for the foreigner residing among you. I am the Lord your God
>
> LEVITICUS 23:22

What would be the result for those that obeyed and shared their bounty? See Deuteronomy 24:19 in the margin and write it in your own words below:

> …so that the Lord your God may bless you in all the work of your hands.
>
> DEUTERONOMY 24:19

Why were the Israelites to do this (Deuteronomy 24:22)?

Because Israel knew what it was to be hungry foreigners, they were to pay it forward to those most vulnerable among them. God had put in place a welfare system of sorts, giving His people a chance to live generously. Their care for the underprivileged would, in turn, mean God would bless them. It was a snowball-effect cycle of provision and blessing.

The famine in Bethlehem was over (Ruth 1:6) and it was harvest time (Ruth 1:22). Industrious Ruth was ready to work to keep her and Naomi's bellies full.

Ruth was a go-getter. God provided plenty of grain for Ruth and Naomi's sustenance, but the check didn't come straight to their mailbox. God didn't plop it in their laps—Ruth would have to go out, and take hold of the blessing.

The same is true for us today. God provides all we need—His word guarantees it. But that doesn't mean life is easy. It doesn't mean everything will fall in our laps. Remember the narrow road? God has provided the way for us, but it's up to us to walk in it. And that, my friend, takes tenacity.

To be crystal clear, we're talking about tenacity in walking out our faith—not earning it. I know it's easy to get confused here, but we're talking about a tenacious response to God's gift of salvation. We're not called to spring into action and work *for* our salvation, but rather work hard *because* of it.

It's precisely because Paul was saved *through no doing of his own* that he wrote about pressing on in Philippians 3 (see the margin). God enabled us to run the race of faith, it's our job to finish strong—storing up treasures in heaven by fully living our faith out here on earth.

In contrast to tenacious industriousness, women that are lazy fall into temptation. 2 Thessalonians 3 says they become, *"idle, disruptive...busybodies."* (verse 11). 1 Timothy 5:13 says that young widows like Ruth are especially susceptible to such

I press on to take hold of that for which Christ Jesus took hold of me. 13 Brothers and sisters, I do not consider myself yet to have taken hold of it. But one thing I do: Forgetting what is behind and straining toward what is ahead, 14 I press on toward the goal to win the prize for which God has called me heavenward in Christ Jesus.

PHILIPPIANS 3:12-14

temptation. It says, *"they get into the habit of being idle and going about from house to house. And not only do they become idlers, but also busybodies who talk nonsense, saying things they ought not to."*

Why do you think the lazy more easily fall into temptation? Reflect on your current circumstances—is there a truth here for you? How does the knowledge about the lazy being more susceptible impact your daily life?

I see the helpfulness of being busy in mothering very little children. Keeping little hands focused on being productive can be half the battle. When my youngest kids want to be my kitchen helpers, I have to quickly come up with tasks—Miri can pour in the oatmeal, Katherine will crack the eggs, Elijah can add the chocolate chips, then Miri will stir. Matthias, can sit in his high chair and chew on a rubber scraper.

If not, before I know it, an egg is dropped on the floor and cracked, two kids are shoving one another for the best spot, the baby grabs the bag of flour and dumps out a white, powdery mound, one child has eaten most of the chocolate—except the mess of it covering his face, and Mama is at her wit's end as a result of all the mayhem.

In the same way, when my own hands are busy with a purposeful project—preparing an extra meal for a new mom, praying with a friend, teaching my children about the Lord—I avoid the mayhem of my own sinful habits. I'm less likely to waste my time falling into the empty pursuits that ensnared the lazy, young widows of old: gossiping about others, or idly scrolling through social media for waaaay too long—when I should be doing something else.

THAT GIRL'S GOT SPUNK!

We know that Ruth was a hard worker—Boaz's field manager reported it. And boy was she.

Upon finishing her first day's work gleaning in the fields, Ruth had gathered and threshed a large amount of barley. Look at Ruth 2:17—how much?

Translated into modern-day terms this would be about 30 lbs of grain. This was way more than expected for a day's work—a great haul.

Yes, Boaz's men had been instructed to be generous with Ruth (2:16), but still Ruth had gathered up the large amount of the stalks, and beat the grain out of them herself. Just like the virtuous woman of Proverbs 31:17, Ruth's arms were strong for her tasks.

Instead, Ruth shows us a picture of what the godly widow described in 1 Timothy 5 is like. How is she described, according to verse 5? Read it in the margin, and notice her tenacity. Underline the ways the widow showed persistence.

Not only was Ruth alone, without a husband or child to help her—she had Naomi dependent upon her. She was working not only for her own provision, but had Naomi's mouth to feed as well. God took notice of her, and provided. In Ruth, God saw a loyal widow with grit, and was ready to give her much more than leftover grain. And God's poised and ready to give us all we need as well—if we keep our eyes on Him.

By coming with Naomi to Bethlehem, Ruth had put the ways of her Moabite childhood behind her, and placed her trust firmly in the God of Israel, the one true God. What promise does Proverbs 3:5-6 have for those who trust in the Lord?

He will **make your paths straight.**
PROVERBS 3:6

He will **guide you** on the right **paths.**
PROVERBS 3:6, HCSB

Ruth the Moabite said to Naomi, 'Let me go to the fields and pick up the leftover grain behind anyone in whose eyes I find favor.' Naomi said to her, 'Go ahead, my daughter." So she went out, entered a field and began to glean behind the harvesters. As it turned out, she was working in a field belonging to Boaz, who was from the clan of Elimelek.
RUTH 2:2-3

When we put our hope fully in the Lord, relying on him alone and surrendering our lives to him, he will lead us in the right path. When we come to a fork in the road—and inevitably, we will—if we're trusting in God, He will direct our path.

At this point in Ruth's story, the Lord was poised and ready to intersect the paths of two Godly people, for both their benefit and His glory.

Fancy Meeting You, Boaz!
Briefly review Ruth 2. Ruth 2:3 tells us, *"as it turned out, she was working in a field belonging to Boaz, who was from the clan of Elimelek."*

The "as it turned out" means that Ruth ended up in Boaz's field unknowingly to her. Naomi and Ruth were just looking for a field of a generous Israelite—they were glad to be able to dumpster dive the leftovers of any benevolent farmer. But Ruth trusted the Lord, and he directed her path to a man whose generosity and provision would be a life-changer for Ruth and Naomi.

Let's get the dirt on this Boaz. Fill in the details below:
- To what family did he belong? (Ruth 2:1)

- What was Boaz's reputation? (Ruth 2:1)

- What does the fact that there was grain to glean in Boaz's field tell us about him? (hint: Deuteronomy 24:19-22)

- Who was Boaz's mother? (Matthew 1:5a)

God had providentially led Ruth to the field of Boaz, a wealthy, God-fearing Israelite who was also the son of a foreign woman. Perhaps his compassion for the poor foreigner Ruth was at least partly due to his own mother's miraculous salvation and acceptance into God's people.

Wandering into Boaz's field was stumbling upon a golden, God-appointed opportunity for Ruth. Boaz happened to be in Naomi's deceased husband's clan (this is what God-directed paths can look like). His field had gleanings left for the poor—a sign not only of his compassion for the poor, but also his obedience to God.

Boaz revealed his true colors throughout Ruth 2 as a generous, merciful protector and provider. He went beyond the letter of the law, providing safety and water for Ruth, in addition to the grain.

So Boaz said to Ruth, 'My daughter, listen to me. Don't go and glean in another field and don't go away from here. Stay here with the women who work for me. Watch the field where the men are harvesting, and follow along after the women. I have told the men not to lay a hand on you. And whenever you are thirsty, go and get a drink from the water jars the men have filled.'"

RUTH 2:8-9

We would do well to take our cues from Boaz. Remember the reputation of Moabite women we discussed in Day One of this week of study? They had historically been a snare used to seduce Israel into idolatry—not someone you'd expect an upstanding citizen like Boaz to take notice of. But God has a way of bringing about his purposes in unexpected places, through unexpected people.

How often do I get tunnel-vision caring for my own, and excuse myself from serving Jesus in unexpected places? But what a beautiful place the world would be if followers of Christ took the time to serve others no matter their reputation. Lord, make our hearts soft to unexpected opportunities to serve you.

Finish reading Ruth 2 (verses 10 and following), and do some gleaning of your own. Record what you find about both Ruth and Boaz.

> Ruth:

> Boaz:

You may have noticed Ruth's humility (vs. 10, 13), good reputation (vs. 11), hard work (vs. 17-18), and obedience (vs. 14, 23). And this passage highlights Boaz's observant respect of Ruth (vs. 11-12), generous provision (vs. 14-16, 20), position in the family (vs. 20), and protection (vs. 21-23).

Jesus assured his followers in Luke 12 that they need not worry about their lives—that God would provide and care for those that trust him. God provided for tenacious Ruth through righteous Boaz, and He still provides today.

Think of a time where God unexpectedly provided a for need you had. It could be financial, but it could also be relational, emotional, or a health need. Record your story briefly below.

Therefore I tell you, do not worry about your life, what you will eat; or about your body, what you will wear. For life is more than food, and the body more than clothes. Consider the ravens: They do not sow or reap, they have no storeroom or barn; yet God feeds them. And how much more valuable you are than birds…For the pagan world runs after all such things, and your Father knows that you need them. But seek his kingdom, and these things will be given to you as well."

LUKE 12:22-24, 30-31

Pray about sharing your story of God's unexpected provision with someone today. If you use social media to share your story, add #significantwomenofthebible to your post. This will help you glean a collection of your stones of remembrance you can look back on later for encouragement.

Ruth experienced God's provision firsthand. She and Naomi were destitute. She was a poor widow in a strange land, and yet God cared for her. Through her tenacious loyalty to Naomi and to Yahweh, Ruth demonstrated that she was seeking first God's kingdom, and God provided for her. He directed her path. Not only would Ruth eat well, but she would go from being a poverty-stricken widow to being a foremother to kings—even a foremother to the King of Kings, Christ himself.

> God directs the paths of those who trust Him, providing all they need as they cling tenaciously to Him.

Share a simple prayer time with the Lord:

- Thank him for his sovereignty in directing your steps
- Ask for the strength to respond to hardship with tenacious faith, rather than bitterness
- Pray for wisdom to know how to apply the lessons from Ruth's life to yours.

Takeaway Truth—"Trust in the Lord with all your heart and lean not on your own understanding; in all your ways submit to him, and he will make your paths straight."
Proverbs 3:5-6

DAY FOUR: MIDNIGHT AT THE THRESHING FLOOR

"May you be richly rewarded by the Lord, the God of Israel, under whose wings you have come to take refuge." Ruth 2:12

Bold Moves

Because of the Levirate Law we discussed in such detail during our Tamar study (Deut 25:5-10), we know that God provided for a sonless widow through her husband's family in Old Testament times—by remarrying her to a relative of her late husband.

Naomi and Ruth were well aware of this law. Naomi had discussed it with Ruth and Orpah in Ruth 1 when she said, *"Return home, my daughters. Why would you come with me? Am I going to have any more sons, who could become your husbands?" Ruth 1:11.*

Naomi was unable to give birth to another son for Ruth to marry, but never lost hope for finding Ruth a husband. In Bethlehem, with kind, generous, wealthy Boaz, Naomi saw a golden opportunity within their grasp. She told Ruth, *"My daughter, I must find a home for you where you will be well provided for."* Ruth 3:1.

Naomi would finally be able to provide Ruth with the security she had longed to provide. During their days in Moab Naomi had told Ruth and Orpah, *"May the Lord grant that each of you will find rest in the home of another husband," Ruth 1:9.*

Mastermind Naomi had a plan. If it worked, at long last, Ruth's tenacity would pay off. God would provide for the widows' every need.

In Ruth 3:3-4 we find the details of her instructions to Ruth.

> Wash, put on perfume, and get dressed in your best clothes. Then go down to the threshing floor, but don't let him know you are there until he has finished eating and drinking. 4 When he lies down, note the place where he is lying. Then go and uncover his feet and lie down. He will tell you what to do.
>
> RUTH 3:3-4

In some ways, Naomi's plan reminds us of Tamar's. Both involved approaching a kinsman redeemer at a celebratory harvest time. For Judah this was sheep shearing (Genesis 38:13), and for Boaz it was grain threshing (Ruth 3:2). Both women were careful to make their appearances just right—Tamar took off her widow's clothes and put on a disguise (Genesis 38:13-14), Ruth put on perfume and her best clothing (Ruth 3:3). Both used the element of surprise—Tamar wearing a disguise (Genesis 38:15-16), Ruth not making her appearance known until midnight (Ruth 3:3-4). And both resulted in an offspring-producing Levirate marriage that in generations would lead to the birth of Christ (Matthew 1:3, 5).

But Ruth and Boaz's encounter would be decidedly different from Judah and Tamar's—as we are about to see for ourselves.

Midnight at the Threshing Floor

I wonder how Ruth might have felt when faced with Naomi's plan. She had already worked so hard to keep she and Naomi afloat. Was she exhausted and ready to throw in the towel? Was she relieved, confident that it would work?

Sometimes, life can be exhausting. Yes, we have the miracles God has done in our past to remind us of His mighty power and motivate us moving forward. Yes, we know that even though the road is narrow and hard to find that God will direct our paths. And yes, we know that it takes God-given tenacity to finish our race of faith. But sometimes we're just. so. tired. How can we manage to endure?

Just think of all that Ruth had been through: the death of her husband, leaving her homeland to migrate to a foreign place, gleaning grain for survival. Thankfully for her, a permanent solution was just around the corner.

But it can be difficult for us when it doesn't seem like the end is in sight. It's like running a half-marathon and coming around the

How can we manage to endure?

...let us throw off everything that hinders and the sin that so easily entangles. And let us run with perseverance the race marked out for us, 2 **fixing our eyes on Jesus**, the pioneer and perfecter of faith. For the joy set before him he endured the cross, scorning its shame, and sat down at the right hand of the throne of God. 3 Consider him who endured such opposition from sinners, so that you will not grow weary and lose heart.
HEBREWS 12:1-3

> No matter what our weariest moments look like, there is always a way to look to Jesus to keep us from losing heart.

bend you're sure is the last—only then learning that the homestretch is around the bend and over another hill.

Or like laboring in childbirth for hours, sure that you'll be dilated enough to push soon—only to learn you've got many painful hours to go.

Sometimes life feels like that—like you've endured so much, you're not sure you have anything left in the tank.

Paul's got a solution for those of us that are world-weary: keep your eyes on the prize. In Hebrews 12, the famous race of faith chapter, Paul encourages us to "fix our eyes on Jesus...so that you will not grow weary and lose heart."

What might fixing your eyes on Christ look like in your weariest moments?

For me, it might be a desperate prayer under my breath when I'm tempted to behave in ways I shouldn't.

For you, perhaps it's fighting for your marriage, filling your mind with encouraging scriptures when everything in you wants to quit—but you realize God will be glorified if you stay.

Or maybe it's wrestling in prayer for that wayward relative—crying out to Jesus on behalf of one who needs to be lifted up in a seemingly hopeless situation.

These are only a few possibilities. No matter what our weariest moments look like, there is always a way to look to Jesus to keep us from losing heart.

"I will do whatever you say," Ruth answered. 6 So she went down to the threshing floor and did everything her mother-in-law told her to do.

RUTH 3:5

 SIGNIFICANT

Ruth persisted, despite the hardships she faced. She showed hardworking humility and kept moving forward.

Upon hearing everything her mother-in-law instructed her to do, Ruth assured Naomi that she'd follow instructions, and according to Ruth 3:5, Ruth was a woman willing to go the distance. She prepared herself, and went to the threshing floor.

Ruth waited patiently in secret until Boaz slept. Then she lay at his feet—a position that was the least scandalous choice for a midnight encounter. To lie at a master's feet was the position of a humble servant. Ruth continued to show humility (Ruth 2:2,7,10) as she acted with integrity.

Unlike Tamar, Ruth's desperate, humble situation has not caused her to abandon her virtue—Ruth is careful in her meeting with Boaz to show as much honor as possible.

Boaz's Opportune Opportunity

Ruth was noticed by Boaz in the middle of the night, and she didn't hesitate to reveal her identity. She introduced herself with her trademark humility—*"I am your servant Ruth" (Ruth 3:9).* Then, she asked for him to provide for her and for Naomi by being their "gaal"—their kinsman-redeemer

In imploring Boaz, Ruth uses his own language from the previous chapter. He had praised her saying, *"May you be richly rewarded by the Lord, the God of Israel, **under whose wings** you have come to take refuge." (Ruth 2:12)* and Ruth implores that Boaz cover her, just as God's wings, saying, *"**Spread the corner of your garment over me**, since you are the kinsman-redeemer of our family."* Both Ruth and Boaz use the Hebrew word "kanaph" in these verses, which can mean "wings," "corner," or "shirt."

God uses this imagery of a protective, redeeming husband, with his people Israel. In Ezekiel 16:8 he said, *"I spread the corner of my garment over you and covered your...body. I gave you my*

WHAT'S WITH THE FEET?

While laying at Boaz's feet was less risqué than other positions, Naomi may have had other reasons for telling Ruth to lay at his feet as well. In ancient Israel, business transactions were solemnized with the feet—by removing a sandal—like a handshake or signature.

Uncovering Boaz's feet would have reminded him of his legal obligation to Ruth and Naomi as a member of Elimelech's family.

You may remember from week 3 of this study, the passage in Deuteronomy 25. In this passage, the widow of an unwilling Levirate removes the sandal of the man and spits in his face after his refusal to redeem her. His family also goes down in history as "the Family of the Unsandaled."

Ruth and Naomi were discreetly reminding Boaz in private of his family's public obligation to care for them.

solemn oath and entered into a covenant with you, declares the Sovereign Lord, and you became mine."

Jesus himself used the beautiful imagery of gathering and protecting his people under his wings in Luke 13:34: *"Jerusalem, Jerusalem...how often I have longed to gather your children together, as a hen gathers her chicks under her wings."*

Covering is a physical symbol of protection and security. In brutal prison camp situations like Nazi Germany, captives are stripped to humiliate them and reveal their vulnerability. In very much the opposite way, the Lord covers us with His protection. Just as God clothed Adam and Eve before sending them off into the fallen world, (Gen 3:21), God, our own redeemer, covers us.

And just as God protected, provided for, and redeemed Ruth—so did Boaz.

Boaz knew that providing for Ruth and Naomi was even more important than preserving his wealth—his generosity had already been evident in his willingness to leave gleanings in his field in obedience to the law. Now Boaz was willing to take his generosity a step further and provide lifelong security for Ruth and Naomi.

> "This kindness is greater than that which you showed earlier: You have not run after the younger men, whether rich or poor. And now, my daughter, don't be afraid. I will do for you all you ask. All the people of my town know that you are a woman of noble character."
>
> RUTH 3:10

Just as Christ commanded his followers in the Sermon on the Mount (Matthew 5-7) to go even further than the laws require, we see time and again in the book of Ruth, Boaz pouring out blessing on the widows Ruth and Naomi above and beyond the law's requirements (Ruth 2:15-16, 3;11,15).

Boaz understood well that his earthly treasure paled in comparison to a heavenly one. Jesus' words in Luke 12 remind us of kindhearted Boaz: *"give to the poor. Provide purses for yourselves that will not wear out, a treasure in heaven that will never fail, where no thief comes near and no moth destroys. For where your treasure is, there your heart will be also" (verse 33).*

In the previous verse, underline how Boaz and others will be rewarded for generosity.

Recognizing Ruth's integrity as a humble, loyal, hard-working young woman of good repute, Boaz knew that he was blessed to have her for a wife. See his praise for Ruth in the margin.

A wife of noble character is her husband's crown…

PROVERBS 12:4

And with the wise words of Boaz—poor, widowed, destitute, Moabite Ruth became the only woman in scripture to be given the distinguished label, "woman of noble character" or in Hebrew, "chayil." Ruth's humble tenacity had fulfilled Naomi's plan. Astute Boaz took the opportunity to gain a wife of noble character, for he knew that *"She is worth far more than rubies" Proverbs 31:10.*

…The Lord does not look at the things people look at. People look at the outward appearance, but the Lord looks at the heart.

1 SAMUEL 16:7

How ironic that a poor, foreign widow from a banished, idolatrous people could place her faith in God and be called "noble" (Ruth 3:10). She went from being a pauper to having the character of a princess. All of Ruth's dogged determination finally paid off. She and Naomi had a secure future.

Wealthy, successful Boaz knew that all the wealth in the world was rubbish compared to a "chayil" woman, whose worth surpassed jewels. The man who possessed wealth aplenty jumped at the chance to marry a migrant. He knew that she, a lowly beggar woman, was really a "crown" (Proverbs 12:4).

If only we would see things so clearly. Think of the people whom you admire. Why do you look up to them? So often we place on a pedestal those that have financial success, fame, attractive looks, and power. If only we could have the eyes of Boaz—or really of the Lord, how much more clearly we would see.

God doesn't desire that we have a flock of Instagram followers, a picture-perfect life, an immaculate home, a manicured garden, the perfect look, high-achieving children, or scale the corporate ladder. He desires a heart dedicated to tenaciously following Him.

> God doesn't desire that we have a picture-perfect life… He desires a heart dedicated to tenaciously following Him.

SHE'S SPEECHLESS

Ruth and Naomi had the right to speak up for themselves (see Deut. 25) but chivalrous Boaz was willing to speak for them. The Hebrew word for widow is derived from the word that means "dumb" or "speechless"—symbolizing that widows no longer had anyone to speak on their behalf. Most widows, that is, but not Ruth and Naomi. God had provided an advocate for them in Boaz.

Just as helpless widows Ruth and Naomi had an advocate in Boaz to speak for them, so we, in our sin, have an advocate in Jesus Christ. 1 John 2:1 says, *"if anybody does sin, we have an advocate with the Father—Jesus Christ, the Righteous One."*

Christ speaks to the Father on our behalf, covering us with his blood and redeeming us from our otherwise hopeless state.

When we overlook others that don't "look the part" we misjudge and miss out on beautiful opportunities. Take singer Susan Boyle, for instance. Growing up a learning-disabled daughter of a miner, Susan didn't look at all like the cookie-cutter idea we all have of a singing sensation. And yet, since her appearance on *Britain's Got Talent*, her singing career has taken off.

When her first album was released, it became Britain's best-selling debut album of all time. Now her net-worth is over 20 million pounds and she's performed for the Queen of England. All from a woman most of us would have dismissed as unlikely to ever make it big.

God sees us clearly. Others may look at us and see only our social class, our appearance, or our reputation. But God (and Boaz) saw tenacious Ruth as a precious crown, and he sees our hearts as well.

> Fixing your eyes on Christ, your Redeemer, keeps you moving forward when the finish line feels far ahead.

Share a simple prayer time with the Lord:

- Thank him for his protection and provision.
- Ask for the strength to endure moments of weariness by teaching you to fix your eyes on Him.
- Pray for eyes to see others accurately—like Boaz saw Ruth, and like the Lord sees us.

Takeaway Truth--"Whoever is kind to the poor lends to the Lord, and he will reward them for what they have done" Proverbs 19:17.

DAY FIVE: THE FAMINE'S FAIRYTALE ENDING

MAIN TEXT:
RUTH 3:12-18
RUTH 4

"Do not fear, for I have redeemed you; I have summoned you by name; you are mine." Isaiah 43:1

Absolute Purity

A midnight meeting at the threshing floor between a young woman and an older bachelor has all the makings of a great scandal—after all, Moabite women were known for their history of seduction. And yet Ruth and Boaz maintain their integrity.

Quite unlike wayward Judah, who was quick to sleep with Tamar, then accuse her of harlotry—we see only the utmost of integrity in Boaz. His behavior toward Ruth that night reflected the admonition in 1 Timothy to treat women with respect. Not only did he treat Ruth properly, but he also took pains to ensure that no one else would get the wrong impression of her.

Boaz knew that Ruth was pure. He had seen the example of purity in her life, and wasn't about to let it be tarnished. Boaz protected both Ruth's purity and her reputation.

Knowing he didn't have first dibs on Ruth (there was another kinsman-redeemer first in line), Boaz cautioned Ruth to be careful to keep their meeting secret. He didn't want to compromise her reputation. He told her, *"No one must know that a woman came to the threshing floor" (Ruth 3:14).*

Boaz gifted her even more grain, saying: "Don't go back to your mother-in-law empty-handed." (Ruth 3:17). Ruth returned to Naomi, and the widows who came had back to Bethlehem "empty" (Ruth 1:21) would now be filled once again—thanks to provider Boaz.

Treat younger men as brothers, older women as mothers, and **younger women as sisters, with absolute purity.**

1 TIMOTHY 5:2

THE COUPON REDEEMER

It's foreign to us to think of people being redeemed, but in our culture, coupon redeeming abounds. And sometimes with hilarious confusion.

A customer had a 20% off coupon for a regular-priced item. The only problem was, the $109 shoes she wanted to buy were on sale for $79. When she tried to use the coupon on the sale shoes, the cashier could not honor it. The coupon stipulated that it could only be used on a regular-priced item.

The agitated customer insisted that the regular price be restored on the item, so that the coupon could be redeemed, or cashed in. When the clerk gave the customer her final price of $87.20, the customer was finally satisfied at receiving her 20% discount, even though the sale price would have been cheaper.

Thankfully our Redeemer's smarter than that.

Things were really looking up for Ruth and Naomi now, thanks to Ruth's steadfastness and Boaz's generous heart. Boaz assured Ruth that later that morning, he would speak to her potentially closer redeemer on her behalf.

Has there been a time in your life when someone stuck up for you and spoke up on your behalf? Or a time when someone failed to advocate on your behalf? How does your experience affect your reading of Ruth's story?

I still remember facing a judge for a traffic violation as a minor. I had been involved in a careless accident—and it had been all my fault. I deserved every reprimand the judge gave. I felt so small and alone. Boy would it have felt good if someone else could have spoken on my behalf.

Boaz Makes it Official

By-the-book Boaz wasted no time in making his marriage to Ruth official.

While the first-in-line kinsman-redeemer was quick to pass on marrying Ruth and redeeming Mahlon's family, Boaz was more than willing to redeem Ruth. And with that short city-gate exchange, Ruth went from being an unwanted, unclaimed widow to a treasured mother of princes.

It's hard to imagine someone in a lowlier state than an impoverished immigrant. But Boaz knew not to judge a book by its cover. Boaz would be blessed beyond measure for his ability to see beyond Ruth's Moabite past. What might we be missing in our own quick-to-judge, preconceived ideas?

Perhaps we're losing out on valuable relationships because we're sure that our next-door neighbor is too busy for us. Maybe we're missing an opportunity to encourage another because the woman at the gym seems to have it all together already. It could be that we're overlooking a chance to spend time with our spouse because we think they've got more important things to do. Let's pray for eyes to see the opportunities for relationships that are all around us.

Our Kinsman-Redeemer

You may stiffen at the thought of a person being redeemed, or ransomed. Redeeming means buying back. We know that slavery is wrong and we don't want to think of being bought or owned. And yet, to Ruth being redeemed meant freedom. To live without her kinsman-redeemer Boaz would mean a life enslaved to poverty and hunger. In being redeemed by Boaz, Ruth would find freedom from poverty and their union would produce spiritual freedom for us in Christ.

Just as wealthy and prosperous Boaz was willing to marry and redeem lowly, Moabite Ruth—so our perfect redeemer Christ has bought our sinful, hopeless souls with his own precious blood.

> For you know that it was not with perishable things such as silver or gold that you were redeemed from the empty way of life handed down to you from your ancestors, but with the precious blood of Christ...
>
> 1 PETER 1:18-19

Pauper to Princess

God would bless the humble Moabite woman beyond her expectations. She would go from her pagan childhood—from a people excluded from the assembly of believers (Deut 23:3), to a woman included in the bloodline of Christ, great-grandmother to the man after God's own heart, king David.

It's likely Ruth had no idea the path God would take her as she tenaciously clung to him. It had been a tough road with grief, migration, and hunger along the way—but Ruth had shown humility and dogged determination. Her enduring faith finally paid off in her happily-ever-after ending with Boaz. Her hungry, empty days were over.

When Boaz married Ruth, God blessed her with one of the greatest blessings of their day. Ruth 4:13 tells us what God gave Ruth. According to this verse, what was this gift?

"...For your daughter-in-law, who loves you and who is better to you than

_____

sons, has given him birth."

RUTH 4:15b

One of the greatest gifts a childless widow could receive on this earth was a son. In him she would be provided with security for her future. Once hopeless, Ruth now had a hope, and a future. Once-empty, Naomi's lap was filled with a warm, wiggling grandson.

The women of the town recognized what a wonderful blessing Ruth had been to her mother-in-law. In a culture that prized sons, they praised Ruth as even more valuable than many sons. Copy the missing word from Ruth 4:15 in the verse in the margin:

We don't always see the happy endings for our stories in this life, but Ruth and Naomi did. Even in their time on earth, the Lord brought beauty from the ashes of their hardship and suffering. And the ripple effect of their happy ending would be felt for generations to come.

The people of Israel recognized that God had provided for once-empty Naomi through kinsman-redeemer Boaz and loyal daughter-in-law Ruth—and her powerful story would be recorded as one of only two books of the Bible bearing a female name.

What could your happy ending be? Perhaps you're in a stage of grief right now, mourning a loss of what you thought might be. Maybe you're journeying with God to unfamiliar territory, and it's a little scary to migrate. Or you might be growing weary working in the field—you're thankful for God's provision, but needing to keep your eyes on Jesus to keep from losing heart.

Be encouraged that despite Ruth's struggles, God saw her through. She wasn't stuck in Moab forever. She didn't always labor in the field. But how can we endure? How can we be women of tenacity when we feel like we can't hold on any longer? If your own happy ending seems far off in the distance, and you're not sure you can make it, you're right. You can't.

Take a lesson from Ruth's own descendant—her great-great-great-great-great grandson King Asa. In 2 Chronicles 16:9, King Asa was told, *"For the eyes of the Lord range throughout the earth to strengthen those whose hearts are fully committed to him."*

That would have been really encouraging for King Asa—if it hadn't been a reprimand. You see, Asa was being scolded for going his own way, instead of depending on God. He had been making strategic treaties with other peoples, and not relying on God. Asa's foolish self-reliance would prove deadly when he became sick, and didn't seek the Lord's help (2 Chronicles 16:12-13).

So, what does this have to do with Ruth, being tenacious, you, and I? Well, Ruth's tenacity wasn't a pull-yourself-up-by-your-bootstraps, tough it out, grit your teeth, keep-moving-forward-at-all-costs tenacity. It was a tenacious clinging to God. We see in Asa's life that self-reliance is deadly, but God-reliance brings victory.

If we're trying to forge ahead on our own, not only will we wear out, but we'll be foolish. We might start to worship at the altar of works. Keeping our eyes on Jesus, we'll be the opposite of Asa. We'll be the ones fully committed to God, found and strengthened by Him.

Because when we stop trying to tough it out and blaze forward in our own strength, God moves on our behalf. It had happened in Asa's family just one generation earlier, during the rule of his father Abijah. In 2 Chronicles 13:18 it says that, led by King Abijah, *"the people of Judah were victorious because they relied on the Lord, the God of their ancestors."*

Let's show *that* kind of tenacity—one that digs deep in God-reliance. If we keep our eyes on Jesus, we won't lose heart. And

> ## If you're not sure you can make it, you're right. You can't.

> …Obed, whose mother was **Ruth**, Obed the father of Jesse, 6 and Jesse the father of King David.
> David was the father of Solomon, whose mother had been Uriah's wife,
> 7 Solomon the father of Rehoboam,
> Rehoboam the father of Abijah,
> Abijah the father of **Asa**
> MATTHEW 1:5-7

> ## Self-reliance is deadly, but God-reliance brings victory.

when we cling to Him, our fairytale ending can be better than any happily ever after we could write.

Because if we try to grit our teeth and work hard in our own strength, we might just get what we want. We might get the house we want, the ministry we want, the job we want, the family we want—but we'd be missing out on the immeasurably more than all we ask or imagine that God wants for us.

Will it look like the fairy-tale ending we picture? Not likely. I doubt Ruth's life turned out exactly as she hoped—I think it was much better than she dreamed.

And as we cling to our God with the tenacity of Ruth, when the road forks, He'll strengthen us for the walk and guide us to a much happier ever after in eternity than we could even dream.

When others see our God-reliance, our eyes-on-the-prize of Christ tenacity, maybe—just maybe—they'll let go of their bootstraps too. They'll stop wearily walking their own way. And together we'll take the right fork and run toward the finish line—toward our happily ever after with Him.

Now to him who is able to do **immeasurably more than all we ask or imagine**, according to his power that is at work within us,

EPHESIANS 3:20

> God's fairytale ending for us is even better than any ending we could write–and He'll give us the strength to reach the goal when we are women of true tenacity, clinging to Him.

Share a simple prayer time with the Lord:

- Thank him for the redemption of your once-hopeless life.
- Ask for His help to have a fully committed heart, strengthened by Him.
- Pray for a heart of God-reliance when your heart grows weary.

Takeaway Truth--*"Then you will know that I, the Lord, am your Redeemer, the Mighty One of Jacob."* Isaiah 60:16

A Tangible Reminder—**Set** out something agricultural—perhaps a toy tractor, a handful of oats, or a picture of a field—as a reminder throughout the week of Ruth's humble beginnings and dogged tenacity.

Pause for Praise—Nice work finishing week 5 of our study! God has much to teach us through his word. In Ruth's life we are reminded that no matter how hopeless our circumstances seem, clinging to God is always worth it. Because of her humble yet tenacious loyalty to God and his people, the Lord took Ruth—a powerless widow from a forbidden people—and made her a mother of princes. We can follow the example of hard-working Ruth who, even through dire circumstances, was willing to give of herself to sustain her otherwise helpless mother-in-law Naomi. And ultimately, we can realize that just like poor, futureless Ruth—we would be without a future except for our own redeemer, Jesus Christ. Before you head to your Bible Study Gathering for this week, take a few moments to meditate on the perfect redemption of our awesome God. I suggest you find the lyric video for Hillsong United's *Empires* on YouTube and watch with a worshipful heart. If you prefer more traditional songs, try *There Is A Redeemer* instead.

God uses mightily those who cling to him with tenacity—no matter their humble beginnings

BATHSHEBA

Invisible to Influential

Significant

DAY ONE: FROM JUDGES TO KINGS

MAIN TEXTS:
Judges 21:25
1 Samuel 8
Luke 18:1-8

"If my people, who are called by my name, will humble themselves and pray and seek my face and turn from their wicked ways, then I will hear from heaven, and I will forgive their sin and will heal their land." 2 Chronicles 7:14

Once Upon a Time in Israel's Dark Ages

During Rahab's life, Joshua and the Israelites conquered Jericho and moved into the Promised Land. It was victory at long last for God's people. But Joshua died, and the judges ruled Israel. Trouble befell God's people.

We learned last week that Ruth and Naomi lived during the time of the judges (Ruth 1:1). Though Ruth and Boaz were both examples of Godly individuals, the Israelite people as a whole struggled greatly during this period.

In Judges, the book of the Bible that chronicles this time in history, we find some of the most brutal, disturbing, dark stories in scripture. A time period that could have been a climactic time of victory and obedience to God was instead characterized by idolatry, disobedience, violence, suffering, captivity, and bloodshed.

Ultimately, there is no happily-ever-after Hollywood ending for the time period of the judges. Any small success of God's people was eclipsed by catastrophic blunders. What we can learn from this dark time in Israel is its overwhelming need for a Savior—a Prince of Peace, a King of Kings who would redeem and lead His people in victory over sin and death.

The epilogue of the book is telling: *"In those days Israel had no king; everyone did as they saw fit."* Judges 21:25. The land ached for a savior.

God's People Throw a Hissy Fit

Rather than patiently, contentedly, and obediently follow the judges that God had put in place until the Messiah came, the

> The land ached for a savior.

Israelites decided they knew the best way forward. They demanded that Samuel appoint a King.

What three reasons do the Israelites give Samuel for their demand? See the verse in the margin.

"You are old, and your sons do not follow your ways; now **appoint a king to lead us**, such as all the other nations have"

1 SAMUEL 8:5

1-

2-

3-

The people demand a king because they no longer want Samuel and his sons to rule as judges. They want to be like all the other peoples surrounding them. Their petulant request sounds just like a sullen teenager's—"but everyone else is doing it!!"

And they could've used the trite response—"if everyone else was jumping off a cliff, would you too?!" But God wasn't going to lecture his disobedient people. He'd give them what they wanted—even if that meant more suffering.

Samuel was hurt by the people of Israel's demand for a king. What action did Samuel take (1 Samuel 8:6)? And what was God's response (verse 7)?

It's sobering to think that God will sometimes give us what we want, even if what we want is not good for us.

God knew that having their own king is not what is best for Israel, and yet He gave His people what they wanted. It is sobering to think that God will sometimes give us what we want, even if what we want is not good for us. At first glance, this doesn't seem to be congruent with who he is. God gives good gifts, right?

Christ says in Matthew 7:7-11, *"Ask and it will be given to you; seek and you will find; knock and the door will be opened to you. For everyone who asks receives; the one who seeks finds; and to the one who knocks, the door will be opened. Which of you, if your son asks for bread, will give him a stone? Or if he asks for a fish, will give him a snake? If you, then, though you are evil, know how to give good gifts to your children, how much more will your Father in heaven give good gifts to those who ask him!"*

Have it Your Way

But Israel was not seeking the Lord when they were begging for a king. Even after God led them out of slavery, through the Red Sea, sustained them in the wilderness, and crumbled the walls of Jericho, they still wouldn't follow His lead. They wanted to have things their way. But God didn't indulge their request without warning—he let them know that their request for a king was foolish.

What did God warn the Israelites would happen, once they got their much-wanted king? Check out 1 Samuel 8:10-17 in the margin. Circle the verb of each sentence that tells what Israel's king will do. Which verb is repeated the most?

Contrast this to Matthew 7:11 above. What does this verse tell us that God will do? What is the verb used?

People take. God gives.

God had solemnly warned Israel that a king would abuse his power, and they would suffer. He would take their sons and daughters. He would take the best of their fields and harvest. He would take their servants and livestock. Rather than be a blessing to them, a king would take advantage of his position and exploit them.

And then they'd be in a world of hurt.

What would happen once Israel suffered under their much-wanted king, according to 1 Samuel 8:18?

Samuel told all the words of the Lord to the people who were asking him for a king. 11 He said, "This is what the king who will reign over you will claim as his rights: **He will take** your sons and make them serve with his chariots and horses, and they will run in front of his chariots. 12 Some **he will assign** to be commanders of thousands and commanders of fifties, and others to plow his ground and reap his harvest, and still others to make weapons of war and equipment for his chariots. 13 **He will take** your daughters to be perfumers and cooks and bakers. 14 **He will take** the best of your fields and vineyards and olive groves and give them to his attendants. 15 **He will take** a tenth of your grain and of your vintage and give it to his officials and attendants. 16 Your male and female servants and the best of your cattle[a] and donkeys **he will take** for his own use. 17 **He will take** a tenth of your flocks, and you yourselves will become his slaves.
1 SAMUEL 8:10-17

CAN PERSISTENCE IN PRAYER BE BAD?

The Parable of the Persistent Widow in Luke 18 always intimidated me. In it, Jesus told the tale of a woman so determined to get what she wants, that she pesters the judge until she gets it.

He used this to illustrate why we should persist in prayer, saying: *"will not God bring about justice for his chosen ones, who cry out to him day and night? Will he keep putting them off? I tell you, he will see that they get justice, and quickly."* (Luke 18:7-8).

"But what if I ask for the wrong things?!" my over-analyzing self can't help but wonder. "What if I end up like Israel when they asked persistently for a king and got it—even though it wasn't good for them?!"

But there is comfort for a worry-wart like me in the words of David. He says, *"Take delight in the Lord, and he will give you the desires of your heart"* in Psalm 37:4. The key here (that Israel missed badly) is *"take delight in the Lord."*

When we are following the Lord, seeking him daily and spending time in his word—He changes us! We are no longer the selfish, corrupt people we once were. Because of this, we needn't worry so much about asking God for the right things.

Yes, Israel received from the Lord an answer to prayer that was ultimately bad for them—but they weren't seeking the Lord. If they had been, they would have heeded his warnings. Actually, they wouldn't have found themselves in such a mess in the first place (1 Samuel 10:19).

Israel had plenty of chances to recant their request, but never did. The fact that God granted their request says more about the hearts of the Israelites than it does about God (1 Samuel 12:17).

As long as we are seeking the Lord wholeheartedly, we need not be anxious about our prayer lives (Romans 8:26).

God would give Israel their king—despite the suffering their request would bring. But because of their disregard for His warnings, they'd be on their own after that. Their cries for help would go unanswered.

This sounds like the wisdom found in Proverbs 1:25-28. It says, *"since you disregard all my advice and do not accept my rebuke, I in turn will laugh when disaster strikes you; I will mock when calamity overtakes you—when calamity overtakes you like a storm, when disaster sweeps over you like a whirlwind, when distress and trouble overwhelm you. 'Then they will call to me but I will not answer; they will look for me but will not find me."*

We cannot be so naïve to think that our foolish choices and requests are without consequence. Our relationship with God will be affected. We can't go our own way and expect God to bless the path of our own selfish choosing.

Maybe this tough love doesn't quite sound like the God you know. After all, isn't He the one with new mercies every morning? How can He also be One who refuses to answer calls of distress?

The key is a heart of repentance. God relented when His people repented.

He is a God of unending mercy. After Solomon had built the temple, God appeared to him, telling him that the key to ending unpleasant consequences was repentant heart. See 2 Chronicles 7:13-15 in the margin.

When Israel suffered because of their own stiff-necked rebellion, God wouldn't hear their cries. But when people turned to God, their prayers were heard.

We may not think of ourselves as foolish and stiff-necked as the people of ancient Israel, but I think their behavior is reason to pause and consider, is the Lord truly the King of my life? Or have I thrown a temper tantrum and gotten the king of my own choice.

Is my heart truly after God's? Or is it in full-on self-preservation mode—do I sit on the throne of my heart? Am I worshipping the idol of self?

Or how about my family. Oh, how I love them—I serve them night and day—there's hardly anything I won't do for them. Could I be that I'm dangerously close to having them on my throne?

What about my health? Am I so interested in my physique—just another workout to get just a little stronger, just a little more fit? Maybe if I carefully watch my diet, I'll look and feel great. But could I be too caught up in it? Am I more concerned with my physical diet than my spiritual one? After all, man doesn't live on bread alone.

What about careers and status? Are we too preoccupied with the money and prestige that comes with our career, or our husband's? How about the validation we receive from those paychecks? Or what about the warm feeling when we hear the "bing" that our Facebook post has gotten another comment. Is my life out of balance, with the need to make my fame great eclipsing the need to make His name great?

God **relented** when His people **repented**.

"When I shut up the heavens so that there is no rain, or command locusts to devour the land or send a plague among my people, 14 if my people, who are called by my name, will humble themselves and pray and seek my face and turn from their wicked ways, then I will hear from heaven, and I will forgive their sin and will heal their land. 15 Now my eyes will be open and my ears attentive to the prayers offered in this place."

2 Chronicles 7:13-15

Maybe none of these scenarios hit the nail exactly on the head for you, but I think you see where I'm heading. When we hear about the Israelite's foolish behavior fussily demanding a king to replace God, their rightful king, we think they're dunces. How could they be so foolish? But maybe it's easier to be foolish than we realize.

Take a moment to jot some things down in the margin that might be vying for the spot of King of your heart. It could be something we've covered, or something completely different. Take a moment to release those things to God, giving Him the spot he deserves as King.

People tend to be so optimistic—sure that whatever bad consequence they've been warned about couldn't possibly happen to them. That's why there have to be all kinds of rules like: don't run with scissors, only walk next to the pool, always cut away from yourself. I think you see my drift. Sure, other people might suffer negative consequences, but that won't happen to me. Until it does.

I see this same sort of reckless disregard for instruction in my children. There's a rule for no running in the house—but inevitably it happens. And, inevitably, someone gets hurt. Or, it's "don't give the baby a spoon," but the baby hollers so loud for a spoon, someone caves and before you know it he's gagging himself. Yikes.

When I was a girl, my sister and I used to ride down the gravel barn bank on our farm in our little red wagon—bottoms in the wagon, and the handle bent back toward us for steering. We squealed with delight as the wind rushed in our face and we gained speed on the downhill. It was great fun.

I was only four, so, naturally, I wasn't allowed the privilege of steering. Only my big sister, Betsy, was qualified for that.

One summer evening a sitter was watching us, and I jumped at the chance to finally do it my way—to be the one to steer. Before I knew it, there I was cruising down the barn bank in the driver's seat. Also before I knew it, I was faceplanting in the gravel. Because of my rebellious spirit, my parents' date was cut short and my face looked like a pepperoni pizza for a few weeks. Ouch. Sometimes we suffer because of our own stubbornness.

But we need not live in fear that each little misstep will bring down God's wrath. Not every request will come with a dire consequence. After all, God's people were well-warned in Samuel's day. They *knew* that in asking for a king they were not only rejecting God, but incredibly foolish. They knew *full-well* what they were doing. And they did it anyway.

Just like a stubborn toddler won't heed his knowing parents, the people of Israel insisted on having their way, despite all of Samuel's warnings.

So God gave Israel their desired king.

And though the kings of His people had moments of triumph and glimmers of greatness, their reigns were also characterized by failures and selfishness. Because Israel desperately needed a much greater King—a King of Kings that would rule in selfless victory and peace. And He'd come from the unlikeliest of ancestors—like Bathsheba.

> But the people refused to listen to Samuel. "No!" they said. "We want a king over us. Then we will be like all the other nations, with a king to lead us and to go out before us and fight our battles."
>
> 1 SAMUEL 8:19-20

> The kings of His people had glimmers of greatness, but their reigns were also characterized by failures. Israel desperately needed a much greater King.

I'm just like the foolish Israelites when I reject God as King of my heart, but thankfully He is quick to relent; God hears my cries once I repent.

Share a simple prayer time with the Lord:

- Ask for ears to hear the ways He's speaking to you through this story of the Israelites' struggles.
- Pray for a heart that wants God's best—not your own way.
- Thank Him for His new mercies—that He hears our prayers when we repent.

Takeaway Truth—"the Lamb will triumph over them because he is Lord of lords and King of kings—and with him will be his called, chosen and faithful followers." Revelation 17:14

MAIN TEXTS:
2 Samuel 11:1-5
1 John 2:15-16

DAY TWO: ONE BAD DECISION LEADS TO ANOTHER

"This is the genealogy of Jesus the Messiah the son of David...David was the father of Solomon, whose mother had been Uriah's wife (Bathsheba)." Matthew 1:1,6

Israel's First Kings

Samuel anointed Saul as Israel's first king. Though handsome and seemingly well-suited for the monarchy, Saul's reign was characterized by his jealousy (1 Sam 18-23), mental instability (1 Sam 16), and disobedience (1 Sam 13, 28)—only to end tragically (1 Sam 31, 1 Chronicles 10).

Handsome David overcame Israel's enemies (1 Sam 17) and Saul's persecution (1 Sam 19), to become king (2 Sam 2, 5). But the shepherd-turned-king, giant-slayer, Psalm-composing, man after God's own heart (Acts 13:22) would have his own deep-seated faults. This is where Bathsheba entered the story.

The Wrong Place, the Wrong Time, the Wrong Decision

Just like so many of the women in our study so far—unloved Leah, forgotten Tamar, impoverished Ruth—Bathsheba seemed to be in the wrong place, at the wrong time when we find her.

Read 2 Samuel 11:1-5. These are the verses in which we first encounter beautiful Bathsheba.

This verse tells us that a sleepless David was wandering around the palace roof one night—but it wasn't just his feet that were wandering, David's eyes were wandering too. The man after God's own heart was playing Peeping Tom, and beautiful young Bathsheba was the target of his watch.

For some reason, as I have imagined this scene playing out, I've always imagined Bathsheba at the very least indiscreet, and at the most a seductress. It had always seemed that Bathsheba was immodestly bathing on her roof—but that's not what the text says.

Who is on the roof, according to verse 2?

And where would a king have usually been this time of year, according to verse 1 of this chapter?

Mighty King David was in the wrong place at the wrong time. Custom dictated that this time of year he'd be in battle with his men. He wasn't expected to be in his palace, and yet while his officers waged war—he remained in the comfort of his home.

And when temptation came calling on the roof that night, David swung open the door and invited it right in. Rather than flee temptation like Joseph fled Potiphar's wife in Genesis 39, David allowed a lustful look to turn into selfish sinful actions. James 4:7 says, *"resist the devil, and he will flee from you."* But instead of averting his eyes and his thoughts from a potentially dangerous scene, David pursued Bathsheba.

Bathsheba's Infamous Bath

But what of this bath? Was Bathsheba wrong for bathing in a location where she could be seen by David? This has always been my quick jump-to-conclusions reading before—that

> And when temptation came calling on the roof that night, David swung open the door and invited it right in.

certainly Bathsheba was being careless in her bathing. Surely, she should share part of the blame.

This could have been the case. Perhaps she knew that her bathing spot was visible from the palace roof.

Perhaps not.

She could have been bathing within the privacy of her home or within her courtyard. David's palace would have been the tallest structure in the city. He'd have had a bird's-eye view that others wouldn't have had. Besides, he was supposed to be at battle.

There isn't anything written in the scripture that paints Bathsheba as culpable—in fact, quite the opposite. That seems to be a conclusion I'd jumped to all on my own.

Bathsheba's bathing was actually a ceremonial cleansing that devout Jewish women would perform after their menstrual cycle (Leviticus 15:19-24). Her bathing was in obedience to the law. 2 Samuel 11:4 says, *"she was purifying herself from her monthly uncleanness."* The text points to her bathing as a sign of her righteousness rather than her immodesty. This makes sense, considering the character of her father and husband.

What did David find out about Bathsheba's family when he inquired about her (verse 3)?

These are the names of David's mighty warriors:… Eliam…and Uriah the Hittite.

2 SAMUEL 23:8, 34, 39

What elite group were these men part of, according to 2 Samuel 23:8, 34, 39?

Bathsheba's father and husband were both men of good character, chosen by David himself as his elite body guards, his "mighty men." The Hebrew word used to describe these men was "gibber," which can be translated as: heroes, valiant men, warriors, mighty ones, champions, outstanding, and strong. Proverbs 30:30 used "gibbor" to describe lions. Ruth 2:1 described man of character Boaz with this word.

But most notably, "gibbor" is used to describe Christ in the prophecies of Isaiah 9:6 that say, *"he will be called Wonderful Counselor, **Mighty** (gibbor) God, Everlasting Father, Prince of Peace."*

Though Bathsheba's father and husband were among these "mighty men" of David, their greatest asset was not their physical strength. Psalm 33:16 assures us that, *"No king is saved by the size of his army; no warrior escapes by his **great strength** (gibbor)."* Instead of boasting in his strength, a mighty man should boast *"that they have the understanding to know me"* *Jeremiah 9:23-24.*

What was David's action after hearing Bathsheba's identity—that she was a daughter and wife of two of his mighty men? Reread verse 4 of 2 Samuel 11 if you need a refresher:

How did David reward the mighty Eliam and Uriah for their faithful service? By sleeping with their daughter and wife. Anyone repulsed by this guy yet? Knowing full well that Bathsheba was Eliam's daughter and Uriah's wife did not deter him in the least from satisfying his lustful desires. Powerful King David would have beautiful Bathsheba—no matter what.

According to 1 John 2:16, where do the "lust of the flesh" and the "lust of the eyes" come from? Circle it in the margin.

On this spiritually dark night, the man after God's own heart had lost his way. You see, even though David had seen Bathsheba that night, the real Bathsheba had been invisible to him. It didn't matter to David that she was Eliam's daughter, or Uriah's wife.

It didn't matter to David that she was his younger sister in the faith. He saw what he wanted, and took it for himself.

Unlike his great-grandfather Boaz who took great pains to protect Ruth's virtue that midnight at the threshing floor so long before, David wasn't thinking of protecting a young woman's purity—he was only thinking of himself. Precious young Bathsheba wasn't what David saw that night—she was invisible to him. All he saw was an object—a way to selfishly satisfy his sinful flesh.

SKIN DEEP

I still remember the moment I realized the skin-deep way we are seen. It was the summer before my 7th grade year, and I was 12 years old. I had just spent the last four years of my life hiding behind awkward glasses, wearing frumpy clothes, and sporting funny-looking hairstyles. I hadn't even given much thought to my appearance. But all-of-a-sudden, I decided that I had an opinion about how I looked.

I was less interested in reading The Boxcar Children, and more interested in primping. The eye doctor prescribed me contacts, I chose my clothing more carefully, and I learned how to style my hair in a more becoming way—it was my very own Princess Diaries, makeover-the-nerd moment.

And while I liked my new, grown-up look, I was far from prepared for the reaction I got.

Sometimes the catcalls and stares from strangers were a bit flattering, but for the most part it was pretty uncomfortable. How could these boys be interested in me if they didn't even know me? It honestly didn't make much sense. Did they really think I'd walk up to their leering gaze, eager for a relationship?

Unfortunately, this is the word we live in. The enemy takes something God created for good—a man being romantically

> The enemy takes something God created for good and changes it into something demeaning and belittling.

interested in a woman—and changes it into something demeaning and belittling. But don't worry. In the end, he doesn't win.

Still, sometimes it feels like our worth is found only in the skin-deep reflection we see when we look in the mirror.

How should we behave when it starts to feel like the blessing of feminine beauty begins to feel like a curse? When it seems like all people see is our appearance, whether good, or bad? How can we be women of influence when people can't seem to get past what's on the outside? This week we'll explore what we can learn from David and Bathsheba's story to help us in our own journey, sorting out what true, Godly feminine influence looks like.

Thankfully, the Lord wasn't done with David or Bathsheba after that dark night—even though their story got worse, before it got better.

> How can we be women of real influence when others can't seem to get past what's on the outside?

Giving in to temptation takes even the Godliest of us farther than we ever should have gone, but God sees the whole picture and waits poised to make our mess a masterpiece.

Share a simple prayer time with the Lord:

- Ask for ears to hear the ways he's speaking to you through this story David's lust and fall
- Pray for a heart that wants God's truth—nothing less.
- Thank Him for the gift of womanhood and ask for His wisdom in living in a skin-deep world.

Modesty is taught as a virtue throughout scripture—and rightly so. Christ's own humility sets an example for us of a humble spirit (Philippians 2:6-8). Even the secular world often repeats the truth that pride comes before a fall (Proverbs 16:18). Our appearance should outwardly echo inner humility. A modest woman takes care to present her physical appearance in a way that is attractive, but not showy.

Bathsheba's own son Solomon taught what a waste it is when an outwardly beautiful woman is indiscreet. In Proverbs 11:22 he wrote: *"Like a gold ring in a pig's snout is a beautiful woman who shows no discretion."*

These scriptures (and many more) teach the importance of modest living. But Bathsheba's story doesn't. Using her story to teach modesty would be what my husband would call, "Right teaching, wrong text"—in other words modesty is definitely a solid Biblical teaching, but not one which is the main teaching of this story.

There is nothing within our 2 Samuel text which tells us that Bathsheba was being immodest. She may have even been fully clothed—as some people in her time were when washing. This is a story about David's lust.

So why are we so quick to jump to the conclusion that Bathsheba was at least partly at fault? Sadly, the answers may lie in the billboards with scantily-clad women plastered on our streets, the sultry models in our tv commercials, and our checkout-line magazines. We have been conditioned to think of women as seductresses—even though we are women ourselves and should know better.

Was Bathsheba trying to seduce King David? Likely not. He wasn't even supposed to be in town. Can we know for sure of her intensions? No. The text doesn't specifically say one way or another (though the Old Testament is often clear when women *are* trying to seduce— think Lot's daughters or Potiphar's wife). We will have to settle with not knowing for sure on this one.

But stay tuned for who the prophet Nathan says God DOES blame for the whole sinful escapade. That we know for sure.

Takeaway Truth—"'Do not be afraid,' Samuel replied. 'You have done all this evil; yet do not turn away from the Lord, but serve the Lord with all your heart.'" 1 Samuel 12:20

MAIN TEXT: 2 Samuel 11:6-12:14

DAY THREE: IT GETS WORSE BEFORE IT GETS BETTER

"If you do what is right, will you not be accepted? But if you do not do what is right, sin is crouching at your door; it desires to have you, but you must rule over it." Genesis 4:7

Down Sin's Slippery Slope

Have you ever been in a situation where your sin snowballed? When one bad choice led to another, led to another? For David a look turned into lust turned into an illicit encounter...but that wasn't even the end of David's slippery slope of sin. His snowball was about to become an avalanche.

Bathsheba became pregnant, and wasted no time in letting King David know. (This wasn't too much of a surprise, considering the time right after a woman's cleansing from her monthly cycle is a very fertile time—and that's exactly when David slept with her.) God allowed her to become pregnant, and the small baby growing in her belly seemed like a big problem for David.

But quick-thinking David had a cover-up plan: bring Uriah home—then he would sleep with Bathsheba and everyone would think the baby was Uriah's. But Uriah refused to go home. Why wouldn't he? Read his explanation in the margin. Why did David's plan backfire?

> 11 Uriah said to David, "The ark and Israel and Judah are staying in tents, and my commander Joab and my lord's men are camped in the open country. How could I go to my house to eat and drink and make love to my wife? As surely as you live, I will not do such a thing!"
>
> 2 SAMUEL 16:11

Uriah couldn't bear to be in the comfort of his own home and with his own wife knowing that the ark of the Lord and his fellow troops were still dwelling uncomfortably in battle. A stark difference from the comfort-seeking, lustful King David who never went to battle to begin with, and slept not only with his own wife, but Uriah's.

Uriah's good character was foiling David's cover-up plan, but David persisted—the next time stooping a little lower. What did David do to Uriah the second night, according to verse 13?

> At David's invitation, he ate and drank with him, and David made him drunk...
>
> 2 SAMUEL 16:13

David was desperate. He so wanted righteous, loyal Uriah to cover up David's own sinful mistake that he was willing to make him drunk. It worked for Lot's daughters, but not for David.

Strike two, David. And the story was on the verge of getting way more sinister.

David sent a message—by Uriah's own loyal hand—that would be Uriah's death sentence. Uriah was to be put in the most heated part of the battle, where he'd surely be killed. David, the man who was unwilling to even set foot in this battle, was now putting one of his most loyal soldiers to death to cover up his own sinful tracks. The plan was executed.

Uriah died—because of David.

Samuel's words of warning to the Israelites rang true through the selfish actions of their king, David (1 Samuel 8). He selfishly took their sons (Uriah) and daughters (Bathsheba).

Romans 6:16 says, *"Don't you know…you are slaves of the one you obey—whether you are slaves to sin, which leads to death, or to obedience, which leads to righteousness?"* David's slavery to sin had led to death—not his own, but Uriah's.

We often believe the lie that God is a kill-joy, ready to make our lives boring with His long list of rules. Wouldn't life be easier and more fun if we could lie, cheat, steal, gossip, and indulge ourselves?

But God is all about true, abundant life. His word teaches us how to live best, and offers us a hedge of protection. Left to ourselves, we would choose destruction. Our selfish, sinful choices leave pain and death in their wake. David's impulsive, unwise decisions were a typhoon of disaster, leaving a path of pain behind them, as we see firsthand in this week's lessons.

Uriah wasn't the one who deserved to die. Who did, according to Leviticus 20:10?

> We often believe the lie that God is a kill-joy… but God is all about true, abundant life.

> If a man commits adultery with another man's wife—with the wife of his neighbor—both the adulterer and the adulteress are to be put to death.
>
> LEVITICUS 20:10

In killing Uriah, David had covered over his own tracks, keeping his adulterous affair unknown to men. His potential accuser was now deceased; no one was left to point out David's sin—or so David thought. But God knew what had happened that sinful night. And He loved David too much to keep the dark secret hidden. The truth would come to light.

Hidden from Man, Not from God

What was the final step of David's cover-up, according to 2 Sam 11:26-27? Read it in the margin, underlining how the Lord felt about David's behavior.

Taking Bathsheba as his own wife and having her bear their child as his son meant David's plan was complete. He was ready to put his selfish mistake behind him, with a new wife and new son.

But God was not pleased, and David's tidy lie was about to unravel. The Proverb wisely written by his own son years later was coming true in David's own life (see margin). God knew about David's sin and cared too much about him to let it slide.

David was keeping up appearances. His dirty secret life of adultery and murder lurked under the façade of his pretend integrity. Outwardly he was trying to project a kingly righteousness, but inwardly he knew—and God knew—the truth.

I wonder how often we do the same, without even thinking about it. We want to put our best foot forward—and that's not always a bad thing. It's ok to spiff up the house a bit before company comes. There's not a problem with being kind and friendly when we're in front of others.

The problem comes when our behavior in front of others is only an act, a mask hiding an unrepentant heart of sin.

When Uriah's wife heard that her husband was dead, she mourned for him. 27 After the time of mourning was over, David had her brought to his house, and she became his wife and bore him a son. But **the thing David had done displeased the Lord.**

2 SAMUEL 11:26-27

A man who commits adultery has no sense; whoever does so destroys himself.

PROVERBS 6:32

Like if I gripe at my kids unreasonably all day at home, but when we're in the church lobby I'm saccharine sweet to them. Or if I speak about leaders with disdain behind their backs, but stand tall and greet them with a smile and firm handshake in person. Or if my heart is rampant with jealousy at everything my friend's got, but I gush to her about how happy I am for her wonderful life. A two-faced life is no way to live.

We need to deal with sin instead of hiding it.

Don't get me wrong—I'm not advocating that we show our nasty, jealous, disrespectful, unkind behaviors for all to see. Not at all. I'm reminding us that we need to recognize and deal with sin instead of hiding it. In order for us to flourish, we must cultivate. Let's get out our garden spade and dig out the root of those sins from our soul. Otherwise the thorny weeds will take over.

Take a few moments of introspection. Gaze into the mirror of your soul. First, reflect on the image you want to project: are you kind? Godly? Humble? Generous? Resourceful? How might others see you? Write the descriptive words that you come up with in the oval mirror to the left, below.

Now, in the mirror on the right, put the things you see in the mirror (and God sees), but that you try to keep hidden from others. Ask the Holy Spirit's help. What are your secret struggles? Your innermost sins that only those closest to you might know? Are you dishonest? Selfish? Jealous? Short tempered? Unkind? Greedy? How do these two mirrors compare?

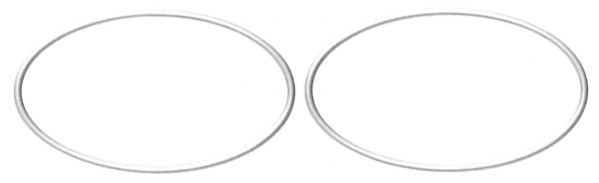

Confess the sinful tendencies of your heart that you've been trying so hard to hide. Ask for the Lord's help in being transformed from the inside out. As you bring each struggle to God and offer it up to Him, cross or scribble out each sinful word on your rightmost mirror, praising Him for the freedom that can only come from bringing the truth to light.

So many years earlier, the prophet Samuel had spoken the truth over David that God saw his heart. When Jesse brought out his strongest, tallest sons, it wasn't any of them God wanted as king. The Lord wasn't interested in looking skin-deep. God wanted the lowly shepherd boy with the right heart to rule.

The shepherd-boy-turned-king had forgotten that truth from so long ago—that God saw deep. He thought he could sweep his sin under the rug and everything would be peachy keen. But hiding the truth wasn't going to fly with the God who cared too much about David to let him keep up the façade. God used the prophet Nathan to call out David. David's sin was going to go public.

Nathan's Fable Reveals David's Folly
Throughout David's reign, the prophet Nathan had been David's advisor. Just as Moses and Aaron had been God's mouthpiece to Pharaoh (Exodus 7:1-2) so Nathan had spoken to David on God's behalf. They had a history together.

Earlier in David's reign, David had wanted to build a temple for the Lord. He had said to Nathan, *"Here I am, living in a house of cedar, while the ark of God remains in a tent." (2 Samuel 7:2).* But God had spoken clearly to Nathan that this was not God's plan. The temple would not be built in David's lifetime. Bold Nathan wasn't afraid to be the bearer of bad news to powerful King David.

Just like Aesop's fables teach children morals by telling life lessons as stories, and Jesus taught through parables, so would

But the Lord said to Samuel, "Do not consider his appearance or his height, for I have rejected him. The Lord does not look at the things people look at. **People look at the outward appearance, but the Lord looks at the heart."**

1 SAMUEL 16:7

"When your days are over and you rest with your ancestors, I will raise up your offspring to succeed you, your own flesh and blood, and I will establish his kingdom. He is the one who will build a house for my Name, and I will establish the throne of his kingdom forever."

2 SAMUEL 7:12-13.

Nathan reveal the blackness of David's own heart through a story.

Review the story Nathan tells David in 2 Samuel 12:1-14.

If David knew anything, he knew sheep. After all, his humble beginnings had been that of a lowly shepherd boy—playing songs on his lyre (1 Samuel 16:17-19) and defending his father's flock from lions and bears (1 Samuel 17:34). He knew intimately the life of one who cares for sheep.

At first Nathan's story seemed like a squabble that Nathan was bringing to David to judge—between a poor shepherd and a selfish aristocrat. A no-brainer. It was easy for David to see the fault of the rich man in Nathan's story.

David was so livid at this injustice that he saw red. The Hebrew words describe his anger as "hot" with his nostrils flaring, his face betraying his passionate emotion at even the thought of such a wrong (2 Sam 12:5).

What a shocking moment when un-repentant David would hear Nathan's convicting words: "You are the man!" (verse 7).

The sin David worked so hard to conceal was now brought to light. The cat was out of the bag. Nathan knew—more importantly God knew—of David's fall.

Why are we so quick to hide our flaws? Humans have been trying in vain to hide from God ever since the Garden of Eden (Genesis 3:8-24). But the truth sets us free.

After more than nine months of secrecy and unrepentance, it was time for David to come clean. The secret burden he carried was revealed. It was the much-needed day of repentance for the man after God's own heart. Tomorrow we'll go deeper into the fallout of David's sin and God calling his bluff.

What about Bathsheba?

In many of the scripture passages we've studied Bathsheba seems to be merely along for the ride while David takes the reigns: first killing her husband, then taking her as his wife. We aren't given the luxury of having her vantage point in these stories—but they are hers nonetheless. She just wasn't given a voice to tell them.

It's difficult to put ourselves in her shoes with all of the difficulties and obstacles she was up against as a result of David's poor decisions. Their life together hit some pretty low points, but ultimately David's repentant heart and Bathsheba's wisdom and humility would be their saving grace.

> God doesn't look skin-deep—we can't hide our secret
> faults from Him—and that's a good thing.

Share a simple prayer time with the Lord:

- Ask for the Lord's help to say, "no" to the sin crouching at your door—before it snowballs
- Pray for a heart that hides nothing from God, revealing even the darkest of hidden corners to Him.
- Thank God for the hope He gives to those who repent.

Takeaway Truth—"Surely the arm of the Lord is not too short to save, nor his ear too dull to hear. But your iniquities have separated you from your God; your sins have hidden his face from you, so that he will not hear. For your hands are stained with blood, your fingers with guilt…The Redeemer will come to Zion, to those in Jacob who repent of their sins," Isaiah 59:1-3, 20

DAY FOUR: THE JOY OF SALVATION

MAIN TEXT:
2 Samuel 12:1-23
Psalm 51

"Then you will know the truth, and the truth will set you free…if the Son sets you free, you will be free indeed." John 8:32,36

Bathsheba the Young Ewe Lamb

Nathan's story about the rich man, poor man, and little ewe lamb shed light on Bathsheba's role in her clandestine affair with David. As an upright prophet of the Lord, Nathan's word could be trusted. The first sentence of 2 Samuel 12:1 tells us why Nathan came to David in the first place. See it in the margin.

The Lord sent Nathan to David. When he came to him, he said, "There were two men in a certain town, one rich and the other poor…"

2 SAMUEL 12:1

Nathan's confrontation of David was in obedience to the Lord—thus the boldness with which he spoke. David was a powerful king, after all.

In Nathan's story, Bathsheba's role is that of the young ewe lamb. How is the lamb described (verse 3)? Circle what you find in the verse printed in the margin.

The lamb is small, and precious—owned by the poor man. It is treasured and treated like family. In the story the lamb and its poor owner are clearly the victims of the rich man's selfishness.

There is no mention of the lamb enticing the rich man to take it—no mention of the lamb's desire to go with the rich man—no mention of the lamb's seductive behavior. Such a storyline would seem absurd. These words of the Lord through the prophet Nathan place the blame for David's downfall squarely on his own shoulders.

Why then are we so quick to want to implicate Bathsheba? Perhaps we don't want to see such a great man fall so far. Perhaps we are products of our own culture.

To put the blame on Bathsheba is reading into things, from scripture we can only say that it is clear that David is at fault. In this story, Bathsheba was the little lamb—a casualty of David's selfishness. And yet, God would take her situation of shame and turn it into something beautiful—if only Bathsheba would continue to cling to Him.

The Truth Sets David Free

Living a lie is exhausting.

David had been living a lie for months—for Bathsheba's entire pregnancy—and surely his unrepentant lifestyle had been exhausting.

According to Isaiah 59 (see the end of yesterday's lesson), our sin separates us from God. We cannot have close fellowship with the Lord if our hearts are not right with Him. We cannot both carry our burden of sin and experience freedom in Christ.

David was a prolific song writer with over 70 of the Psalms credited to him. But there are no known Psalms written by David during Bathsheba's pregnancy. In the months that he failed to repent and come to terms with his acts of adultery and premeditated murder he didn't write one. It's hard to praise the Lord when you're living a lie.

Afterwards David wrote about his lack of repentance in Psalm 32:3-5: *"When I kept silent, my bones wasted away through my groaning all day long. For day and night your hand was heavy on me; my strength was sapped as in the heat of summer."*

David had gone to such great lengths to cover up his guilt, but all the while **the best thing was for his sin to be revealed**. He had feared the death sentence his actions could have brought upon him at Uriah's accusation, but how much more should he have feared the blackness of his soul. In Luke 12:4-5 Jesus taught this very concept. Write the concept in your own words here:

Nathan's words were just the wake-up call David needed. Just as Tamar's revelation of her own identity caused a turning point of repentance in Judah's life, so the Lord's harsh rebuke through the prophet Nathan brought heart-change for David.

Record David's humble words from 2 Samuel 12:13 upon realizing the depth of his guilt:

What is Nathan's immediate response, speaking as God's mouthpiece (from that same verse)?

> It's hard to praise the Lord when you're living a lie.

"I tell you, my friends, do not be afraid of those who kill the body and after that can do no more. 5 But I will show you whom you should fear: **Fear him who, after your body has been killed, has authority to throw you into hell.** Yes, I tell you, fear him.

LUKE 12:4-5

Then David said to Nathan, "I have sinned against the Lord." Nathan replied, "The Lord has taken away your sin. You are not going to die.

2 SAMUEL 12:13

Therefore, there is now no condemnation for those who are in Christ Jesus, 2 because through Christ Jesus the law of the Spirit who gives life has set you free from the law of sin and death.

ROMANS 8:1-2

Just like that, the burden of guilt and sin David bore for months was lifted.

And with his newfound repentance, David penned one of his most beautiful Psalms. Read Psalm 51, recording your favorite verse(s) below. If you are artsy, feel free to use pretty calligraphy, snap a pic and share with the rest of us on social media so we can enjoy too:

Does the completeness of David's repentance and God's forgiveness blow you away? After all that ugly sin and exhausting cover up? Take a moment to review the verse(s) you copied above one more time, rejoicing in the joy of God's salvation.

Joy Comes in the Mourning

Do not be deceived: God cannot be mocked. A man reaps what he sows.

GALATIANS 6:7

God had extended his divine grace to David upon his repentance, and David's eternal soul would be saved (2 Samuel 12:13b). But the after-effects of David's sin would still send shockwaves through his family for the rest of their lives on earth.

While God is rich in mercy, it does not mean he will remove all of the consequences of our sin.

According to Nathan, David's family would publicly suffer greatly (verses 10-12) and his and Bathsheba's child would die (verse 14). And sure enough, the child became sick. The depth of David's repentance is evident in his fasting a prayer on the child's behalf—but it was not God's will for the child to live. He died (2 Samuel 12:16-18).

David was mourning his sinful actions and their painful after-effects. Bathsheba was mourning the death of her firstborn son. David and Bathsheba's later-born son, wise King Solomon, would one day write, *"There is a time for everything, and a season for every activity under the heavens: a time to be born and a time to die... a time to weep and a time to laugh, a time to mourn and a time to dance" (Ecclesiastes 3:1-2, 4).*

David's reaction reminds us of Job. What did David do after hearing the news of his child's death, according to 2 Samuel 12:20 that Job also did upon hearing the news of the death of his children in Job 1:20-21? See the verses in the margin.

Would you find it difficult to worship in the wake of such a loss? I've never grieved child's death, but I think despair, not worship, might be my knee-jerk reaction.

Bathsheba had suffered so much. Her simple life as Uriah's wife had been turned upside down. Sucked into an affair, impregnated, widowed, remarried, giving birth, and now losing her only son. She had been put through the wringer, and we don't even know if she wanted any of it. Throughout this narrative, she's not given much of a voice—she's mostly silent. But her time would come.

We know Bathsheba's beauty was great enough to tempt King David into a sin spiral. We also know that other beautiful women tried to leverage their womanly wiles to get what they wanted in ancient times. We don't see this manipulative behavior from

Though God is rich in mercy, it does not mean he will remove all of the consequences of our sin.

Then David got up from the ground. After he had washed, put on lotions and changed his clothes, he went into the house of the Lord and **worshiped**.
2 SAMUEL 12:20

...It collapsed on them and they are dead, and I am the only one who has escaped to tell you!" 20 At this, Job got up and tore his robe and shaved his head. Then **he fell to the ground in worship** 21 and said: "Naked I came from my mother's womb, and naked I will depart. The Lord gave and the Lord has taken away; may the name of the Lord be praised."
JOB 1:19b-21

Bathsheba, but Potiphar's wife (Genesis 39), Delilah (Judges 16), and Herodias (Mark 6) tried their hand at using their looks to get their way.

In our day we're encouraged to "take the bull by the horns" and "be the master of your own destiny." There are ways we women can attempt to control and influence others that are less-than-godly. Our anything-goes culture says it's fine—"you do you."

Take a few minutes right now for a quick heart check. How are you trying to control or influence others using wrong ways? Are you guilt-tripping your children or your subordinates at work? Are you nagging your husband? Are you giving your parents the cold-shoulder to manipulate them into something?

Or maybe the ways you negatively influence others isn't even intentional. Does your worrywart tendency show up in your children? How about negativity—do you drag down your spouse by complaining?

> A Godly woman lives intentionally—realizing the importance of her influence over others, both for good and harm.

A Godly woman lives intentionally—realizing the importance of her influence over others, both for good and harm. Take stock using the following list. Which of these ways might you be influencing those around you negatively—whether intentional or not. Circle your struggles.

Complaining

Worrying

Manipulating

Deceiving

Cultivating bad habits

Being prideful

Quick tempered

Gossiping

Laziness

Being argumentative

Go back through the above list, brainstorming a positive alternative to each negative behavior you circled. For example, next to "complaining," you could list "gratefulness."

Many of these sins can seem innocent or small because they're common, yet when we participate in them it can send shockwaves of negative influence to those around us, without us even realizing it. Other times we are tempted to take control and purposely influence situations using our looks, reputation, money, or status.

Often, we must rest in God's timing—like Bathsheba. Bathsheba would have her day of influence, but not by using her captivating beauty in sinister ways. She'd use humility and wisdom as Godly powers of persuasion for His purposes instead.

The once-powerless Bathsheba would become a power-player in the royal family line. God took a situation that first brought grief and loss and redeemed it for Bathsheba's—and all of humanity's—gain.

> God took a situation that first brought grief and loss and redeemed it for our gain.

> In real repentance we experience both the depth of despair and the joy of salvation—freeing us from the sins we tried to hide and enabling us to become women of Godly influence.

Share a simple prayer time with the Lord:

- Ask for the strength to live in the truth, instead of falling to the temptation of hiding in lies.
- Pray to be a Godly influence, rather than a negative one.

- Thank God for the chance for a better future—no matter the suffering in your past.

Takeaway Truth—"Cleanse me with hyssop, and I will be clean; wash me, and I will be whiter than snow. Let me hear joy and gladness; let the bones you have crushed rejoice." Psalm 51:7-8

MAIN TEXT:
2 Samuel 12:24-25
1 Kings 1

DAY FIVE: INVISIBLE TO INFLUENTIAL

"He has sent me to bind up the brokenhearted...to comfort all who mourn...to bestow on them a crown of beauty instead of ashes, the oil of joy instead of mourning." Isaiah 61:1b,2b,3b

The Rainbow Baby

After so much loss, so much grief, so much tumult in her life—things would finally settle down for Bathsheba. Comfort was growing in her womb. More than small fingers and toes, more than tiny kicks and hiccups—Bathsheba's belly nurtured the promise of a brighter future.

Barren and childless women in ancient Israel despaired—we've seen this over and over in the stories we've studied: first Sarah (thus, the Hagar ordeal), then Rachel (thus her jealousy of Leah), then Tamar (thus her desperate plan for an heir), then Naomi (and her grief at losing all of her sons). With no children a woman had no chance for becoming a foremother to the long-awaited Messiah—the ultimate accomplishment for any Jewish woman.

Even in our modern culture, infant loss is devastating—how much more devastating when that infant loss means not only losing your precious baby, but missing out on your chance at the ultimate purpose for your life: being the foremother to the Christ. Bathsheba's loss of her firstborn would have cut deep— but God gave her a rainbow baby.

Read 2 Samuel 2:24-25 in the margin.

After an infant loss, families often call their next child a "Rainbow Baby." Bathsheba and David's next child truly was the rainbow at the end of the storm. David had repented of his sin, and was reconciled to God.

The couple had felt the depths of grief at the loss of their first child. Now God gave them the precious gift of Solomon, a name that means "peace" (Shalom)—a child God loved who'd be known as "beloved by the Lord." The birth of Solomon would be the final symbol of God's complete forgiveness and restoration in the lives of David and Bathsheba.

The Wisest of Kings

David took care to instruct his son before he died. Underline David's recipe for a successful reign in 1 Chronicles 22:12-13 in the margin.

David encouraged Solomon to be wise. He knew that the success of Solomon's reign hinged on his obedience to the Lord. Solomon took his father's words to heart. See how Solomon echoed his father's words years later, in Proverbs 4:3-5:

*"(my father) taught me, and he said to me, 'Take hold of my words with all your heart; keep my commands, and you will live. **Get wisdom, get understanding**; do not forget my words or turn away from them.'"*

Solomon listened to his father. When the Lord appeared to him, Solomon knew just how to respond—thanks to the pro-tip from David.

Solomon asked God for wisdom to rule well. Because of Solomon's unselfish request, the Lord blessed his socks off. The

24 Then David comforted his wife Bathsheba, and he went to her and made love to her. She gave birth to a son, and they named him Solomon. The Lord loved him; 25 and because the Lord loved him, he sent word through Nathan the prophet to name him Jedidiah.

2 SAMUEL 2:24-25

Only may the Lord give you wisdom and understanding, and give you charge concerning Israel, that you may keep the law of the Lord your God. 13 Then you will prosper, if you take care to fulfill the statutes and judgments with which the Lord charged Moses concerning Israel. Be strong and of good courage; do not fear nor be dismayed.

1 CHRON. 22:12-13 NKJV

On Day 3 of this week's study, we learned that David had wanted to build a temple for the ark of the Lord, but Nathan delivered the message from God that it was not David that He wanted to build his temple—that honor would rest on David's son Solomon.

Although David longed to build a glorious temple for the Lord, he accepted God's instructions that his son be the one to build it. He set Solomon up for success, making preparations before his death. David explained to Solomon what the Lord had revealed to him in 1 Chronicles 22:7-10. What was God's word to David?

David's hands had shed much blood. He had seen battle, and warfare, and even committed murder. But the Lord wanted his temple built by a man of peace—and that's exactly what Solomon's name meant.

story is found in 2 Chronicles 1:7-12 (also recorded in 1 Kings 3). God made Solomon the wisest, richest, most famous king in all of history. He rubbed shoulders with the Queen of Sheba and received more than a billion dollars of gold each year.

You may have already known this.

But what you might not have known is that without Bathsheba's bold influence, Solomon wouldn't have reigned even for a day. You see, David and Solomon weren't the only wise ones in the family.

Voiceless Bathsheba Becomes a Critical Woman of Influence

So far, our knowledge of Bathsheba has mostly been gleaned second-hand from stories about King David. Young Bathsheba was the typical woman of her day. Though married to one of David's mighty men, she did not have power.

In the passages we've covered already, her only words were her message to David—*"I am pregnant" (2 Sam 11:5)*. Nathan likened her to a lamb, stolen against her master's will. More like a piece of property than a treasured child of God.

But the once powerless, voiceless young woman came a long way. With God's help, Bathsheba's voice was heard. And she became Queen Mother to the most legendary human king in all of history.

Bathsheba knew God's plan for her son Solomon to reign over Israel—but it would take boldness and influence for things to go according to that plan.

One of the catastrophic consequences of David's sinful affair with Bathsheba was division within his own household. Nathan had warned David that God had said, *"the sword will never depart from your house, because you despised me and took the wife of Uriah the Hittite to be your own." 2 Samuel 12:10.*

One such division required Bathsheba to take action.

In the first chapter of 1 Kings, David was very old—so old that his power-hungry son Adonijah plotted to steal the kingdom from the rightful next king, his brother Solomon. He hoped to pull a fast one on his elderly father.

Adonijah rallied the support of many men, some of which had been close to his father David—like Joab the army commander and Abiathar the priest. The men were even treasonous to the point of calling Adonijah king.

But Nathan and Bathsheba knew this was not God's will for his people. God had chosen Solomon to reign. It was time for Bathsheba to use her influence as the King's wife to curb Adonijah's rebellion.

Bathsheba's appearance before King David is recorded in 1 Kings 1:11-35. How did Bathsheba use her influence to bring about Solomon's rightful reign?

> Then Bathsheba bowed down with her face to the ground, prostrating herself before the king, and said, "May my lord King David live forever!"
>
> 1 KINGS 1:31

Bathsheba bowed before the king—a position of humility—and told him about Adonijah's behavior. She gave details about who was siding with Adonijah, letting David know the severity of the situation. Like the Proverbs 31 woman, Bathsheba spoke with wisdom. She reminded David that Solomon was the rightful heir to his throne.

When it mattered most, Bathsheba spoke up. She was a woman of influence. With humility and wisdom, following Nathan's lead, Bathsheba saved the kingdom from the poor leadership of selfish Adonijah.

When it mattered most, Bathsheba was a woman of influence.

Bathsheba's plea to David was successful. David anointed Solomon—Israel's rightful king. Thanks to Bathsheba's bold request, Israel enjoyed the reign of prosperous, wise, peaceful King Solomon. And the Lord's temple would finally be built.

By taking a posture of humility, following the advice of Godly Nathan, and choosing her words wisely, Bathsheba became an example for us to follow. And David who once saw only skin-deep heeded her wise words, saving the kingdom.

Do you have a situation in your life that you feel God calling you to influence? At home? At work? In your community? Maybe you're frustrated that others don't take you seriously or won't see your point of view. Take your cues from Bathsheba before you dive in. Jot down ways you can:

Take a posture of humility—

Follow the advice of the Godly—

Choose your words wisely—

> Humbling myself, taking the time to consult scripture, and choosing my words carefully give me much greater odds for success.

I haven't had whole kingdoms to salvage, but there have been a few times John and I have disagreed strongly about a family decision. Going into the conversation hastily, without prayer, and being sure I'm right is usually a big disaster. Humbling myself, taking the time to consult scripture or a Godly friend, and choosing my words carefully give me much greater odds for success.

The Hand that Rocked the Cradle of the Richest Wisest Ruler

Bathsheba was Queen Mother of the richest, wisest, most famous king in all of history. A once powerless, voiceless woman was now in a position of influence. She crowned Solomon on his wedding day (Song of Songs 3:11) and sat at Solomon's right hand (1 Kings 2:19). The son she raised recognized her part in his successful reign.

Wise Solomon would follow in his father's footsteps, penning large portions of scripture. While his father's were words of praise, Solomon's would be words of wisdom: Proverbs, Ecclesiastes, Song of Songs. Solomon recognized the importance of heeding his mother's wisdom. Notice the verses in the margin that wise Solomon wrote, circling his references to mothers:

Catch a theme there? Solomon knew that listening to his mother Bathsheba's teaching was of utmost importance. He knew that her guidance was invaluable—*"the way of life."* The wisest man in all of history knew that the hand that rocked his cradle had a key part in who he had become.

One can only imagine the precious relationship between Solomon and his mother, as reflected in the respect and admiration in these verses. It is clear that Solomon greatly valued his mother Bathsheba.

Yes, Bathsheba had her important moment of influence before King David when Solomon's reign and the building of the temple hung in the balance. Our big moments of influence are important.

But perhaps just as important were her daily moments of influence as she raised her son. Part of being a woman of influence for the Lord is embracing the roles of influence in which the Lord has already placed you.

Sometimes it feels like we need a grandiose platform to make a real impact. Like we need to be on television, or have 50,000 Facebook followers, or write 17 books to be women of influence. But when we stop striving for the roles we don't have, and start living faithfully in our lives now, God grows our influence in only ways He knows.

When Bathsheba bounced baby Solomon on her knee, she didn't know the words of wisdom she taught him could one day end up in the scriptures, learned by billions of people for thousands of years to come.

Might there be an unforeseen way the King of your heart is calling you to be a woman of influence? Is he calling you to have

"Listen, my son, to your father's instruction and **do not forsake your mother's teaching.** They are a garland to grace your head and a chain to adorn your neck."

PROVERBS 1:8-9

"My son, keep your father's command and **do not forsake your mother's teaching.** Bind them always on your heart; fasten them around your neck. When you walk, they will guide you; when you sleep, they will watch over you; when you awake, they will speak to you. For this command is a lamp, this teaching is a light, and correction and instruction are the way to life."

PROVERBS 6:20-23

Not every moment of influence needs to be flashy—in fact it's likely most of them aren't.

that baby? Coach that team? Take that job? Volunteer in a church position? Reach out to a certain neighbor? Serve someone needy? Or Maybe it's as simple as cooking supper. **Not every moment of influence needs to be flashy**—in fact it's likely most of them aren't. Let's pray for the Holy Spirit's guidance to the opportunities for influence already around us.

One of the most sobering places I often think of influence is at funerals. There's something about a person's time on earth being done that helps me hit the pause button on my own life and get perspective.

Certain funerals celebrate the influence the person has had in a genuinely special way. I'm not talking about a twisting line of people or crowded pews. Those can certainly be the case—but I'm talking about a glimmer in someone's eyes. The tearful smiles, the babbling babies—something intangible about a race well run. And one thing I've noticed is that these special funerals are usually celebrating the most seemingly ordinary people—of great influence.

God had taken a beautiful, stolen little lamb and made her Queen Mother to the most powerful, wise human ruler on earth. A voiceless, powerless young woman had become influential and been given a voice through her scripture-writing son. Bathsheba may not have realized—that wasn't even the best of it!

Repentant David, Beautiful Bathsheba, and wise Solomon would be part of an even bigger story than an opulent earthly kingdom. They'd be part of the bloodline that brought the long-awaited, desperately-needed Messiah.

Bathsheba had seen firsthand in David's dark soul the dire need for redemption from our sins. Complete forgiveness and restorations for the dark affair was symbolized in the birth of baby Solomon, but an even greater forgiveness for all who would choose Him would come through another precious babe—the Christ child.

Just as Bathsheba rose from her invisible state to that of royalty, so Christ has made us royalty. 1 John 3:1 and Galatians 3:26 say that we are God's children—we too are royalty. In a kingdom even *greater* than Solomon's.

> A true woman of influence speaks careful words humbly, with wisdom, at the right time—intentionally embracing the opportunities put before her by the King of her heart.

Share a simple prayer time with the Lord:

- Thank him for the good work he is carrying to completion in you—that he has taken you from powerless to daughter of the King of Kings.
- Ask for God to grant you his wisdom.
- Pray that you would be a good influence over others.

Takeaway Truth--"The Teacher searched to find just the right words, and what he wrote was upright and true...here is the conclusion of the matter: Fear God and keep his commandments, for this is the duty of all mankind." Ecclesiastes 12:10, 13

A Tangible Reminder—Set out a special piece of jewelry, or perhaps a child's dress-up tiara to remind you of your place in the King of Kings' royal family. As you see it throughout the week, think of Bathsheba and how the Lord took her life—once full of grief and loss—and brought her to a place of power, influence, and honor. Let others know about your symbol and what it means by posting it on social media with #significantwomenofthebible #stonesofremembrance. Or jot down your thoughts in the "Significant Encounters With God" section and share your reflections with a friend. Take a minute to look over your past posts over the course of this study. God is good!

Pause for Praise—We have completed all of the homework for our study! Woo hoo!! God always has so much to say to us through his word. I hope you have treasured it. Take some time to reflect on what these weeks of study have meant to you. Perhaps you were **encouraged**—maybe you felt like your past actions or your current circumstances meant God wasn't planning on using you. But after seeing God use Sarah the bully, or forgotten Tamar, or impoverished Ruth you now know that God is not bound by our failures or circumstances. Our pasts don't determine our futures. Perhaps you were **convicted**— maybe you had always puffed up with pride when thinking of these women of Jesus' bloodline before (after all Rahab *was* a harlot). But after seeing them close-up maybe you realized their faith was as great or greater than your own. Maybe you needed a reminder to examine your own heart. Perhaps you were **humbled** when you realized the good our God brought from such broken women—all for His glory and our salvation. Perhaps it wrought praise in your heart! Before you head to your Bible Study Gathering for this week, take a few moments to meditate on the good God who sits on the throne of your heart. I suggest you find the lyric video for Kutless's *King of My Heart* on YouTube and watch with a worshipful heart. If you prefer more traditional songs, try *Come Thou Fount* instead.

God-given opportunities for influence are
all around us.

CONCLUSION: WE ARE CHRIST'S SIGNIFICANT OTHER

"'For this reason a man will leave his father and mother and be united to his wife, and the two will become one flesh.' This is a profound mystery—but I am talking about Christ and the church."
Ephesians 5:31-32

But What About Me?

Now that we've wrapped up our six weeks of studying women in Jesus' bloodline, perhaps you're left wondering: "what about me?"

Maybe you're thinking about how far removed your life is from these women. Perhaps the distance of years and miles seems too great a separation to span. After all, Christ has already come—we can't also be his foremothers.

But God will to continue to teach us through the lives of these women—if we will only listen. Second Timothy 3:16 assures us there are many lessons to learn from scripture. It tells us that, *"All Scripture is God-breathed and is useful for teaching, rebuking, correcting and training in righteousness."*

While it's true that you and I can't be Significant by being Christ's foremothers, we have an equally special opportunity— to be his significant other. Throughout the Bible, God uses the example of a husband and wife to illustrate the relationship between Christ and his church (see Ephesians 5).

> God will to continue to teach us through His word—if we will only listen.

In fact, in Old Testament times, God called the prophet Hosea to marry a harlot to illustrate God's longsuffering love for his people (Hosea 1:2). Some of the heart-wrenching verses from the book of Hosea show us just how significant we are to our heavenly bridegroom, Christ—despite our own unfaithfulness.

Listen to the love of our God dripping from His own words in this passage from Hosea 2:

> 14 "Therefore I am now going to allure her;
> I will lead her into the wilderness
> and speak tenderly to her.
> 15 There I will give her back her vineyards,
> and will make the Valley of Achor (trouble) a door of
> hope...
> 16 "In that day," declares the Lord,
> "you will call me 'my husband';
> you will no longer call me 'my master'
> 17 I will remove the names of the Baals from her lips;
> no longer will their names be invoked...
> 19 I will betroth you to me forever;
> I will betroth you in righteousness and justice,
> In love and compassion.
> 20 I will betroth you in faithfulness,
> and you will acknowledge the Lord"

We may not be able to be the mother to Christ, but we are His bride. I pray that our hearts would respond to Him in praise—I find Sarah Reeve's cover of Phil Wickham's *You're Beautiful* to be especially poignant, the traditional hymn *The Love of God* is also fitting.

Now what? What do we do?

Surrender All to Become Significant

Perhaps now you're thinking, "ok, I get it—God loves me, and to Him I'm significant. Now what? What do I *do*?" After all, we studied that true faith is evident in our actions—like Abraham laying Isaac on the altar and Rahab welcoming the spies.

The final story I'd like to leave you with comes from my own life, a few years ago (originally published on rachelrisner.com):

God was calling me to a ministry—one for which I was woefully unprepared. He wanted me to organize, teach, and lead a mom's ministry.

I had been to plenty of Bible studies, and loved them! But led one? Never. Surely I was misunderstanding the Lord's leading.

And yet, the call was clear. I was to move forward.

He took me to Mark 12:41-43, the story of a poor widow.

Jesus and his disciples watched as religious people gave their offerings. The rich came with huge sums, their coins jangling loudly as they dropped into the collection box—a telltale sign of their lavish gifts.

Then came an impoverished widow. She had only two of the least valuable coins of all—equal to only a fraction of a day's wages. Barely making a sound, she dropped her meager amount. It was all she had to give (Luke 21:4). But according to Jesus, she had outgiven them all.

And then, it clicked. God didn't expect me to be the most polished speaker. He didn't expect me to be the perfect leader. He didn't expect of me anything I couldn't give. He only expected my all—even if it was not very much to give.

In weakness and fear I prayed, "Lord, if you want this to work, it's going to have to be your doing!" And an amazing thing happened. It worked.

Not every phone call to organize the ministry was a success, not every idea I pursued was a slam-dunk. But with a little

41 Jesus sat down opposite the place where the offerings were put and watched the crowd putting their money into the temple treasury. Many rich people threw in large amounts. 42 But a poor widow came and put in two very small copper coins, worth only a few cents.

43 Calling his disciples to him, Jesus said, "Truly I tell you, **this poor widow has put more into the treasury than all the others.**

MARK 12:41-43

He only expected what I could give.

persistence, the doors flew open. God was making a way for this ministry! It was going to happen.

Seeds were planted, and lives were encouraged—through God's power alone. And in it all, God taught me about His faithfulness. He taught me about my weakness, and His strength. Paul's words rang true in my soul, *"For when I am weak, then I am strong." (2 Cor 12:10).*

But sometimes I forget. Sometimes I find myself right back where I started: white-knuckling my fears, my worries, my time and meager talents, my own plans once again. I snatch back those things I'm called to joyfully surrender.

And I must remember the lesson of the widow—I may not have much to offer, but when I surrender it all, it's the greatest gift I can give.

So be significant through surrender. Follow him with abandon. God wants all of you—and that's the greatest gift you can give Him. It may not be easy. But it will be worth it—and it's the only way to live a life that is truly *Significant*.

Pressing On

We've wrapped up our study, and done plenty of digging. Now it's time to cultivate, and plant. With some purposeful planning we can move forward on God's path for us, making the most from the knowledge we've gained.

The Christian life can start to feel overwhelming when we tell ourselves, "there's so much I can do to live for the Lord, where do I begin?" Let's begin by prayerfully looking over the following list of some of the lessons we've learned.

Pay special attention to areas where you are particularly weak, or that seem especially applicable to the circumstances of your

> Follow him with abandon. God wants all of you—and that's the greatest gift you can give Him.

life now. Star or circle those areas, and ask the Lord for your help in giving Him lordship and following Him in that area of your life. Which one(s) is the Lord calling you to zoom in on right now? Flip back through this workbook, or see the list below:

Sarah—**God makes beauty from our mess**. A woman of true beauty trusts the Lord—letting go of her own way of doing things, and living with an attitude of respect for others.

Leah—**God is worthy of our praise** because He loves and accepts us, even when others don't. A woman of true worship chooses to leave a legacy of victorious praise—giving God glory despite disappointment and discouragement.

Tamar—**God has shown great mercy to us**—that we can show to others. A woman of true mercy can melt hard hearts, turning the tides of evil for good, and bringing repentance to the wayward.

Rahab—**God's salvation gives us courageous hope**. A woman of true courage doesn't dwell in her crumbling Jericho, she recognizes her need for Christ and places her hope in Him alone.

Ruth—**God's provision strengthens our tenacity**. A woman of true tenacity clings to God through difficult times, finally reaching His fairytale ending come true.

Bathsheba—**God made us to be women of influence**. A true woman of influence speaks wise words humbly, embracing each opportunity put before her by the King of her heart.

Beauty, Praise, Mercy, Courage, Tenacity, Influence—which is God calling you to walk in today?

Significant

ENCOUNTERS WITH GOD

Record your stones of remembrance here—or online with #significantwomenofthebible—noting the times and ways in which God has shown Himself faithful to you and your family. Do this both when prompted during the study, and also on your own.

Review these pages or your posts regularly to remind yourself (and those around you) of all the good things He has done.

"In the future when your descendants ask their parents, 'What do these stones mean?' **tell them…so that all the peoples of the earth might know that the hand of the Lord is powerful** and so that you might always fear the Lord your God."

JOSHUA 4:21b-22a, 24

Significant
ENCOUNTERS WITH GOD

I will give thanks to you, Lord, with all my heart; **I will tell** of all your wonderful deeds.

PSALM 9:1

I will sing the Lord's praise, for he has been good to me.

PSALM 13:6

Significant
ENCOUNTERS WITH GOD

Let those who fear
the Lord say: "His
love endures
forever."

PSALM 118:4

Significant
ENCOUNTERS WITH GOD

Give praise to the Lord, proclaim his name; **make known among the nations** what he has done.

1 CHRONICLES 16:8

Significant
ENCOUNTERS WITH GOD

I will declare your
name to my
brothers and sisters;
in the assembly I
will sing your
praises.

HEBREWS 2:12

Resources

FREEBIE ADD ONS FOR NEXT-LEVEL BIBLE STUDY

- Video teaching—Stream six free lessons (one per week) with lesson notes online anytime at: www.rachelrisner.com/significantvideolessons

- Promotional goodies—Grab attractive, ready-made images and catchy blurbs for promoting your own Significant study group at: www.rachelrisner.com/significantpromogoodies

- Women's Ministry Pro-tips—Nab my free e-book on leveraging the powerful tool of social media for your local women's ministry at: www.rachelrisner.com/facebookforwomensministry

- RachelRisner.com—Find encouraging posts, book giveaways, shareable images, a chance to subscribe, pics of my family, and more goodies on my blog at www.rachelrisner.com

Been blessed? Pass the blessing on!

If you've been blessed by the *Significant* Bible study, please spread the word. After all, who doesn't love good news?! Here are five specific ways you can catch the vision and help other women learn for themselves about being truly *Significant*.

1. Word of Mouth—one of the most powerful ways you can let others know about this study is also the simplest—talk about it! Whether in person, by text, or on social media, you can spread the word to other women in your circle of influence. If the study helped you, it's likely to help them. **Let them know**.

2. Leave a Review—reviews at online retailers are worth more than their weight in gold. **Leaving yours would be a huge boost**. Reader reviews lend credibility and visibility to books. If you leave a simple review (even just one sentence), it helps online shoppers find this study, and have a better idea if it's right for them. Go to the *Significant* book page on Amazon or GoodReads to leave your review. Simple as that! (If you can't figure it out, reach out to me at www.rachelrisner.com/contact/ and I'll help). Seriously—if you leave a review, I will be on Cloud 9.

3. Lead a group—leading your own group study of *Significant* is an awesome way to pay forward what God has taught you through the study. **Prayerfully consider if God's calling you to this step today.**

4. Give feedback—I would be glad to hear any feedback you have after doing this study. I am all about giving our best to God, and that means being willing to hear it all—the good, the bad, and the ugly. If you let me know feedback on your experience in this study it gives me the chance to tweak it and make it better. It also helps me learn and grow as a Bible study writer and be better equipped to write the next one.

5. Pray—Best for last! My heart and prayer is that everything about this study gets women closer to God through His word. I'm thrilled and humbled with the impact it's had so far. Will you pray that God would continue to use it? *"So is my word that goes out from my mouth: It will not return to me empty, but will accomplish what I desire and achieve the purpose for which I sent it." Isaiah 55:11*

Thanks to each of you for walking with me on this journey.
I have to say, your impact on my life is…well…*Significant.*

Made in the USA
Las Vegas, NV
17 June 2022

50370941R00142